Penguin Book 2717
Len Deighton's London Dossier

Len Deighton was born in London in 1929. At the age of seventeen he became a photographer attached to the R.A.F. Special Investigation Branch. After his discharge in 1949 he did a variety of jobs including working in a railway marshalling yard and in 1952 won a scholarship to the Royal College of Art, London. After graduating in 1955, Deighton, with characteristic unpredictability, joined B.O.A.C. as a steward. Deighton resigned from B.O.A.C in the summer of 1956 (anticipating by one week his almost certain dismissal for an innocent involvement with a gold-smuggling organization based in Hong Kong) and embarked on yet another circumnavigation of the world, this time financed out of his earnings as a designer and illustrator. In 1960 he became art director of an advertising agency.

Deighton's first novel, *The Ipcress File*, was published in the autumn of 1962, and was an immediate and spectacular success.

In 1963 Deighton's second book, *Horse Under Water*, appeared and confirmed his reputation as one of the most talented novelists to emerge since the war.

He has since written *Funeral in Berlin* (now, like *The Ipcress File*, a successful film), *Billion Dollar Brain* and *An Expensive Place to Die*.

During the past four years he produced a weekly illustrated guide to cooking for the *Observer* and has published two books on the subject, *Action Cookbook* and *Où est le Garlic*.

Although Deighton travels thousands of miles each year accumulating information for his books, London remains the place he enjoys most deeply.

Len Deighton's London Dossier

Penguin Books

Penguin Books Ltd, Harmondsworth,
Middlesex, England
Penguin Books Inc., 3300 Clipper Mill Road,
Baltimore, Md 21211, U.S.A.
Penguin Books Australia Ltd, Ringwood,
Victoria, Australia

First published 1967
Copyright © Trinity Travel Ltd, 1967

Made and printed in Great Britain by
Hazell Watson & Viney Ltd
Aylesbury, Bucks
Set in Intertype Times

Contents

Acknowledgements

A couple of years ago I opened my big mouth at lunch and instead of putting food into it I spoke. I suggested that Cape and Penguin publish a 'real London guidebook'. Choose a dozen or so residents who really know the town and let them be biased and contradictory on their own subject. The book should not be re-edited into a homogenized and anonymous whole, I said, but remain provocative and personal.

Two long years later the London Dossier is complete. It's been a tough project. You'll find plenty of arguments and overlapping contradictions among the experts who share their lifetime in London with you. We all hope you will find it useful and amusing.

I can't list the very large number of people involved in this complex enterprise but personally I say thanks to Tom Maschler of Cape, Tony Godwin, Tony Richardson and Richard Holme of Penguin, and Continuum Ltd who have nursed the project through its many troubles. John Crusemann edited the book with a diplomacy tempered with ruthlessness and Nigel Lloyd was a sub-editor who tempered his ruthlessness with diplomacy. John Owens and Ysabele de Ranitz attended to endless amounts of checking and research. Finally I say thank you to the contributors themselves. Thank you all.

Basic London

London is a large commercial and industrial city, at latitude
51° 30′ and no longitude at all. London is 26½ miles wide,
18 miles across and occupied by 8,186,830 human beings of
various shapes, sizes and sexes the last time we counted. A
large proportion of the town is ill-lit, grimy and not worth
a visit. At its lowest part (the underground railway) it is 192 ft
below ground and its tallest building, the G.P.O. tower, is
620 ft high. (It is, incidentally, crowded, dirty and not pleasant
to visit.) The London public transport system, which covers
2,000 square miles, varies from the excellent at mid-morning
and mid-afternoon to the frantic rush hours and is virtually
non-existent after midnight. Ideally a tourist should find a
hotel near to Piccadilly Circus, for this is the heart of tourists'
London.

I well remember motoring right across London with two
Moroccan visitors who spoke no English. I was in the driver's
seat, also in a foul temper. I counted them saying *'C'est énorme'*
twenty-seven times before we got clear of the suburbs. That
was three years ago. Now, perhaps, you'll never get clear of the
suburbs. So pay no heed to that smart guy who has found a
really cheap hotel just a short bus ride from the centre of the
city. Either you'll spend the evenings in deserted Chinese
restaurants or you'll be arguing about fares with avaricious
taxi men.

London is the heart of Britain. Perhaps it's the most
important city in the world, for no other capital is at once
the largest town, the most important seaport, and the financial
and business centre. London is also Britain's cultural centre:
the place with the most theatres, cinemas, ballet, concerts,

opera and museums. In addition it is the film capital and TV production centre. Because it is such a complexity of things, begin by buying a map of central London. Petrol stations have the cheapest: Esso ones are clearest. To find addresses in central or outer London most people use an *A to Z* atlas and street index. It costs 3s. 6d. and, although the print is tiny, it is easy to use. A map of the Underground railway and bus maps are available at any Underground station. London Transport also runs a 24-hour telephone travel advice service at A B B 1234. To discover the events of the week buy a copy of *What's On* or *Where to Go*, two surprisingly similar publications that list everything from sermons to striptease.

The electricity supply emits 240 volts and 50 cycles and is efficient except for the large variety of plugs and sockets, none of which will fit any apparatus you own. The telephone system is well-meaning and polite but below expectations unless you come from France. The telegraph service is good for connexions to overseas addresses but extraordinarily bad for local communications. The telegram delivery service does in fact cease from about 6 p.m. until 8 a.m., so that between those hours all British inhabitants not on the phone are incommunicado.

The temperature varies from an average low temperature in winter of 35° (2° C.) to a pleasant 70° (21° C.) in the best part of summer. July is the warmest month, and averages only 63°F (17°C.), with August and June a not very close second and third. January is the coldest month, with February, December and March hard on its heels. The most pronounced feature of its climate in general is its wetness. November, January and February get the prize for rain, but there is no regular drought, so come equipped with a raincoat or buy one here. Burberry, 18 Haymarket, s w 1, would be my choice, but most West End shops keep a rack full. Rain is accepted by the Londoner as an inescapable fact of life like shaving, contraception and income tax. Most things continue to function during rain, and the visitor is well advised to do likewise. Take a walk in the rain, and note how it keeps the city sweet-smelling and diffuses the light in a way that adds to the beauty and conceals the squalor.

No city can provide a more varied cross-section of humanity than London does. Thomas Dekker, a sixteenth-century dramatist, said:

Foot by foot and elbow by elbow shall you see walking the knight, the gull, the gallant, the upstart, the gentleman, the clown, the captain, the apple-squire, the lawyer, the usurer, the citizen, the bankrupt, the scholar, the beggar, the doctor, the idiot, the ruffian, the cheater, the Puritan, the cut throat.

A present-day stroller will rub elbows with company more varied still, for the captain might be from Nigeria, the lawyer from Winnipeg, the doctor from the Punjab, the knight from Canberra and the idiot from Hollywood.

On your first morning take a sightseeing bus and dispose of the guide-book sights in one go. The British Travel Association's tourist information centre will tell you about sightseeing in most foreign languages. The centre is at 64 St James's Street, s w 1 (M A Y 9191), but it keeps office hours and on Saturday afternoons and Sundays does not open at all. While you are there buy a copy of *Coming Events in Britain*, also get *This Month in London*.

Our researchers sometimes found the British Travel information centre impatient with foreign-speaking inquiries and rather uncooperative with English-speaking ones, but they do have the information if you can get it. Just three doors along from there is Map House, which specializes in maps and guides.

It is important to have hotel accommodation booked before your arrival because the tourist hotels in London, as in all big cities, are fairly full all the time. If you are desperate phone M A Y 5414, the London Hotels Information Service at 20 Upper Brook Street, W 1. Incidentally, it's the expensive rooms which go first, the cheapest last.

Because continental hotels are primarily concerned about police checks, an unmarried couple booking into a double room abroad should put their true names on the card. (In practice one card signed by the man is usually all they ask for.) British hotels, on the other hand (being primarily concerned

with the proprieties), prefer you to write Mr and Mrs even if
you are sinning. Any public hotel suggesting that a couple are
unmarried runs the risk – should it be wrong – of paying hefty
damages. So does a public hotel refusing a room to anyone if,
at the time, it has rooms free. The litigation is made easier for
the couple by their being a witness to each other. All public
hotels will therefore back down when faced by an irate liar.

British nationals have no cards of identity so there is no need
to hand your passport over to any hotel employee. As a rule it's
the crummier sort of hotels who want to get their stubby
peasant fingers on their clients' passports, presumably to
prevent them doing a moonlight with the hotel cutlery.

Hotel laundry services vary greatly, one Park Lane hotel's
idea of a priority express laundry service being 'ready the day
after tomorrow'. Many hotels sub-contract to a laundry that
gives them a large mark-up rather than to the fastest and most
efficient. In other words, you will usually do better – if only
marginally – in quality and price by using a local luxury
laundry service rather than your hotel's.

Hotels will also mark up the price of your telephone calls.
Many hotels consider that a 100 per cent increase is reasonable.
I don't, but I'd rather pay it than get involved with the
G.P.O. telephone service.

If you are intending to stay for a prolonged time you could
live in a club (ask the travel centre about clubs that provide
accommodation) or rent a flat or house. For this you will need
to talk to an estate agent or buy some suitable publication that
advertises them. *Daltons Weekly* is a possible source, so is the
London *Evening Standard* if you buy it early and phone right
away. Lots of agencies also advertise there, and in fact some of
the choicest flats advertised are really bait put there by sharp
agents who want to get you on their books and mail you
addresses. Sharp agents might be your best bet, so don't avoid
them on that account.

Just in case you come from some strange foreign country
where the house agents feel they should earn their fees by
driving you to see the premises they have on offer, let me tell
you that these London fellows consider that their work finishes
when they write down the address for you.

Another way of solving the problem is to share a flat. This is a very popular way of keeping expenses down, and there are Australians in London who are living eight to a room (and letting landlords get away with exorbitant rents) in order to live near Earls Court. What a strange reason. Many London flats are so large you can share them without being thrown into the lap of your flatmates. If on the other hand you want to be thrown into a lap this may be your big chance. Contact Share-a-Flat at 175 Piccadilly, w 1: it is just around the corner from the British Travel centre. Another firm doing the same operation is Flatsharers Register at 11 Beauchamp Place, s w 3 (a short bus ride away). It is no use phoning either place: they want to see you. They charge you your share of the first week's rent. They will put you in touch with people who already have a flat and need someone to share the expenses. Some of them will want you to share the cooking and electricity while others will be organized to give you a self-contained room and key, and forget you exist from rent day to rent day. Either way round, this might be a good way for a newly arrived visitor to get a ready-made circle of friends and enemies.

The square shape of a London taxi is almost as typical a London landmark as coppers' helmets and double-decker buses. The design is controlled by law. They must have a small turning circle for U-turns in traffic and are inspected periodically for cleanliness and mechanical condition, so if you see a direly battered one it will certainly be a student's runabout bought very cheaply after it failed its test. Once inside you'll find you have generous headroom and a glass partition to give you a chance of private conversation. What's more, the driver is forbidden by law to have an interior mirror so that he can't see what's going on on the back seat. Still think the design's old-fashioned?

All London cab drivers have passed a test in the geography of London streets, known as 'the knowledge'. The meter will register charges at the rate of 2s. for three fifths of a mile, then 6d. for every three tenths of a mile. In addition to this the driver has his own part of the meter which he can operate by hand. This registers extras. Extras are passengers additional to the

hirer, prams, animals, parcels of very large size indeed
and luggage that is put next to the driver instead of inside with
the passenger. After midnight there is an extra charge of 1s.
The driver puts all money from extras into his own pocket
and thus is keen for extra people and luggage. A group of
people or a railway porter (implication of much luggage) has a
far better chance of attracting a taxi than does 'a single pin'
or single passenger. Therefore when hailing a cab, stand near
people or luggage if there are any near by. For journeys over
six miles a cab driver can charge anything he wishes, but if he
doesn't make this clear and state his price *before* the journey
starts you need only pay the meter price.

Taxi drivers, even if the 'For Hire' sign is lighted, are not
legally soliciting custom unless their wheels are stopped. Late
at night taxis will move slowly towards would-be hirers
with the cabbie anxiously asking their destination. Wait until
he stops, get in, then tell him the address to which you wish
to go.

Taxi drivers have sometimes told me strange stories, such as
that they (1) do not go south of the river, (2) do not go into
the City, (3) are on their way home but forgot to switch the
'For Hire' sign off, (4) charge double fare after four miles.
Such story-tellers are a minority in the cab trade, as are the
drivers who prefer to idle at London Airport and then charge
an extraordinary fare (about £3 10s. or twice what it is likely to
be on the meter) from an unsuspecting visitor rather than do a
normal day's work. Don't take a taxi from the airport; take the
airline bus or if you prefer it a hire car; it will be cheaper than
a cab and you won't have the driver arguing with you either.
When using London taxis, remember: providing that it is
standing (whether on a rank or not), and is not actually hired,
the regulations state that a taxicab must take you to any place
within the Metropolitan Police District or City of London that
is not more than six miles from the place where it was hired
(although to prevent you taking him round in circles the driver's
obligation ends after one hour). A refusal to take you is an
offence.

A cab rank is not a cab driver's car park. If you are hiring a
cab from a rank, the drivers of the first two vehicles there are

obliged to be '. . . with their cab and available for hiring immediately'.

You might also bear in mind that the regulations (specifically the Act of 1853, s. 17) say, 'It is an offence for a driver to demand *or take* more than the proper fare.' The italics are mine.

In case of difficulty or disagreement give the taxi driver your name and address but no money. Take his badge number and refer the matter to the Public Carriage Office at 15 Penton Street, N 1. This, however, is to look on the black side. The London taxi driver can be good-natured and helpful. Some taxis are radio-controlled. Owner Drivers' Radio Taxi Service at L O R 1133 have always given me good service as have Radio Taxi Service (London) at M O U 3232.

All London taxis disappear from London's West End between about 5 p.m. and 6 p.m. Please make a note of that highly inconvenient fact. I am told that they go away to change drivers. I asked, 'Why not change drivers at some time other than rush hour?' That would not be fair apparently: one driver or the other would get that peak period when everyone is looking for a taxi.

I call A B B 1234 every time before setting out on a bus trip. London buses are cheap, and they are like rolling grandstands, but they are not easy to understand. You can get a bus map at any Underground station. If you're clever, perhaps you'll be able to make more sense of the bus maps than I can.

It seems to me that most Londoners are only familiar with the buses they use to go to work, and the cinema, and maybe to Aunty Flo's for tea on Sunday. Outside of that, they're as ignorant as any visitor. But they'll never admit it.

Never ask a *group* of people for advice about bus routes. They'll all have contradictory theories, most of them wrong. And since there's no way of knowing who is right you will just get confused.

If in doubt about bus routes, go to a bus stop, wait for a bus and ask the conductor. If he isn't on the step (he could be upstairs collecting fares) get on the bus and ask him. He'll advise you and drop you at the next stop without selling you a ticket. A lot of bus conductors are Jamaicans, and very sunny fellows they are.

But if you've got the family with you, leaping on and off buses can be more of a drag than it's worth. The conventional approach is to read the information printed on the panel attached to the bus stop. It tells you the routes of the buses that stop there. It mentions only the landmarks, so use your *A to Z* to locate a landmark near your objective.

The grid immediately under the bus stop sign gives the numbers of the buses that stop there. A bus stop with the word 'Request' on it means you'll have to stick out your hand to stop the bus. Similarly, when approaching such a stop (they're red with a white crossed circle on them) on a bus you have to ring the bell once to get it to stop.

If you're wildly keen on buses, get yourself a Master Ticket for £3 from London Transport Head Office, St James's Park Station, s w 1 (sold to overseas visitors only). It entitles you to unlimited travel on London buses and tubes for seven days.

Don't go by bus between 8 and 10 in the morning or 4 and 6 in the evening. They're jammed. Don't expect to find them late in the evening.

That goes for the Underground, too; it closes at about midnight. The British invented the underground railway in 1863. It got pretty smoky down there, so soon after they invented the electric tube train. During the day and evening the Underground is the fastest way of getting around. It isn't scenic and it can be stuffy, but a New Yorker will find it clean in comparison with the subway. And safe. The only hazard you may encounter is somebody falling over you after too much beer late on Friday or at a weekend.

Anyone will find the Underground map easy to follow. The only thing that throws me is the Inner Circle Line. It actually does go round in a circle. I suppose this gives me a false sense of security. I expect to land where I want to go eventually, regardless of which way I start out. So I would, if I always got on a Circle Line train. But there are other trains, District Line trains, which run through some of the Circle stations. The only visible difference between the one and the other is a little label on the front of the train. So look for it. There are also illuminated boards which forecast which trains are going

to arrive at which platform in what order, but I've been known
to run down the stairs and jump on a train without
bothering to look.

If you're going to return to the same tube station you start
from, buy a return ticket. It saves queueing up twice. Tear it in
half. Keep the bit with an R in the corner for the trip back and
give the other bit up at the end of the first leg.

Quite often at stations like Piccadilly there are great
serpentine queues of people waiting to buy tickets. If you
dislike queueing as much as I do you'll buy a ticket from a
machine. If it's the right one so much the better. If it isn't,
never mind. It'll get you past the barrier without risk of
prosecution. Offer to pay any excess required to the ticket
collector at your destination. You won't get an argument, your
ticket proves where you got on the train.

For the really intrepid sightseer Savile's Cycle Stores (165
York Road, Battersea, s w 11) will let you have a bicycle for £1
a week, and £1 down payment.

Londoners prefer to travel on the Underground: it's clean,
quick and simple to understand, although at rush hour it can
get crowded to the point where passengers abandon the whole
idea and go to the nearest pub for a drink. Pubs open – artfully
enough – when evening rush-hour is at its peak moment. For
the visitor, walking and taxis, with the occasional bus, would
be my system. Parking is murder.

Once upon a time there were in London Town men called
Parking Attendants; elderly fellows who wore metal armbands
and for a fee supervised the parked cars in the squares and
parking places. Then someone heard that across the sea in
America the parking meter was in use. Although they were ugly
pieces of street furniture that caused congestion and cracked
ribs on crowded pavements they did have one great advantage:
it was no longer necessary to employ all those old Parking
Attendants. For these meters had been expressly designed so
that a red indicator would catch the attention of any passing
police car or patrolman who could pause long enough to write
out a parking ticket before proceeding with his normal duties.

So at colossal expense our streets were lined with
plantations of meters like stunted metal saplings that

never bloom. But the critics of automation also had a victory, for regiments of Parking Attendants were also recruited. Now they were fitted out in smart uniforms with yellow bands round their hats and special canvas bags to hold their sandwiches. They were given a new name too: Parking Wardens. The change in name signified the essence of the new relationship with the motorist, for these men were not there to attend him but to command him. Now everyone was satisfied: the meters were there to save manpower and the men were there to look after the meters. A truly British compromise had been reached.

Unless you are really devoted to vehicular brawling you are best advised to avoid self-drive. Stick to taxicabs. There are also many mini-cab firms in London. Their phone numbers change frequently because the taxi driver's hobby is to pester them with hoax calls, but the mini-cab has become a permanent feature of the London scene in spite of opposition. Mini-cabs are available only by phone. Ask at your hotel for the phone number of a mini-cab company they recommend; if they don't know, ask in another hotel. Mini-cabs will drive you anywhere, but prefer journeys over two miles. A typical mini-cab company charges a 7s. 6d. minimum for five miles, then 2s. a mile. London Airport to town is £2 5s. 0d. They are available by the hour – for £1 an hour – and that is the best way to do the last-minute shopping and sightseeing in style.

Another way to do last-minute sightseeing is to go to London Airport on a sightseeing coach. They depart from Victoria Coach station and take you through the West End, the City and Dockland. Some trips go also via Windsor and Hampton Court. For details and times ask London Transport, A B B 5600. For a new slant on London take a horse ride through Hyde Park; L. G. Blum, 32 Grosvenor Crescent Mews, s w 1 (B E L 6846) will give tuition in riding and has well-behaved ponies for young people.

Teenagers

Jane Wilson

Born in 1939 and spent the Second World War quietly on Exmoor wearing a small pair of hobnailed boots. Thereafter attended character-forming grammar school in London. Learned a lot about behaviour of teenage girls, and very little about anything else. Left school with plans to become nightclub hostess in South America. Became waitress in Brighton. Became desperate. Took correspondence course in Eng. Lit. and became undergraduate at Oxford. Met amazing number of fresh-faced maladjusted youths, worked hard, got good useless degrees. Returned to real world and took secretarial course. Monstrous error. Got job as secretary on glossy magazine. Wrote glossy articles and was promoted. Became frivolous, rich and blasé. Went to America to suffer, explore and write book. Would like to be very old, very famous, and look like Edith Sitwell.

Young Londoners are resilient and fast on their feet. They may be dangerously self-conscious, but when the voyeurs arrive they move out next day. Reporting on their activities is therefore difficult – by the time you read this it may have become a Domesday record of establishments sunk without a trace. But London will still be a good place to be. It's a comfortable city if you are an ageing, insolvent hipster; and if you're young, reasonably decorative, and either talented or rich, there's no point in going anywhere else. It's all here. To describe this all as 'swinging', 'groovy' or 'fab' gives the wrong impression. Londoners don't rush about twittering and raving and ricocheting off one another as they swarm headlong to the next 'in' arena. When some well-known trendsetters got together and opened a large discothèque opposite Madame Tussaud's they called it The In Place. The idea was that ordinary people should be allowed to mingle with the mighty. It was an immediate and spectacular flop. Londoners are not that dim.

Young Londoners fall into two main groups which are divided by the usual distinctions of age, occupation and money. First there are the teenagers, referred to generically as 'mods'. Clearly some are modder than others, but if you watch the crowd scenes in the various television programmes devoted to pop, you will get a general idea of the current fashions in this group. (Boys on these programmes whose fancy dress appears to be fancier than most, and girls of immodest appearance, are probably not mods at all but specially hired to give colour to the proceedings.) Mods like to look as much like one another as possible, and their girls are rather demure. Elder mods are sometimes as old as twenty-two. No one knows what happens to old mods because we haven't had a whole generation of them yet. Presumably they marry, have children, and settle down to form the backbone of England.

Mods continue to earn more than their parents ever did when young, and they spend their money almost exclusively on pop records and clothes. The correct attitude in this group is exceedingly cool, almost blank. The younger girls may scream occasionally at the pop group of their choice, and the boys may have the odd Saturday night or Bank Holiday punch-up, but emotional behaviour or any kind of frolicking is otherwise unseemly. They are not strictly chaste – but the girls are preparing for a white wedding. Mods don't go to bistros, they prefer the Golden Egg type of restaurant. Wherever you see gigantic orange light fittings and décor which looks like one huge fruit machine, you will know that the mods are inside eating square meals in round buns. Mods' night-life ends around midnight during the week. They have nine-to-five jobs and live at home, so they don't go to the expensive late-night discothèques.

The mods are responsible, as principal consumers, for the progress of pop music, and the tabernacle and heart of London's blood-music is the Marquee Club at 90 Wardour Street, w 1. The entrance is murky and the air inside is hot, damp and salty. If you really like pop music and can survive in unconditioned air, you should investigate this place.

This is how it goes. First, the words: I TAKE WHAT I
WANT GIRL, I TAKE WHAT I WANT. Swaying in the sul-
phurous spotlight is a fake-blond Ganymede figure with a
Birmingham accent. His shirt is striped in pink, purple and
scarlet and he is a great big sexy cream-cake, bold, voluptuous
and disgusting. The guitarists, hipless forked youths whose con-
cave chests are filled by their instruments, begin to throb with
full sound. Their guitars have umbilical flexes which stretch
behind them, taut and horizontal, to the amplifiers at the back
of the stage. Ganymede advances like an odalisque between
the parallel flexes. He is doing his Salome bit, winding himself
up in his microphone cord as he sings. Suddenly he goes ape,
shambling about in a crouch with his lips puckered into a Mick
Jagger sink-plunger. Then once again the repetitive, aggressive
lyric and the room becomes one huge, shuddering decibel.

This is ritual and the audience sits in rows, attentive. The
groups come from all over England, and if they make it at the
Marquee, that's the big break. The management here has recording studios and can help and promote a favoured group.
The hipless boys from Birmingham have gone over about
seventy per cent this evening, but their bass guitarist is ill and
they have to stop early.

'YEA! THAT WAS BRUTAL!!' a gnome in a blazer is
yelling into a microphone as they switch off, unplug and leave.

'WE CERTAINLY DIDN'T MAKE A MISTAKE
SIGNING THEM UP – DID WE?'

He has a breathless line in euphoric incoherence, and he is
old enough to have done National Service. The best kind of
beat club compère is someone with whom absolutely no one in
the audience can identify. If they can, they start shouting at
him. There is only some mild whistling and stamping. 'You're
a lovely audience tonight. All full of loveliness.' Some of the
faces in the audience are very beautiful – 15-year-olds untouched by anything more than cool fan emotion. No one
screams here, they don't even smile. You can see the fantasies
in their eyes, but there isn't time to speak between numbers. No
one dances much. The groups have an *act*, they are not dance
bands.

The Marquee moved about three years ago from its old

premises in Oxford Street to this new larger outfit. In Oxford Street they used to announce every night how many people were in the club. 'LADIES AND GENTLEMEN – TONIGHT, AN ALL-TIME RECORD! THERE ARE 874 OF US IN HERE!' The Stones, in the days when they really were dirty, had their first central London club engagement at the old Marquee. Rhythm'n Blues in England began there with the late Cyril Davis, who died a few years ago from pneumonia after being stranded in the rain on the way to a gig somewhere. His music was much harsher and harder than anything around now, and the Marquee then was not exactly fashionable. There were always a lot of old, ugly and unexplained people around. Some nights the rucksack-beard-and-bedding-roll group would arrive from hitching in some unknown Thumb Country, and there was usually a sort of habitué circle of Negroes with hip flasks dancing up in front of the bandstand.

The Negroes have moved on now to the Flamingo and All-Nighter Club in Lower Wardour Street, home of Georgie Fame and The Blue Flames, and Zoot Money and The Big Roll Band. The hitch-hikers have disappeared altogether from the beat-club scene. They were the extremist end of the Rocker tribe, which is now almost extinct. But you can still see the nomads in Trafalgar Square outside the National Gallery on a summer afternoon. They are filthy and hairy and lost, and they sit there nursing their blistered feet after a trek from God knows where. Most of them grow out of it and get over it, but they suffer for their art and make a change sometimes from the neat little mass-produced mods.

These mods, the ones who care more about The Look than The Sound, congregate nightly at a place called Tiles just a block down Oxford Street from Tottenham Court Road. The music of Steve Darbishire and the Yum Yum Band, or of Everett of England, or the Anteeks, is relayed out into the street via speakers placed in neighbouring shop doorways. Inside they dance actively, and spend their money in the night-time shops built in the maze of corridors that surround the main dance floor. The birds' clothes shop is called Plumage, and if you're not a success on arrival you can nip in there and come out again in something new.

On nights when there's no live music they still crowd up near the bandstand and listen to the patter of the tiny D.J. But they dance less and inspect one another's clothing more. The girls gather in serious little groups and tell one another the price of things, and the boys go peacocking around catching their own reflections in the glass swing doors. Wall-to-wall mirrors in this welter of narcissism would send the sales of plumage for both sexes up by 50 per cent – or bring the whole enterprise to a halt.

Before Tiles opened at the beginning of 1966, the mod stronghold was a smaller, merrier place, but like the old Marquee it became too small. The Scene (a name that was then original) was in a rambling cellar off Archer Street. This was where The Animals began. To get to it you had to go through a car-park which became a kind of mods' West Side Story playground. There was always trouble there, and once some of the cars caught fire. In the spring and summer of 1964 the boys at the club were very violent and they also wore eye make-up which they carried around in small plain purses. They danced together in groups, and for a while it looked as if they might go over the top; but it was just a phase. Fashions and styles of dancing were then incredibly volatile, and there were hot-lines buzzing all over London with what was happening where. A small American in a racoon skin jacket went down to The Scene one night then, and he jived. No one knew what was happening at first, and they stood around in worried groups wondering how they had missed out on this particular development. Then they heard him order a hot-dog, and the whole club visibly relaxed.

Before the sharp end of the British rag trade caught on to what was required, mod fashions evolved in a curious untraceable way, mostly in the south and east of London where there were enterprising tailors and shoemakers who had once catered for the Teddy Boys and could still produce goods to order from customers' own messy sketches. The kids had the money and they knew what they wanted. When manufacturers like the all-apparelling John Stephen of Carnaby Street began to meet the demand, the old native Streatham styles disappeared. What individualism there is left now in the clothes worn at mod clubs comes from the art schools. There, it's P V C Bermuda shorts one week, and Hebridean tweed culottes the next. Fashion editors, when they can't think what to do next, descend on the Royal College of Art Fashion School and get a lot of photographs of student Rory Mulholland in his midnight blue crêpe de chine bowling outfit.

For a preview of the astonishments ahead in music, manners, and clothes the Royal College of Art dances cannot be bettered. These occur once a fortnight during term time, and the boys on the door reckon that if you know enough to find out what night the dance is on, you know enough to be allowed in. The Golden Youth inside are often depressingly beautiful and always astonishingly arrogant, so if you are over twenty-five and insecure, don't bother. R.C.A. fashions are about a year to eighteen months ahead of anywhere else in London, but they do sometimes rush off at a tangent. Suddenly last summer, for instance, the entire college – from stained glass to graphics – burst forth in a terrible rash of West Coast surfers' Americana. Overnight all the hairy people acquired pin-head crewcuts, and for three long months there were infinite variations on a theme of sneakers, cryptically emblazoned T-shirt, and a kind of cotton ice-cream seller's suit.

These students were pioneer customers in Carnaby Street, but they hardly ever go there now. The best men's clothes are once again to be had from individual tailors, and reasonably good stuff is stocked in the boutique sections of big shops such as Austin Reed and Simpson. Mr Stephen's shops have been so influential and his styles have been so copied, that his clothes have ceased to be particularly remarkable. Mary Quant has suffered the same fate. Carnaby Street clothes have a natural built-in obsolescence, but they have also certain disturbing auto-destructive qualities which become apparent after any continuous wear.

The whole industry began nine or ten years ago with a couple of small shops which did a brisk trade in black leather swimming trunks and mustard suedette trousers with scalloped bottoms. The windows of these shops were usually decorated with colour photographs of teenage body-builders wearing pale blue 'posing garments'. The assistants within were an amazing bevy of lads swift to measure the inside leg of the most casual tie-purchaser. Compared to the exotica that these shops sold, the stock of John Stephen's nine shops has become positively conservative. There is only the occasional pair of two-tone trousers (mauve at the front and pea-green at the back), or one or two multicoloured patchwork suede jackets.

But the street is interesting and becomes a kind of teenagers' Play Street when the mods arrive from all over London on Saturdays. It is narrow, about 150 yards long, and lies between Regent Street and the store-room fag-ends of the orthodox rag trade area of Soho. Top Twenty sounds pour from the doorways of Lord John, Adam w 1., Tre Camp and the Carna B Hive. The most remarkable feature of these shops is their fitting rooms. Boys try on trousers two inches too tight from every angle in merry little pink and orange pagodas, and one of the girls' boutiques has leering male pin-ups on its cubicle walls. You undress surrounded by life-size photographs of hirsute youths striking daft attitudes in their underpants. Interestingly none of the models chosen for this particular gimmick look like pop singers. Perhaps customers would have fainted in their petticoats. The girls' boutiques were added unto Carnaby Street when someone noticed that the boys brought their girls with them on Saturdays. Palisades and Tuffin & Foale are good, but watch out for flashy, expensive rubbish elsewhere.

Apart from the clothes shops Carnaby Street has two rather musty pubs, a health-food shop where you can buy booklets entitled *Raw Juice Therapy* by John B. Lust, an austere progressive toyshop which sells top-quality building blocks in natural wood, a place called the Button Queen which sells beautiful old buttons, and a big glorified junkshop named Gear. This is the place to go if you want a lot of old furniture with the varnish stripped off. Immediately inside you will see a good butcher's chopping block which has been irrationally converted into a bad unevenly surfaced table. Above this will be a quasi-Victorian sign saying DO NOT SPIT. On the floor there is probably an old bedpan full of paper flowers and a free-standing *art nouveau* coal stove freshly painted with white Valspar. The whole shop is a triumph of pretentious tartiness, a much more advanced version of many basically similar establishments in the Portobello Road. The mod dollies wander about with enigmatic expressions on their faces. Are they imagining their mothers' cut moquette three-piece suites replaced by several rickety rocking chairs and a revamped William Morris-covered chaise longue?

Carnaby Street is for serious clothes-buying and for cruising around a bit to see what everyone else is wearing. But the street is really too short for the satisfactory display of astonishing garments. Once you've been the length in your purple and yellow striped Mongolian lamb coat – that's it. Everybody has taken note, and if you hang about thereafter the proper air of nonchalance is lost. New clothes are anyway bought principally to wear in the evenings at mod clubs, and last month's clothes are worn during the day and to work. A kind of all-our-yesterdays mod fashion show can be seen during the working week at lunch in a place called Chips With Everything. This is a Lyons restaurant at 88 Chancery Lane and it serves automated permutations of eggs, beans, sausages, bacon and chips. The décor was conceived, according to the designer, in terms of a 'pin-table aesthetic' – so everything is neon-lit in combinations of egg yellow, ketchup red, and electric blue, and deafening music is provided by a giant jukebox. This is where the working City mod goes for his mid-day transfusion of R'n B. [*The restaurant is closing as we go to press. L. D.*]

Chips With Everything, Carnaby Street, the Marquee, and Tiles are the main central London locations where mods congregate in large numbers. All are worth investigating, and nobody minds so long as you don't behave as though you're visiting a zoo. Mod clubs and beat ballrooms in the suburbs are something else. Here there is some xenophobia, and a definitely *local* feeling, so it is as well to have a talent for merging with the woodwork.

The Streatham Locarno, for instance, and the Wimbledon Palais de Danse can get quite tough, as you will realize from the number of bouncers wafting around in dinner jackets. Surburban mods are, if anything, even cooler than the West End habitués, and they take their pleasures somewhat dourly. The atmosphere in the biggest beat ballroom of them all, the Orchid at Purley, is curiously dignified and restrained. This is one of the Mecca string of ballrooms and it is easily the most overwhelming. It's a long pilgrimage out there, but the décor makes it worth while. The place is huge. Every plastic flower is lit from within by a coloured bulb, the Fish and Chix bar is surrounded by life-size swaying plastic palm trees, the Blue Grotto milk bar has cement stalactites hanging from the ceiling, and in the Wine Bar you sit on barrels around a waterfall. The gents is called the Stag Room and the ladies is the Palace of Beauty, where fifty-five individual dressing tables are provided 'for London's Loveliest Ladies'. 'Steady Rings' and harmonicas are available at a shop called the Beatique, and in the Olde Inne there is a photograph of Benny Hill inscribed 'Mecca Night Of It And Come Dancing'.

These ballrooms in South London differ from the West End clubs in that conversation is possible. They are too big to be entirely saturated by the music. So a lot of the boys go simply to talk, and drink at the Revolving Lager Bar, and watch the girls dancing together. Any pairing off or picking up is done very late – in the last half-hour – or outside afterwards. A couple of years ago all mods of any substance had scooters which they decorated first with quantities of chromium, then with fur, and finally stripped down to bare mechanical essentials. The best mod vehicle currently is a van, partly because pop groups have vans to carry their gear around with them, and partly because the van has social uses as well. In the cloakroom at the Orchid you can hear the girls warning, or advising, one another as to who has or hasn't got a mattress in the back of his van.

Mods don't drink much. To become jolly and gregarious, and to fall around in a disorganized fashion in your best clothes, is not their idea of a good time. (Nor are they all full to the brim with pills – despite all the fuss about 'Purple Hearts' two years ago.) Outside the ballroom mods go mostly to those pubs which have premises for a beat club of some sort. There are at least a hundred such pubs in and around London. The pop papers mentioned at the end of this chapter give listings of these places, though many advertise themselves mostly by fly-posters. The groups that play the circuit are usually beginners, noisy, enthusiastic and often pretty terrible. They are usually called

something like 'Captain Fog and the Fantoms'. Near closing
time in these club-pubs the clientele tends to become boisterous
and the Carnaby Street veneer may slip a bit. There are fewer
bouncers than there are at the big ballrooms, but more rules.
There is, for instance, often a sign outside which says something like this: 'Collars and ties – No jeans or leathers – No
girls in trousers – No unusual dress.' The Rolling Stones would
not be allowed in.

The most 'in' discothèque is invariably the one which has
most pop stars on its membership list, whereas the best beat
clubs are the ones which have them performing on the stage.
Beat clubs simply provide entertainment which everybody
watches, but discothèques provide a lot of pretty people who
watch each other. Annabel's club is the smartest discothèque
in London, but it is a bit too restrained and expensive to be
the most popular. Its exclusiveness has, however, given it some
permanence – and you can also get decent food there. It is in
Berkeley Square, at 44, beneath the Clermont, a gambling
club. (Young Londoners do not usually go to such places.
They have a core membership of rich older Londoners and
are also patronized by charter-plane loads of Americans who
come over for a change from Las Vegas.)

The Ad Lib, off Leicester Square, was *the* original discothèque, but its popularity waned, and in the end it had to
close down because of complaints about noise – or so they
said. After that, 'in' places were the Scotch of St James's, and
very briefly the Cromwellian. At the time of writing Dolly's
Club at 57 Jermyn Street is the place to go – but it may not be
by next week. There is no security at all for these places. Last
year one London magazine reported that the Beatles were no
longer to be seen at a particular discothèque. The establishment in question immediately sent the editor a stiffly worded
letter threatening legal action unless this assertion was withdrawn. There is nothing more depressing than a discothèque
recently deserted by the pack leaders.

While it lasts the proprietor of whatever club is 'in' makes
a fortune. Dolly's sends regular chatty letters to its members
thanking them 'for making the club what it is today'. But it is
sensibly taking thought for the morrow and opening a deli-

catessen and a restaurant just around the corner. The truth is
that there are not enough regular discothèque-goers to support more than one or two profitable establishments. These
never really get going till at least midnight; you must either be
a member, which costs about 5 gns., or a member's guest, and
there is usually a minimum cover charge of about £1. One
might suppose, from the amount of publicity given to discothèques, that large sections of Young London never get to
bed before 4 a.m., but it's possible to live through several days
in London without encountering a single soul who has ever
set foot in a discothèque. If you never set foot in one either
what you will have missed will simply be the sight of London's
richest and/or prettiest youth at play.

Dolly's is simply a long dark room with coats at one end
and loos at the other. There's no real food and no gambling,
but there's plenty of drink and dancing. The service is quick,
the receptionist is Chinese, the manager is quiet and good-
looking, and the music is continuous and assaulting. All
conversation is mouth-to-ear. If you wear a Little Black
Dress or a sober suit you will just be invisible. Gleaming
through the gloom are Mick Jagger's white trousers. He is
doing a developed version of his stage wiggle which, in
time, could be most damaging to his lower three vertebrae. A
first rule in these clubs is that all celebrities are ignored, unless
you happen to come with them or they really are your best
friends. A hopeful young man recently announced that he
planned to open the Ultimate Discothèque for In People – of
whom he estimated there were no more than 1,000 in London.
They were, he said, 'the kind of people who can live with the
Beatles'. What he meant by this was that if Paul McCartney
happens to be sitting at the next table to you at Dolly's you
do *not* zoom over and ask for his autograph. He has come for
a little privacy. There is a certain amount of swanning around
and everyone wants to see and be seen, but if more than about
twenty per cent just want to see, and sit there gaping, the
thing is spoilt. Any kind of dancing is O.K. so long as it is
controlled and economical of space. Prancing and swirling
are not favoured, and callisthenic self-expression just em-
barrasses everyone. A discothèque is a discothèque is a

discothèque. There are much more elaborate ones in New York, but what distinguishes the best London ones is their style. The lighting and the music must be right, and then the people bring everything else.

Girls' clothes for wearing in these clubs are bought in Mayfair and Knightsbridge boutiques if you're rich, or in the King's Road ones if you are just like everyone else. This area was once the inexpensive and slightly inaccessible province of an amiable mixture of arty rich and bohemian poor. Ten years ago the Chelsea Set – a nasty and roaring offshoot of the deb world – moved in and opened up the stretch of the King's Road which extends from Sloane Square to the Six Bells, where Oakley Street turns down to the river. Prices went up, new restaurants opened, and the post-war bohemians were pushed gradually down towards World's End and cisalpine Fulham. Then Mary Quant opened the first Bazaar, Jaeger moved in with a new branch, and the dollies arrived on Saturdays to shop. Boutiques have proliferated ever since and include, at this moment, Top Gear, Countdown, The Shop, Granny Takes a Trip, Hung on You (men), Susan Locke Boutique and 430.

The success of the boutiques depends upon the originality of their stock and their relaxed atmosphere. Not only is there no hard sell, it is sometimes difficult to get any attention at all. The girls who work in them are invariably depressingly pretty, and manage to look always as if they are doing someone a favour by just holding the fort for an hour or two. They sit at the back somewhere reading magazines, entertaining their friends, or telephoning interminably about special autumn orders of astrakhan mini-spats. Boutique clothes are not mass-produced and are therefore expensive, stitch for stitch. They usually come from small collections produced by new designers whose heads are seething with fresh and astonishing images of elegance. They are sometimes very badly made and somewhat experimental in shape, so it is inadvisable to shop in boutiques if you are looking a mess and feeling indecisive.

Carnaby Street mushroomed suddenly and the only reason for its existence is as a showplace for new clothes. But the

King's Road has always been one of the pleasantest streets in London and had a jolly 'village' atmosphere long before the boutiques or the dollies arrived. It has lots of good little green-grocers and ironmongers, a Boots and a Woolworth's – without which no shopping street is complete. Along its mile-and-a-half length there are art and antique shops, public swimming baths and libraries, colleges and schools, three cinemas, eight or nine pubs and innumerable cafés and restaurants. Good pubs for the gregarious are the Chelsea Potter and the Australian (which is in Milner Street just off the King's Road, about 300 yards down from Sloane Square on the right). Anyone in search of anything in the way of company can usually find it at the Potter. The atmosphere is rowdy and moderately decadent; entertaining so long as you don't get involved. Don't ever go to the bottle parties which move off from here after closing time at week-ends. They're quite terrible. The Australian is best at summer weekends when both bars expand right across the street and the whole road is jammed with patrons' sports cars. Then it's all very 'golden youth'. At other times the bars are full of dogs and men in Harris tweed.

Selected eating houses, working down from Sloane Square, include the Kenco Coffee House, the Chelsea Kitchen, Alexander's, 259, the Casserole and Le Rêve. The Kenco is a surprising meeting-place. It looks like a particularly square olde tea shoppe where you might expect to see only middle-aged ladies in hats munching macaroons. Nevertheless this is where everyone goes for coffee because the seats are comfortable and the uniformed waitresses are indulgent. The Casserole, down towards World's End, is simply a superior bistro – *very* superior since Nureyev started coming. It's not cheap and the waiters tend to lean their dainty hips against the table while taking your order. Still, it's quite a merry establishment. Membership of the Gigolo Club downstairs is exclusively male, so don't go down there if you like women. The Chelsea Kitchen, near the Kenco, is remarkably cheap and reasonably good – 10s. will get you two solid courses and carafe wine. But never stay after the pubs shut or you will be surrounded by boring drunks demanding moussaka and chips. The management and staff here are French and the clientele includes some exotic *au pair* girls.

Linguists wishing to meet *au pair* girls might do worse than to hang about the pram park inside Peter Jones department store in Sloane Square. Otherwise *the* London club for these girls is the Rheingold at 361 Oxford Street, where according to the membership blurb 'the unescorted lady may feel completely at her ease'. The Rheingold is very foreign and in-group – the notice boards in the foyer are covered with multilingual messages and announcements. It is one of the hardest clubs in London to get into. You must be a member, and the management insists that you really do have to be proposed and seconded by current members. It's not, as is usual, just a formality. The police check the Rheingold fairly regularly to make sure that alien minors are not being corrupted, so the nervous caution of the management is understandable.

Cinemas popular with Young Londoners are the King's Road Classic, and the Paris Pullman in Drayton Gardens, where there is a remarkable tradition of audience participation during bad films. There is also the Hampstead Everyman – though it does tend to show the Maxim Gorky Trilogy once every three months – the two excellent Academy Cinemas in Oxford Street, and the arty-tarty National Film Theatre on South Bank.

The two youngest and most experimental theatres in London are the Royal Court in Sloane Square and the London Traverse Company at the Jeannetta Cochrane Theatre in Holborn. The Traverse stages lunchtime entertainments for sandwich-eating office workers, rush-hour matinées for commuters who want to avoid the worst of the squash, and late-night try-out programmes for the Way Out. The Traverse seems to have links of sympathy with a new bookshop called Indica in Mason's Yard right next to the Scotch of St James's. Here you can buy good new books, doubtful *avant garde* books, the *Los Angeles Free Press*, and quantities of enigmatic home-printed verse – and your purchases will be wrapped in paper with a design by Paul McCartney. He is one of the backers of the shop, together with Marianne Faithful's husband, John Dunbar, and Peter Asher, brother of Jane. Interesting bookshops are few and far apart in London, but you probably won't go to read.

Informative about Young London, and sometimes readable, are the following publications:

Melody Maker *New Musical Express*	Principal weekly pop journals – report the pop, jazz and folk worlds.
Rave *Teenscene* *Petticoat*	Best of the under-18s' pop-feature magazines. Deluge of interviews with pop-stars and close attention to what's in and what's out. Readers generally referred to as 'fans'. Tough agony columns deal with topics such as unmarried motherhood and rape.
What's On 'Briefing' section of the *Observer*	Weekly information about cinemas, theatres, restaurants, art galleries, etc.
Town *Queen*	London-oriented glossies. First has good monthly guide for restaurants and useful men's clothes section. Second is fortnightly and has spectacular women's fashion and dull society gossip.

Puddings and pies

London can provide food as fine as any in the world. If you want *haute cuisine française* or genuine German cooking then this is no town to be in, but if your tastes run to jellied eels, boiled beef or heavy dumplings then read on. You might have a delightful surprise if you are prepared to face English food with an open mind and mouth. Instead of central heating the English have puddings. They have suet puddings and steamed puddings, cabinet puddings and chocolate puddings, puddings with treacle and puddings with marmalade. They have stout white puddings crammed with currants and raisins, and other fruit, so that more people know a Dalmatian as a 'plum-pudding dog' than know its correct name. English puddings are eaten to keep out the cold and at Christmas the great maestro of puddings comes to the table flaming and splendid. What a shame that so many visitors try them in the middle of summer when few Englishmen would choose to eat them.

The English have not developed one of the world's great cuisines – they have not had to. Plenty of excellent beef, pork and lamb have long been available. In spite of the fact that only fine meat can be roasted, and that roasting is an extravagant way to cook, roast meat has always been the Englishman's first choice. Sunday lunch must be roast meat, it's almost an English law. It still is No. 1 favourite today, according to a recent survey. Simple food – beef, mutton, crab, plaice and sole accompanied by incredible amounts of bread, potatoes, salads and greens – is the English style of eating.

Pies are another British favourite: not only fruit pies, but steak-and-kidney pies, made ideally with flaky pastry, crisp and buttery and golden brown. The Great Fire of London in 1666 broke out in Pudding Lane but the statue that celebrates its end is on Pie Corner.

English cooking is based upon plenty and quality, but this truth is only apparent if you eat in private houses or the best country hotels. The Englishman has no talent for running restaurants. The best restaurants in London are run by foreigners and they cannot be expected to offer English food. So the Londoner at work eats foreign food (curry was in fact third choice in the survey mentioned above). He'll also detour for Italian or Cantonese food.

'Boiled Beef and carrots, that's the stuff for your darby kell, makes you fit and it keeps you well', went the words of the old music-hall song as near as I can remember them. The only places now making boiled beef available to your darby kellies, or bellies, are the Jewish salt-beef bars, and very good they are too, but I do miss my carrots, and my steamed potatoes and dumplings and onions boiled whole around the meat. Still, I can always cook it myself, and that is what a lot of Londoners do. The standard of cooking in middle-class London homes has long since overtaken the average restaurant which, beset by labour costs, rents and licensing laws, has not yet realized that the raw materials are such a small factor of the total cost that it does not pay to buy anything but the best. The next best thing to home cooking might be cooked food from tempting delicatessens. Very few London delis have a place to sit, so eat in the park, or on the top of a bus, or if all else fails in the gloomy – but dry – depths of an Underground station. But don't try eating it in a café, that's just for Paris; here the waiters turn nasty. If they have waitresses, well that's something for the two of you to work out together.

Not long ago I was honoured to be present when one London restaurant proprietor – Tom Benson of Parke's restaurant – cooked a meal for Mario of the Trattoria Terrazza. It was superb, and Mario, congratulating him, said that the menu at the Terrazza had been used as model for almost all the Italian restaurants in London but that Tom's menu could not be copied. Tom Benson is one of the very few proprietors who cook. To see what Mario meant go to Parke's at 4 Beauchamp Place, s w 3 (k e n 1390). It's superb but it's sometimes booked up a couple of days in advance, so book early. Mario's own restaurant – the Terrazza – is in Soho at 19 Romilly Street, w 1 (g e r 8991).

If I was ever consigned to a desert island and could take only one thing with me I would take the Terrazza and all its staff; for then I would have friends, food and home, and wouldn't try too hard to be rescued.

Not only will many London restaurants let you order at 11 or 12 in the evening but it is the most civilized city in the world for lingering late over brandy and cigars. Alvaro was the manager of the Trat until he left to start his own place. Alvaro's is in Chelsea at 124 King's Road, and gets so crowded that unlike most London restaurants there is no menu outside nor any clue except the word Alvaro, and what's more, his phone number is ex-directory. It is k e n 6296.

As would be expected, the rivalry between Alvaro's noisy but tiny restaurant and its prototype the grand Terrazza was quiet but intense during the first few months of operation. Friends were divided, protagonists of each establishment became quite bitter in their arguments. At that time I had to leave England for a month and thus both restaurants were convinced that I had gone over to the enemy. Soon after Alvaro's first opened, a large group of Alvaro's old friends had a meal there. There was exquisite pasta – cooked by Alvaro's aunt who works in the kitchen – and chicken baked in clay; wine from Alvaro's father's home village and then coffee, grappa ruta and cigars, all served with untiring and cheerful attentiveness. When it got to 3.30 a.m. with none of the diners making any movement to go, Ken Adam, sitting at the head of the long table leaned across to Alvaro and said, 'You know, Alvaro, when we stay as late as this at the Trat ...'

'Yes,' said Alvaro, expecting to hear a lavish compliment and thanks.

'... Mario or Franco always sends over a free drink,' said Ken blandly.

In the very heart of Soho on the corner of Old Compton

Street and Dean Street is the Colombino d'Oro. It provides
Italian home cooking at its best. Just say you are hungry and
leave the rest to them. As in all Italian restaurants the greatest
compliment you can gain is not having a spoon for the pasta;
Italians eat it with only a fork.

Some of London's Indian food is outstanding. For anyone
who thinks curries are reheated meat stews with raisin and
apple pieces in them Indian food will be a revelation. There is
(as far as I know) no really good book about Indian food
available in English, so go eat some while you are here.

Indian food can mean either food from that particular
political region or from anywhere on the whole Indian
sub-continent, part of which is now called Pakistan. During
the Indo–Pakistan war many Pakistani restaurants, which for
the sake of simplicity had been happy to sell their curries as
'Indian Food', hastily replaced their signs for ones that said
'Pakistani Food'. The Indian and Pakistani restaurant
proprietors' trade association hastily concluded a
non-aggression pact among their members and you'll notice
that many restaurants compromise nowadays with 'Indo–Pak
Food' signs.

A Hindu restaurant serves only vegetarian dishes and they
will sometimes add the word 'vegetarian' to their sign. These
are the only true Indian restaurants and you will find them in
and around Gower Street where there are many Indian
students. The Saruna Hotel in Great Russell Street is a genuine
Indian restaurant, but that doesn't mean that you will enjoy the
food there more than the food in some of the less genuine ones.
In these Hindu vegetarian restaurants you'll eat *bhajjis*, a curry
of fried vegetables. There are hundreds of varieties. *Brinjal* is
the word for aubergine (egg plant) and a *brinjal bhajji* is one of
the most popular. Taste also the wheat cakes if they have them,
and the very, very sweet desserts.

However you won't find many restaurants have vegetarian
Hindu menus. Most curry restaurants are owned by
Pakistanis. On the menu there are all manner of regional dishes
but most of them will be Madrasi or Southern Indian in
character. Madras curries are wet in texture and very strong in

flavour. They are served with rice, which helps to make the wet
curry manageable. With Indian food the meat and sauce is put
on to the rice (whereas with Chinese food sauces and rice
are kept apart so that the rice is solid enough to eat with
chopsticks). These southern curries are cooked in vegetable
oils, not *ghee*.

Punjabi or Northern Indian food is cooked in animal fat –
such as *ghee* – and served with various flat unleavened breads
and lots of lentils. Sometimes there will be no rice at all, for rice
is grown only in regions where the rivers flood, and just as
certain regional Chinese cooking is without rice, so is some
Punjabi cooking.

The Ashoka, 22 Cranbourn Street, w c 2 (t e m 5936)
specializes in Punjabi cooking.

Unlike Hindu cooking, Pakistani menus have lots of meat
(although not pork, of course), their favourite being mutton and
lamb. Lamb kebabs are usually on the menu somewhere. The
curries are inclined to be dry in texture. Pakistani cooking does
not emphasize rice as strongly as some other regions do. When
rice is served it is often mixed with pieces of meat, almonds,
poultry and vegetables and heaped up decoratively. These dishes
are called *pilaus*. A *birianee* is an assembly of a *pilau* and a
meat dish. Both *pilaus* and *birianees* were brought to India by
the Mongols and in fact one great recipe is called
Moglai birianee.

Many Pakistani dishes have their origin in Persian cooking,
and the Parsees (descendants of ancient Persians who fled from
the Arab conquests of the eighth century) brought, and still
have, some of the most complex and sophisticated dishes in the
whole range of Indo–Pak cooking. *Dhansak* (it can be chicken
or mutton *dhansak*) is a good example of Parsee cooking; it is
served in a lentil sauce that is almost sweet in flavour. Parsees
speak Gujarati and this word sometimes appears on menus to
indicate a Parsee dish.

Jamshid restaurant (mentioned below) serves Parsee dishes.

Most Indo–Pak restaurants have Pakistani owners, red velvet
wallpaper, stars on the ceiling and undrinkable coffee. They will
almost always supply food to be taken away if you go there
with containers. The food is normally eaten with a spoon and

fork although in India or Pakistan it would be scooped up with a folded *chapatti* – a bread pancake – and a little of the *chapatti* eaten at each mouthful. Most inhabitants of that under-nourished sub-continent would have nothing to scoop up except a platter of boiled lentils (*dhall*) which is a high-protein food, easy to grow.

Pappadoms are plate-sized wafer-thin pancakes, not unlike giant potato crisps. Nibble them before, after, or during a meal, or crumble them over it. *Parrattas* are fatty *chapattis*; both of these items come from North India and Pakistan. If you order them it is incorrect to order a plate of rice too, although no one will be very surprised. A small *chapatti* with a savoury filling is called a *puri*.

With your *parrattas* or *chapattis* order a couple of curries. I have selected the most common words found on menus but obviously the waiter will help you choose your meal if you'd like help.

Bhajji is a fried vegetable curry.

Kebab can mean anything from meat balls to meat on skewers. Restaurants, to make their customers happy, usually serve kebab Arab style (lamb, onion, etc., on a metal skewer) rather than unusual Pakistani recipes.

Bhoona means a dryish style of curry. You'll see *bhoona* chicken written on menus but a mutton *bhoona* is usually called by its Pakistani name, *Bhoona ghosht*.

Kooftahs are meat balls or fish balls in curry sauce. Sometimes spelt *Kufta* or *Koftah*.

Korma (or *Quormah*) is the one to have if you want a mild curry. These are always marinaded in curd (a little like yoghurt) before they are cooked.

Madras. This word is just there to warn you that this curry is quite hot.

Vindaloo. This is a very hot and very rich curry cooked in a slow oven. Like most very hot curries it is southern in origin.

With your curry dish order some *sambals*, which are pickle-like side dishes based on uncooked fruit or vegetables.

A *foogath* is a similar dish but it is cooked.

A *bhurta* is a mashed-vegetable side dish.

Don't drink wine with your curry. A light cold beer tastes

good with it but strict Moslems and Hindus never drink
alcohol and would probably have lime juice or lemonade. For
real authenticity do the same. One last tip: if you take some
curry that is too hot for you don't sip at your drink, it will
make you feel hotter, take a mouthful of rice or *chapatti*.
Better still, ask to have some fresh bananas on the table and
take a bite on those.

Among my favourite Indian restaurants is Jamshid at
6 Glendower Place, s w 7, very close to South Kensington
Underground station. It's a very small restaurant, so book early
(k n i 2309). For excellent Indian food to take away (they
supply foil packs and containers), try the Agra, 135 Whitfield
Street, w 1. Order from e u s 8833 if you like, but they take
only ten minutes for many dishes.

Until very recently almost all Chinese food on sale here was
Cantonese because Canton was the part of China that abutted
the Crown Colony of Hong Kong. Now there are many Chinese
restaurants selling other types of Chinese food, such as the
Kuo Yuan at 217 High Road, Willesden Green, n w 10
(w i l 2297). Allow an extra few minutes for the taxi ride; this
one is not in the centre of town. The food is Pekin and the
cook used to be at the Chinese Embassy, so it's rather special.

There are also a number of Greek restaurants here run by
Greek Cypriots. Because of the bitter feeling and fighting in
Cyprus, some Greek restaurants will not write 'Turkish
coffee' on their menus. Luckily some of the best ones don't
have menus so it doesn't arise. 'Coffee?' they ask. I just nod.

Greek food of tip-top style, quality and expense is served
at the White Tower, 1 Percy Street, w 1 (m u s 8141).

For details of hundreds more restaurants, hotels and pubs
buy the *Egon Ronay B M C Guide* (25s.) at any bookshop. It
gives details and ratings of hotels, restaurants and pubs for
the whole of Britain, as also does Raymond Postgate's excellent
Good Food Guide (18s.) to which readers send their reports.

Food

Adrian Bailey

Born 1928, in St Albans, Hertfordshire, under the sign of Aquarius. Moved home sixteen times and went to six schools. Two of these were art schools, admirable for their complement of girls, excellent for their total lack of *esprit de corps* and discipline.

Finds self-discipline immensely difficult. Cannot bear people who will not concede that there is more than one point of view. Hates all forms of competitive sport with the sole exception of judo. Has worked as a labourer, a barman, a bookshop assistant, a caretaker, a Post Office clerk, a film extra, a male model, a photographer, a copywriter, illustrator and journalist. Would like to go to Japan for six months. Likes almost all women, music and animals, cooking and drinking, travelling and driving.

French cuisine, like the French themselves, prefers to stay in France; it is simply not an exportable commodity. The big-name, high-class London restaurants often flourish blanket-size menus, full of beautifully written exaggerations. The restaurants are dulled with an atmosphere of middle-aged complacency. The staff, cooks, waiters and the maître d'hotel are rarely French, often Swiss, Austrian or Italian, yet they drop sibilant gallicisms like hot rivets plunging in a pail of water. One might occasionally meet with a place run by a rogue Frenchman who would never have made a cook anyway, even in France, but my main complaint is that when a restaurant succeeds in producing a fair imitation of French cuisine, they charge far in excess of their achievement. However, all is not lost. The best places to eat at are the less expensive restaurants, and pubs. There are many in London which I will recommend with the greatest of pleasure. The Italian restaurants, some Italians tell me, are often better than those in Italy. The Trattoria Terrazza in Romilly

Street, Soho, known to its regulars as the 'Trat', is friendly, bustling, even exciting. Mario and Franco, who own the Terrazza and that richer confection in Mayfair, the Tiberio, sit astride their two restaurants like anticipatory holiday makers on a tandem. The Terrazza is not too expensive, the food is good, and the welcome is genuine.

Pasta has almost become the staple diet of Londoners. Spaghetti, ravioli and lasagne are featured on the menus of many non-Italian restaurants, and even in pubs. Londoners who have never been to Italy are nonchalantly dextrous with a forkful of gleaming spaghetti al pesto. Some of them even learn enough *cucina*-Italian to convey the impression that they know much more. '*Due cafe neri,*' one hears them command, 'and may we have another carafe of *vino rosso*?' '*Vino rosso!*' shouts the waiter, accenting the words and loving the sound they make, '*e due neri!*'

Italian has crept into our everyday conversation; words like *grazie* and *ciao* are now part of the English language. We too have our *dolce vita*, and we love our Italian restaurants. The Osteria San Lorenzo in Beauchamp Place is generally so crowded that you should book well in advance. The structure of an Italian home is based on family solidarity. Like other restaurants of its type, the San Lorenzo is a family business and we are its children. This is home cooking of a high standard; it is also remarkably inexpensive. Walter Mariti's restaurant, the Pontevecchio, at the Earls Court end of Brompton Road, Alvaro's and Don Luigi, both in the King's Road, Chelsea, are all bright, gay and cheerful places to spend an evening.

Many London pubs serve good, simple food at good, simple prices. At the Hand and Flower, opposite Olympia, there is always something to eat and one frequently receives a personal welcome from the owner, Mr Jack Levy, or from his son, an almost unheard-of courtesy in a pub. The restaurant upstairs specializes in oysters, jugged hare and grills. The oysters, Mr Levy told me, were X-rayed to ensure perfection, and they arrived every morning by train from Whitstable. The Hand and Flower also provides breakfasts for non-residents, from 9 to 10.30 on Sundays and 8 to 9.30 on weekdays. Another pub-restaurant where oysters and English cooking are a speciality is

De Hems in Macclesfield Street, Soho, where the walls are entirely covered in oyster shells. Bentley's in Swallow Street, off Piccadilly, apart from having an oyster bar, also sells lobster bisque freshly tinned, fresh oysters, lobsters and smoked salmon to take home. Emberson's in Shepherd Street, Mayfair, is a free vintner. Like Gordon's Wine House in Villiers Street, near Charing Cross tube station, it has an age-old charter which allows it to sell drink without the usual licence, and it is not obliged to keep to specified trading hours. Unlike Gordon's, Emberson's has an oyster bar, and here one can choose from a variety of seafood and a wide selection of wines. Emberson's also has a fine vintage 1950 Cockburn port, if you don't mind paying 12s. 6d. a glass for it.

London abounds in seafood restaurants: Wheeler's, Prunier's, Cunningham's, Scott's, Overton's, Wilton's, Sheekey's. Which are the best? I must confess to not knowing; I adore fish, yet I cannot make up my mind and can do little to help you to make up yours. Try Manzi's or Sheekey's. Manzi's ground-floor restaurant in Leicester Street, called the House of Hamburger, is open from noon until midnight. Sheekey's, in St Martin's Court off Charing Cross Road, gets so crowded that you may have to share a table. The huge portions of steamed white fish – turbot, halibut and sole – are simple and excellent. This is really a lunch or pre-theatre restaurant, since it closes at 8.30 p.m., and specializes in Whitstable oysters and lobsters from the Orkneys – fresh daily.

Sheekey's may intercept its consignment of lobsters off the train at King's Cross, but most fish is cleared at Billingsgate Market. This market is so old that it has its place in folk literature. Smithfield and the Borough markets are pretty old, too, but not as old as Billingsgate. Smithfield, once called 'Smoothfield', was the centre for such pursuits as archery, jousting, public floggings and executions, and became a meat market in 1615. But Billingsgate was there before the Romans came. It was the first port of London, called Belin's Gate in the fifth century, and faced the Saxon military barracks at Suthringageweorc across the river, now named Southwark, where you'll find the Borough Market.

At six o'clock in the morning the Billingsgate bell goes clang!

and the market opens. The entire area below the Monument –
Fish Hill and Pudding Lane – becomes alive with white-coated,
wooden-hatted porters. Above the market hall a tall iron chimney stretches a thread of black smoke taut against the early sky.
Inside the market are live lobsters from Whitby, Prussian blue,
packed in wood shavings; live crabs, zodiac, pink and doomed;
eels in their galvanized trays, eels with a jellied destiny, lubri-
cated, cartilaginous and tortile, by rail from a Dutch or Irish
eel boat; mackerel from Newlyn, stiff rainbow-hued mackerel
with bright eyes; cod, hake, turbot and whiting from Hull,
Fleetwood, Aberdeen and Bridlington. Huge fish, headless butts,
packed in ice; a buyer bends down and looks under the gills to
see if it's fresh.

Over the river at the Borough Market you can have a rum
and coffee in the Wheatsheaf, Stoney Street, at six in the morning (it is allowed an extended licence for the porters) if you
don't look too much like a tourist – and buy a hundredweight
of Jersey cauliflower or broccoli. The market begins at the top
of Southwark Street, full of hop merchants and wine cellars,
including Becky's Dive Bar, the oldest Free House in London.
The brewers buy most of their hops from this street; the Hop
Marketing Board has its headquarters here and the local telephone exchange for Southwark and the Borough is H O P, for
this reason.

The markets of London thrive like mad, and no wonder.
London's stable population, plus the passing tourist trade, has a
voracious appetite. Each year we eat an average of 53 lb. a head
of beef and veal, and about 26 lb. of mutton and lamb. Britain
imports over 370,000 tons of beef and veal in addition to our
own produce. Londoners eat more fruit and green vegetables
than do people anywhere else in the country. Every day Londoners boil, poach, fry and scramble, over eight million eggs.
London waits in hungry anticipation, fork poised, while express
trains and road transport rush a thousand tons of potatoes from
Lincolnshire, broccoli from Cornwall, brussels sprouts from
Bedford, frozen peas from Norfolk, and perhaps 6,000 tons of
butter and bacon from Ireland, which also sends us 7,000,000
gallons of Guinness a year. There are ten main markets which
feed London, not counting the railway terminus markets like

King's Cross and Somertown, held in Ossulston Street and in York Way, N W 1, where the potatoes arrive every day from Spalding in Lnicolnshire. There used to be others: Cheapside was a market for the west of London, Eastcheap for the east. Milk Street was a milk market, Bread Street sold bread. Hence too Honey Lane, Pudding Lane, Poultry, Beer Street and Friday Street, where fish was sold on Fridays. Leadenhall market, perhaps the smallest and certainly the prettiest in London, still exists to retail poultry and fish. Leadenhall's cream-and-maroon-painted Victorian ironwork, erected in 1881 at a cost of £99,000, is a vaulted ventricle in the beating heart of the City and is worth going to see just before lunch, for you are in chop-house land. The chop houses are there for one purpose only: to feed financiers, press barons, captains of industry and lesser mortals (bowler hat, furled umbrella) during the frantic lunch-hour. The waitresses call you 'dear' and serve you so fast that they could probably fill a table four times in one hour. Dickens again; the George and Vulture in St Michael's Alley, off Cornhill, built in 1661, has a speciality called Pickwick pudding, for Dickens used to come here and to Simpson's chop house just round the corner, to eat steak-and-kidney pie with his ale.

If you were to follow the behaviour of Dickens over a week you would be drunk on Monday, an alcoholic on Tuesday and dead by Friday. Simpson's little bow-windowed entrance at 38½ Cornhill is delightful, and worth a visit, even if you go merely to look at it, since the food is definitely for the English taste – the meat is always good, the veg rarely. It's the same with the other Simpson's, the famous one in the Strand, *the* place to go for lunch; but if you do, be sure and have a double portion of roast beef or saddle of lamb, and don't forget to tip the carver a couple of shillings. The vegetables leave much to be desired, but the Stilton is worth having, likewise the apple pie. There are three restaurants that serve traditional English food and are so well patronized, particularly by Americans, that success has blunted the fine edge of excellence. They are still, however, worth visiting, although booking is essential. One is a pub, the Cheshire Cheese in Fleet Street, famous for its beefsteak pudding, the other two are restaurants in the grand manner:

Simpson's in the Strand and Rule's in nearby Maiden Lane. Rule's is Edwardian Theatrical, where the play's the thing, and so is the steak-and-kidney pie. All three are closed on Sunday.

The chop houses and wine bars in the City would reward months of study, but one lunch-hour under the shadow of St Michael's Church, Cornhill, is worth while. Here is almost a village: the church, a little square, Simpson's, the George and Vulture, and the Jamaica Wine House. Here in 1652 stood London's first coffee house, at the sign of the Pasqua Rosee's Head. In the wine house you can digest a slice of history, and wash it down with a glass of vintage port. When it was a coffee house there used to be a box on the wall inscribed, 'To insure promptness', since abbreviated to TIP – the birth of the gratuity. In most London restaurants it is customary to tip between 10 and 12 per cent for services rendered, and correspondingly less if you consider that service hasn't been rendered at all.

City pubs have as much claim to your attention as the chop houses. The Olde Dr Butler's Head in Mason's Avenue, just off Coleman Street, is a good place to go for lunch, especially if you like Pimm's, which is a speciality here. Another pub with a reputation for good food is Ye Olde Watling in Watling Street. Most City eating-places don't bother to open during the evening or the weekend; all the trade has gone home and there's a lot of competition from the West End, where some of the restaurants are open all night.

Indian restaurants stay open late; and many are open all day, every day of the year except Christmas. They are open during our national holidays, and theirs: right through Easter, August Bank Holiday and Ramadan. Your time is their time; the service is always willing if not completely efficient – although one is rarely bugged by the petty irritations which haunt our restaurants: dishes in Indian restaurants are rarely 'off' the menu. The décor is curious though. The interiors look like a Bombay wallpaper showroom; there's often a different pattern on each wall and one for the ceiling. They are an uncertain mixture of East and West, an odd blend of Simla and Surbiton. But the food is great, genuine Maharajah Indian, and something that I miss terribly if I am away from England for long. If you like really hot curry, ask for a Vindaloo or a Madras curry. Dhansak and Korma curries are much milder, containing little or no chilli at all; yellow rice, *chapattis*, *pappadoms* and *dhall* are essentials. Wine doesn't go with curry: beer or water is best. The kind of food that Punjabi Maharajahs ate in Peshawar and Rawalpindi in the old North-West Frontier Province is served at the Tandoori restaurant, 153 Fulham Road, sw3. The interior bears little resemblance to the Punjab, but the food is unusual and very good. There is a set meal should the complexity of the menu confuse you, or ask the owners to guide you through the menu.

Stay out all night and, if you are hungry at four in the morning, there is a special à la carte menu at the Barrie Room, Kensington Palace Hotel, until 7 a.m. More or less opposite, the Maze Coffee House under the Royal Garden Hotel has an all-night service. You can have a hamburger à l'anglaise at the Wimpy bar in the Earls Court Road, open all night; a steak and more at the Steak Encore in Leicester Square, also open all night. The Elegant Bistro, 272 Brompton Road, sw3, not far from South Kensington Underground, is a restaurant where one can order the meal with the universal appeal – steak, salad, wine, cheese and coffee – until 1 a.m.; there seem to be any number of people who prefer to eat in the early hours of the morning. Breakfast is served at Guys n' Dolls in the King's Road, Chelsea, from 10 a.m. right up until it becomes lunch. The West London Air Terminal runs a 24-hour service for early and late birds. The Lyons Corner Houses in Coventry Street and the Strand will cook bacon and eggs for you from 7.30 a.m. to 11 p.m. including Sundays. Dawn arrivals at Victoria Station can breakfast at the Chicken Inn, open from 5.30 a.m. including Sundays. The King's Restaurant at 235 King's Road, sw3, is open for breakfast *only on Sunday*; you can sit around until the pubs open at noon when you might care to follow the crowd to the Queen's Elm or Finch's in the Fulham Road.

In England, Sunday lunch is a ritual. The men go to the pub and drink pints of beer while the women stay home and cook the roast, a vast selection of vegetables, perhaps a Yorkshire pudding, and a filling dessert with custard. The men return home with a mighty hunger, eat everything in sight, and then pass out under the Sunday newspaper. Among restaurants that provide Sunday lunch and dinner are the Belvedere, set in Holland Park and surrounded by trees and gardens; Lyons Corner Houses, which have excellent roast beef; the Hand and Flower opposite Olympia; and the majority of Steak Houses. If you are going to lunch *en famille* and want a restaurant in the grand style, try the Empress at 15 Berkeley Street, w 1; they make a special point of catering for children and serve half portions. The restaurant in the Zoo at Regent's Park also caters for family lunches, and is open on Sunday, but will not accept bookings, so you may have to queue.

The physiology of the English Sunday will one day undergo a welcome change, but until then the Shops Act makes it impossible to buy fish and chips to take away and eat. Every other day of the week fish-and-chip shops, national as cricket, exude a beckoning aroma of batter-clad fried fish, pickled onions, vinegar and fat-impregnated newspaper: an aroma that should be caught and canned for the delight of expatriate Englishmen abroad.

Another national characteristic, as indigenous to London as a Saturday night knees-up in the boozer, are the jellied-eel, whelk, cockle and mussel stalls. There's usually one in Cambridge Circus, white-lit by naphtha lamp, where the *aficionados* eat jellied eels with a hunk of white bread, and spit the bones on the pavement. King among the shellfish-stall owners is Tubby Isaacs, who operates one of his many stalls in Goulston Street, opposite the Hoop and Grapes in Whitechapel. If you don't like standing on a street corner while eating your eels, there are plenty of eel and pie shops all over South London and the East End. The pies are usually meat pies cooked on the premises. The eels are eaten stewed with a parsley-flavoured 'liquor' poured over them, or jellied in bowls. Until recently there was an eel and pie shop in the Elephant and Castle, run by a friend of mine, which had traditional pew seats, zinc counter, mirrored walls and staircase. All the fine old shops are fast disappearing to make way for new buildings and car parks; the one in Brixton Market has now gone, but Joyce's at 20 Tower Bridge Road, s E 1, by the Bricklayers' Arms, still exists, as it has done for well over a hundred years. For the modern version try Arment's at 278 Walworth Road, S E 17, or Lou Hart's seafood restaurant at 294.

The finest smoked salmon comes from Wentworth Street behind Bloom's kosher restaurant in Whitechapel. If you are Jewish, you may like to know that Wentworth and Old Montague Streets have many shops selling Jewish specialities. This area is Saltbeefsville, but if you hunger after gefillte fish or latkes when in Soho, try Grahame's Sea Fare restaurant in Poland Street, Folman's in Noel Street, or, for a salt-beef sandwich, the Nosh Bar in Windmill Street.

Sandwich shops abound to feed the mid-day lunch-hungries who haven't the time or money for more than a snack. The Kahawa Coffee House in Brook Street, Mayfair, sells sandwiches made with wholemeal bread; very good they are too. Benoît Bulcke, the continental butcher in Old Compton Street, Soho, makes marvellous beef or pork sandwiches, and also ones with unusual fillings like game pâté, rillettes, and goose liver. Le Petit Café in Stafford Street, just off Bond Street, an Italian restaurant with a French name, has a window full of luscious sandwiches and also a restaurant upstairs which is cheap, quick and good; I remember its oeufs sur le plat sizzling in butter served with crisp French bread. The Catherine Wheel, a pub in Church Street, Kensington, makes the best roast beef sandwiches I've ever had – thick slices of rare beef between wholemeal bread.

At the Moka Bar in Greek Street, London's first espresso coffee house, you can get a plate of really excellent spaghetti, rigatoni, tagliatelle or ravioli and afterwards a slice of cheesecake and a cup of strong espresso coffee. You may have to stand to eat because space is limited, but they will serve you as fast as you can eat. Just around the corner in Old Compton Street the Pasticceria Amalfi gives a fairly fast service, but gets very crowded at lunch-time, and the tuna-fish salad or pizzas are worth having. The Kebab and Homous Restaurant, 95 Charlotte Street, sells, not unnaturally, kebab, and also a bread called 'pita' that looks like an oven glove and is usually stuffed with meat, raw onions and tomatoes. Castell beer goes well with it.

The Hungry Horse in the Fulham Road, which also has a

pie-shop where you can buy pies to take home, serves huge portions of classic English puddings and pies: steak-and-kidney puddings and pies, Queen's pudding, Dorothy's pudding and bread-and-butter pudding. Dieters beware!

For vegetarians there is the Cranks' Salad Table in Carnaby Street or the Vega in Whitcomb Street by Leicester Square; neither restaurant has a licence to sell drink, by the way. The London Health Centre in Baker Street has branches in Finchley Road and Kensington Church Street, where one can buy vegetarian specialities.

You can buy a complete cook-it-yourself *couscous* kit from Roche in Old Compton Street, which even sells those big, tasty French tomatoes, when in season. You can eat Malay Satay in the Singapore restaurant in Allen Street, w 8, and a number of shops in Soho sell tinned chocolate-coated ants or snake steaks. One exception: you can't buy real French bread in London, it simply isn't the same; but anyone will tell you that the ice-cream in the Marine Ice Cream Parlour at the bottom of Haverstock Hill, Chalk Farm, is the best outside Italy.

Derry & Toms in Kensington High Street is the only store in Europe with a garden (ornamental pond, goldfish, ducks, tree-shaded inglenooks, fountains) on the roof, and a panoramic view over London. The restaurant serves morning coffee, lunch and tea, and is licensed. Access to the roof garden costs one shilling, the money goes to charity; the visit is worthwhile. It is closed Saturday afternoon and Sunday.

A number of firms are famous for their chocolates. At Charbonnel et Walker of Bond Street you can order a box of chocolates containing an appropriate personal message, in moulded chocolate, such as 'Thanks for a lovely weekend.' Ackermans, 43 Kensington Church Street, w 8, also make hand-made chocolates, and special boxes of chocolates for diabetics. Searcy Tansley, 19 Sloane Street, s w 1, make marvellous bittersweet after-dinner mints, and when you go there remember that they make the finest treacle tarts outside the farmhouse kitchen. Searcy also make up special dishes, like coq au vin or lemon soufflé, to order.

Dial E M P ress 5121, and the Home Meal Delivery Service will provide you, usually within the hour, with a hot, ready-to-eat duck à l'orange and a bottle of Mateus rosé, well chilled. The service operates every day of the year, and it has over a hundred items on the menu. Nick's Diner has an even more ambitious selection: the service is called Movable Feasts, FLA 1022, and will provide a complete three-course meal for six people, as it did once for me, sending along some salmon profiterolles and dish of lamb Provençal. But remember, they require at least a day's notice.

If you go to eat at Nick's Diner, 88 Ifield Road, SW 10, the fillet of beef en croûte is a speciality worth trying. This is the only restaurant where I can accept the description of dishes on the menu. It makes no false claims; if they say the dishes are good, they usually *are* good.

The tea most commonly drunk in England is Indian, served with milk and sugar. It is a beverage that lubricates the entire nation, and can usually be commanded at any hour of the day or night; indeed, many people cannot get out of bed until they have had a cup of tea.

Most of the big hotels serve tea, notably the Ritz and Claridge's, where there is sometimes a piano trio to play such tea-time numbers as 'Fascination' or a selection from *Rose Marie*. It's so reminiscent of between-the-wars insouciance as to be almost unbearable. Tea is served gracefully and with ritual. The cakes are miniature, the sandwiches fine as porcelain and the atmosphere tranquil. Fortnum & Mason's, which should be treated with the respect due to all national monuments, also serves tea. Then of course there's Fuller's in Regent Street, or Bendick's in Wigmore Street. Gloriette opposite Harrods and Maison Bertaux in Greek Street, Soho, both serve tea or coffee plus a selection of the most tempting carbohydrates ever devised. Most of the big stores serve tea, and the Ceylon Tea Centre in Lower Regent Street or the India Tea Centre in Oxford Street can hardly be expected to serve anything else. Tea of the English home-made cake variety can be had at the House of Peter up at the north end of Gloucester Road – country teashop oak tables, sponge cake and macaroons. Maison Bertaux and Gloriette are open on Saturday afternoon but closed on Sunday. Most of the teashops in central London are closed on Sunday, but the House of Peter is open, and so is

Daquise, a Polish restaurant that serves delicious continental pastries, at 20 Thurloe Street, South Kensington.

Kenco Coffee Houses have sprung up all over the place. Most of them are licensed, and serve such items as Quiche Lorraine or frankfurters with potato salad, a selection of hamburgers, spaghetti and a variety of salads. They serve breakfast, tea and supper and the standard is uniformly good. The one in Kensington High Street specializes in Breton crêpes and omelettes. They all serve many varieties of coffee and tea.

Most of the steak houses, like Peter Evans, Angus or the London Steak Houses, have the same menu at all their branches. You can have potted shrimps, smoked fish or perhaps pâté, steak or chops, baked jacket potato and salad, followed by cheese or fruit pie. These are simple, well run and pleasant restaurants and very reasonable – especially for the carafe wines.

There are several bright stars in the London firmament which exert a strong gravitational pull on the public. Apart from such supernovae as Alvaro's, with Alvaro at the centre of gravity, there is Nick's Diner, run by Nick Clarke; Parke's in Beauchamp Place spins around Tom Benson; and a new north star is Robert Carrier's very pretty restaurant at 2 Camden Passage, Islington, which was booked up for months in advance, even before it opened. I had the first meal ever served there; the high standard gives me good reason to predict its continuing success. That may sound a trifle pompous, but at the time of writing Carrier's is in its infancy, and I am very hopeful that my judgement is neither inaccurate nor premature.

I don't know how many restaurants there are per head of the population, but they all get pretty crowded, especially at lunchtime; so, except for the large multiple eating places like Lyons Corner Houses, it is best to book. Since Somerset Maugham said, 'If you want to eat well in England, have breakfast three times a day,' London has changed. It has now become a place where food is something that you can eat, something that you can enjoy and something that you may even remember.

Here are some useful telephone numbers:

Ackermans, WES 4359
Alvaro's, KEN 6296
Arment's, ROD 9414

Belvedere, W E S 4641
Bendick's, W E L 7272
Bentley's, R E G 4756
Blooms, B I S 6001

Carrier, Robert, C A N 5353
Catherine Wheel, W E S 3259
Charbonnel et Walker, M A Y 4396
Cheshire Cheese, F L E 9129
Chicken Inn, Victoria, V I C 6535
Claridge's, M A Y 8860
Crank's Salad Table, G E R 9431

Daquise, K E N 6117
Derry & Toms, W E S 8181
De Hems, G E R 2494
Don Luigi, S L O 3023

Elegant Bistro, K N I 1668
Emberson's, G R O 1906
Empress, M A Y 6126

Folman's, G E R 2250
Fortnum & Mason, R E G 8040
Fuller's (Regent Street), R E G 4948

George and Vulture, H O P 4561
Grahame's Sea Fare, G E R 3788
Guys n' Dolls, K N I 1873

Hand & Flower, F U L 1000
Hart, Lou, R O D 9947
House of Peter, K N I 6744
Hungry Horse, F L A 7757

Kahawa Coffee House, M A Y 2730
Kebab & Homous, M U S 3144
Kenco (Kensington High Street), W E S 8121
King's Restaurant, F L A 2417

Lyons Corner House (Coventry Street), G E R 7431
Lyons Corner House (Strand), W H I 7373

Manzi's, G E R 5131
Maze Coffee House, W E S 8000
Moka Bar, G E R 6858

Nick's Diner, FLA 0930
Nosh Bar, GER 9518

Osteria San Lorenzo, KNI 1074

Parke's, KEN 1390
Pasticceria Amalfi, GER 7284
Pontevecchio, FRE 9082

Ritz, HYD 8181
Roche, GER 4588
Rule's, TEM 5314

Searcy Tansley, KNI 3344
Sheekey's, TEM 4118
Simpson's (Cornhill), MAN 8901
Simpson's (Strand), 836–9112
Singapore Restaurant, WES 5854
Steak Encore, WHI 4828

Tandoori Restaurant, 589–7749
Tiberio, MAY 3561
Trattoria Terrazza, GER 8991

Vega, WHI 9612

West London Air Terminal (restaurant), FRO 4224

Ye Olde Watling, CIT 6235

Zoo (restaurant), PRI 3544

Quenching your thirst

One of the greatest disappointments for visitors to Britain is the price of Scotch whisky. One expects watches to be cheapest in Switzerland – they aren't – and cameras to be dirt cheap in Japan – they are – but panting, thirsty visitors determined to recoup their fares by an endless flow of cheap whisky feel angry and cheated. In fact there are few places on earth where whisky – or any other alcohol – is as expensive as it is in Britain. So stick to beer. Many pubs serve cheese, sausages and pork pie and keep food prices down to encourage drinking customers in the lunch hour.

Pubs have doors marked 'public' where the furnishings are the simplest of wooden seats with sawdust on the floor. In the public bar the beer is at its cheapest. Other doors marked 'saloon' or even posher 'lounge' – have soft chintzy décor and a penny or two on the prices. 'Jug and bottle' is a counter for selling bottled beer where they will fill your jug with beer so there is no charge on the bottle. 'Off Licence' is sometimes a part of a pub or sometimes a separate shop. In either case it's a place where alcohol can be bought but not consumed. It has a licence for alcohol to be sold for consumption off the premises.

If you are looking for the best value available in cooked lunches, try asking at the public bar counter of a pub. Very often they will give you a handful of bent cutlery and an excellent hot, meat-and-two-veg-style, meal. It will come across the counter and there'll be no salt, pepper, service, or tablecloth and sometimes not even a table, but it will probably be superb value for money. Food served in pubs is subsidized by the breweries.

Pubs are a curious institution. Professor Higgins said that any Englishman's accent will make some other Englishman despise him. And any Englishman's pub will also make some other Englishman despise him.

One man's 'snuggery' is another man's chi-chi. The cheerful atmosphere that will make one man glow down to his chukka boots will make another incandescent with rage. As a visitor you might want to tour a selection of pubs, but few Londoners truly enjoy doing so. They go to the pubs they like and to them remain ever faithful. Perhaps the most easily disliked pubs in London are the completely phoney ones like the 'Cockney Pride' behind Piccadilly, but there are, according to Adrian Bailey, another 6,999 pubs in London, of which he chooses one or two.

Drink

Adrian Bailey

London stretches her red-brick fingers into the country gardens of the Home Counties until even the suburban becomes urban. Sprawling across the Thames from Kingston to Erith Causeway, her face is lined with streets and richly freckled by over 7,000 pubs.

For me, eleven o'clock in the morning is the best time to get the atmosphere of a pub. You may well have the bar all to yourself, or share it with one quietly desperate stout-drinker who has been leaning with recusant pressure on the doors of the public bar, waiting for opening time.

Order a half-pint of best bitter, preferably drawn from the wood. Sip it contemplatively, taste it as one tastes wine, for here is the best beer in the world, full-flavoured and strong. The stout-drinker will have downed a pint by now and pushed his glass, brown froth clinging, across the bar for a refill. He can't wait, but you can. Indeed you must, for you are on the edge of discovery. The full awakening, the rich reward of your perseverance, may take time to develop, like under-exposed film.

I have seen people, when introduced to their first glass of bitter, pull a wry face and give a convulsive shudder, 'Ugh! I don't like it.' They haven't given themselves, or the beer, a chance. Do they expect it to taste like Empire Nutty Oloroso? English beer has taken centuries to perfect; the palate needs – *deserves* – to be trained in appreciation. If, finally, you decide that bitter is not for you, don't despair. Each to his own taste. Try mild ale, dark and sweeter than bitter, or, if you can find a pub that keeps it, try Burton, sometimes called 'Old'. This is a strong, dark and sweet draught beer, similar to stout and often mixed in the glass with mild ale when it becomes a popular winter drink in the public bar, known as 'Old and Mild'. Burton is difficult to find in southern England, and may one day disappear altogether, like porter or like the old 'Shrub' which I last saw in the wine cellar of the Cedars Hotel, West Kensington, in 1945. Burton is traditionally brewed at Burton-on-Trent in the Midlands, although many London breweries make a Burton-type ale. Truman's Burton, a real Burton-brewed ale, can be found at the Duke of St Albans, Swaine's Lane, Highgate, and at the Assembly House, 292 Kentish Road, Kentish Town. Most pubs sell Burton only from mid-October to March, so be sure of the season.

Nearly all pubs, with few exceptions, open in the morning at 11, close at 3 in the afternoon (Sundays 12 until 2), open again at 5.30 and close at 11 p.m. (Sundays 7 until 10.30). This complex arrangement of licensing hours, which must be learned like a mathematical table, exasperates the English and puzzles foreigners, who are unable to understand why we put up with something that we so plainly dislike.

Londoners sometimes refer to pubs, vulgarly, as 'Boozers'. Pub is short for Public House, but why Boozer? Booze came from the Middle English word 'bousen', which was sixteenth-century thieves' cant, taken from the Dutch word 'busen', and the German 'bausen', meaning to drink to excess. Beer and ale are Old English words that nowadays mean the same thing – any malt-fermented alcohol drink. Ale once meant a beer without hops. Bitter, flavoured with hops to give a slightly bitter taste, is a beer, and mild ale, also flavoured with hops, is a beer.

Every morning, in every pub, the bar staff or the cellarman has to 'bottle up', that is, replenish the depleted shelves of bottled beer from the cellar. When the pub opens you will find a well-stocked selection aligned on the shelves with pride and precision, like a company of soldiers in dress uniform. They shine cleanly, these bottles, a bright highlight staring from the warm brown glass; crown caps, each a different colour according to the type of beer: yellow for pale ale, red for brown ale, green or blue for stout. Some of the soldiers are from different regiments: Charrington's Toby Ale; Ind Coope's Double Diamond (works wonders); Guinness (is good for you); Ben Truman (more hops); Watney's (what we want is); Stingo, Red Barrel,

Dairymaid Stout; John Courage (in Courage houses the cognos-
centi call for J.C.); Barclay Wine; powerful Colne Spring Ale
brewed by Ind Coope; and the formidable Courage Imperial
Russian Stout, reputed to be the strongest bottled beer ever
brewed; try a glass when you visit a Courage house.

Most bottled beers are quite lively and highly carbonated,
especially pale ale, which is why you will see the barmaid tilting
the glass to meet the neck of the bottle; it avoids too frothy a
head. Otherwise you have to stick your nose in three inches of
cold froth before you get to the beer. Another beer which has
now disappeared is Reid's Stout. When my father was tenant
of the Stanley Arms, Pimlico, flattened by a bomb during the
war and recently rebuilt (the pub, not my father), Reid's Stout
was the favourite tipple in the public bar. He used to display a
baby's feeding bottle with a Reid's label stuck on the side
'because,' he said, 'my customers were weaned on it.'

You have to live in a pub, as I did, to really appreciate the
changes in mood and atmosphere, which vary each hour of the
day. Before opening time there is a beautiful, virgin aroma of
freshness, an inimitable pub-perfume mixture of hops and malt,
spirits and polish with perhaps a faint touch of violet-scented
air-freshener. This is my boyhood nostalgia. Spilt ale, dried
and sugar-sticky. The beer 'engines' and the black ebony (or
sometimes rare coloured ceramic) pump handles that draw the
beer through red rubber-jointed glass pipes (which jump with
a reflex when the pumps are pulled) from a barrel in the cellar
and up through the bar floor. Shifting those barrels, or carrying
crates of bottled beer – twelve bottles to a crate – up from the
cellar is hard work. This is why the leather-aproned brewer's
draymen sink two pints each of draught ale at nine in the
morning.

London has more than a thousand tiny, back-street pubs that
have barely changed in a century. You will never find all of
them, and neither will I, for it would take more than a lifetime.
Many are well hidden and jealously guarded by a handful of
customers who always remain faithful, and refer to their
favourite pub as 'my local'.

Each pub is an individual, just as you are an individual, just
as you are extrovert or introvert, boisterious or aloof and

sophisticated, bawdy or reflective. Some are quick to reveal their personality, like the punch-up pubs in Camden Town, Praed Street and the Harrow Road. On a Saturday noon, when the crushed, empty pay-packets are scuffed underfoot in the public bar, a fist in the face is as satisfying as a pint of draught stout – if you are Irish.

The character of the customer reflects the character of the pub. There are boating pubs like the London Apprentice at Isleworth, decorated with sculls, pennants and navigation lights, or the City Barge, Strand-on-the-Green, Kew; there are pubs for airline pilots and globe-trotters, like the Goat in Stafford Street, w 1; there are pubs for humorists, like the Punch Tavern in Fleet Street, and pubs for printers, like the Printer's Devil in Fetter Lane. There are painters' pubs, writers' pubs, dockers' pubs, market pubs, theatrical pubs, police and lawyers' pubs. The riverside pubs along the Thames embellish London like a necklace of pearls: the London Apprentice, the City Barge and the Bull's Head at Strand-on-the-Green, the Black Lion and the Dove at Hammersmith, the Anchor at Bankside and the all-too-famous Prospect of Whitby at Wapping.

There are pubs in London so old that it's a miracle they have survived. Charrington the brewers have spared no expense to keep the old Hoop and Grapes from falling into Aldgate High Street. Built in the thirteenth century, this ancient monument is now strengthened with hidden steel supports to prevent it sinking to its knees under the heel of time. The Olde Wine Shades is in Martin Lane, just off Cannon Street by London Bridge; it is the only City tavern to survive the baker-shop blaze in Pudding Lane – the Great Fire of London – and remains virtually unchanged since 1663. Motes of static dust filter the light that pales through the old windows; the light contours a formless shadow into a club chair, a bouquet of bowler hats by the door, a block of books on the mantelshelf: Lloyd's *Shipping Register* for 1930, Foote's *Handbook for Spies*, *Bernard Spilsbury – His Life and Cases*, the *Law List*. Pepys sipped a glass of port in the Wine Shades while carpenters varnished the new interior, while brown rats spawned the Black Death in the Eastcheap sewers, while British redcoats fought the Dutch settlers along Manhattan's Fifth Avenue – still called New Amsterdam. Old, old varnish, black and creaking joints. Rich ruby port and thin, pale sherry, burgundies and clarets. A feeling of sanctuary. If the phone rings it's not likely to be for you.

Don't confuse Martin Lane with St Martin's Lane, which runs parallel to the Charing Cross Road. Halfway down St Martin's Lane is a pub so famous that a mere mention seems like over-indulgence – the Salisbury. Lush, plush, glass, brass. Victorian voluptuous. Hurried, busy and usually crowded. If the phone rings it may be for you. Not many people live around St Martin's Lane, but the Salisbury has its regulars because it is a cathedral in the episcopate of theatreland. Actors, film directors, script-writers, advertising men, sophisticates and darlings of the arts charge their personalites with draught Guinness or a glass of wine. The Salisbury is there for you to go and see, like an expensively dressed woman who adores to be admired. Even the graffiti in the toilet can be Chaucerian.

Some publicans specialize. The Admiral Codrington in Mossop Street, Chelsea, the interior of which resembles a Bavarian dream of an English pub, keeps more than a hundred different whiskies; the Bell and Crown at Strand-on-the Green keeps seventy-six. The landlord of the Chelsea Potter in the King's Road, Chelsea, claims to have the largest variety of aperitifs and spirits in London, including such exotica as tequila and saké, and keeps forty different wines to serve by the glass. The majority of London's pubs were slow to adopt the now common practice of selling wine by the glass, for the brewers would rather have them sell beer. Not long ago one was apt to be regarded with the suspicion generally reserved for foreigners if one requested wine in a pub. 'Better go to a restaurant and have a meal if you want wine,' was the advice. Nowadays anything goes. There are vodka pubs and schnapps pubs and champagne pubs. The Cask and Glass, behind Watney's brewery offices, Palace Street, Victoria, is a neat, well-kept, fresh little pub which keeps quarter bottles of champagne in an ice-bucket on the bar, port and sherry are from the wood, and there are twenty-six different wines by the glass. Owing to the proximity of Watney's it is, naturally, a Watney 'tied' house, used by Watney executives.

That decorative glass Victorian gem, the Bunch of Grapes,

on the corner of Yeoman's Row, s w 3, has Holstein lager on draught, worth remembering in the summer; Henekeys in the Portobello Road (don't go there on a Saturday unless you like crowds) has a large steaming copper kettle for hot rum or whisky punch, worth remembering in the winter. There is just one old cider house left in London, and that's Weston's, part of an inflorescence of dwellings rapidly going to seed on the stem of the Harrow Road. Go to Weston's and drink a glass of 'rough' draught cider before this last Victorian flower is plucked by the property developers. I recently appealed to the brewers, the G.L.C. and the Victorian Society on behalf of the Widow's Son, 75 Devons Road, Bow, one of the finest late Regency pubs in London and in danger of being demolished. There is nothing quite like it in the whole of London; the Widow's Son is almost unchanged, untouched and original. It has a real atmosphere of gaslight, 1830s East End. Devons Road begins just by Bow Church, in the Mile End Road, and finding this pub is a trifle difficult, but worth the trouble. Hanging from the ceiling is an age-blackened basket of Easter hot-cross buns, and hanging with them a legend: 'A cottage once stood on the site now occupied by the pub.' In the cottage lived a widow whose son – a sailor – was due to arrive home on Good Friday. She put a hot-cross bun aside for him, but he never returned. Each year she kept a bun, and the ritual collection grew. The pub has carried on the tradition since 1820, and each Good Friday a sailor adds a bun to the collection. The evidence of the buns hanging from the ceiling supports this legend, yet no one seems to have drawn attention to the fact that a Widow's Son is also a term applied to freemasons.

A London pub unrevealed by the finger of fame is the Beehive in Railway Side, White Hart Lane, Barnes. It is so well hidden and protected by its obscurity that it has remained original. This tiny pub, one bar, an ivy-covered porch outside offering a bleak view over a vegetable garden to the railway, has a cosy interior with the atmosphere of a country cottage. A hundred years ago this was a district of market gardens. On a flat area of land called Westfields, from where Beverley Brook joined the main artery of the Thames to White Hart Lane, plots of vegetables portioned the land with green geometry. The market gardeners, dressed in smocks, bent their backs to raise black, earth-coated potatoes and long, green beans. Here stood a cottage which was also run as an alehouse, for digging potatoes is thirsty work. The cottage was rebuilt in about 1860 as a public house and is now owned by Watney's. In the bar you can play a game of shove ha'penny with one of the locals, who will win hands down, or just stand with a glass of ale and watch the trains go by. Shove ha'penny is hardly a game poised on a razor's edge of sin and depravity, but you may learn something; you may learn that to accurately place a number of small brass discs in the appropriate sections of a polished board with a masterly flick of the wrist can earn the player a pint of ale – and a step toward immortality.

The renaissance of the pub as a place of entertainment has been a huge success and a surprise to everyone, especially the brewers, who feared the rivalry of coffee bars and television. So now we have entertainment pubs – big, noisy, brassy boozers, where the beat-groups play, like the City Arms in West Ferry Road, E 14. It is packed solid to the doors most nights and especially at weekends, with young East Enders and crowds of tourists. The Waterman's Arms, further down the road in Glengarnock Avenue, is definitely more upstage and almost pure English music hall, all over again. This is a complete evening's entertainment if you've got the stamina and a spare set of eardrums, but they should be considered as out-of-town attractions; it is an intense drag to go there by public transport, so go by car.

The East End of London is a treasure trove of beautiful, unexplored pubs. Even the famous ones still have much to offer. The Grapes in Narrow Street, E 14, has a balcony overlooking the river and also the inevitable connexion with Charles Dickens, who appears to have visited nearly every pub in England and must have had a liver like a hydro-electric pumping station. The Town of Ramsgate, by Wapping Old Stairs, where the fish boats from Ramsgate used to unload, has its connexion with Judge Jeffreys, who was captured there by a lynch-mob while trying to escape, disguised as a sailor.

Nearly every old London pub has a slice of history and literary association. The painter George Moreland used to drink at the Bull on North Hill, Highgate. The recently well-restored Jack Straw's Castle in Hampstead has its connexions with the highwayman Dick Turpin, likewise the Spaniards on the way to Highgate; the Cheshire Cheese in Fleet Street, which today dispenses steak-and-kidney pudding to American tourists, once served pudding and ale to Dr Johnson; Shakespeare is sometimes performed in the yard of the George at Southwark, and Conan Doyle had Sir Henry Baskerville stay at the Northumberland Hotel, now called the Sherlock Holmes. G. K. Chesterton may have had a pint or two in the Scarsdale, Edwardes Square, although this is mere surmise. More recently Dylan Thomas and Brendan Behan dropped poetic pearls, and tears, into their beer in the York Minster, *my* local in Dean Street, Soho.

Many fine pubs get ruined – or so it seems to me. The Greyhound in Kensington Square, which once had a lovely old Victorian mahogany billiard-room, and an atmosphere to match, has recently been 'improved'. So has the Black Horse in Rathbone Place; the hand-painted glass and old bar fittings have been replaced by a modern interior. Ye Olde Castle, in Battersea High Street, built when Elizabeth I was still on the throne, was recently destroyed to make way for a block of flats! The building which has replaced the old pub may, in a few hundred years, be considered an architectural gem, but I doubt it, I very much doubt it. The Olde Castle was an unclassified ancient monument, its destruction a monument of thoughtless urban planning. Very few modern pub interiors seduce me into staying longer than ten minutes. A curious paradox emerges: why destroy original material like the Greyhound when, less than a half-mile away in the Earls Court Road, the Pembroke Arms has had its saloon bar changed from the 1930s back to the 1860s and its name to the Hansom Cab? The bar panelling and superstructure in the Greyhound was of real mahogany and chestnut, but in the Hansom Cab the capitals on the columns are made of plaster! The Champion in Wells Street is far more deceptive, yet this Victorian bar is just fourteen years old; the Cockney Pride in Jermyn Street recently opened its doors for the first time, and looks like a film set for a Lupino Lane musical.

Pubs are part of the skeletal structure of English social life –

yours and mine. We go to a pub for a drink, a meal, conversation, because we are happy or because we are sad, because we want company or because we wish to be alone. There is nothing like a pub, and there are no successful imitations. Where else could you find a place like Henekeys Long Bar in Holborn, that lofty manor hall with a catwalk high among the vats, and a tricorn fire without a chimney?

The Olde Mitre Tavern in Ely Place, Hatton Garden, has a cherry tree in one corner of the bar, closes at 10 p.m., doesn't open on Sunday and is a *part of Cambridgeshire*. Ely Place has been, since the fourteenth century, the town residence of the Bishops of Ely and as such part of the Bishops' territory; accurately the Mitre isn't a London pub at all.

The wedge-shaped Black Friar seems to support one end of Blackfriars railway bridge. Trains rumble overhead while *art nouveau* friars, going about their daily tasks in copper relief on marble, admonish us and criticize our conceits: 'Finery is foolery', or 'Haste is slow', and 'Industry is all'. The Black Friar is a free house, not tied to a specific brewer, and permitted to sell any brand of beer.

The Red Lion in Duke of York Street is a precious gem set in the architectural bijouterie of St James's. Here is a perfectly proportioned Victorian pub in miniature. Everything is here, the rich, varnished mahogany and etched, decorative glass – oriel, pilaster, cyma and prism.

Look at London's pubs and savour their unique qualities. Londoners make a special point of going to pubs as far afield as Greenwich or Isleworth because, like our friends, each pub has a different face.

It is not easy to nominate the twelve best pubs in London. Excluding many that seem to have a better claim to inclusion, like the Cheshire Cheese in Fleet Street, these are the ones which I chose: The Beehive, Barnes; the Black Friar; the Bunch of Grapes on the corner of Yeoman's Row; Henekeys Long Bar, Holborn; Jack Straw's Castle, Hampstead Heath; the London Apprentice, Isleworth; the Mitre Tavern, Ely Place; the Red Lion, St James's; the Salisbury in St Martin's Lane; the Widow's Son, Bow; the Olde Wine Shades, Martin Lane; the York Minster, Soho.

Whatever the pub, remember that you must pay for each drink or round of drinks when served, and that customers never, ever tip when served a drink, unless by a waiter serving tables in a saloon bar, when it is customary to give him anything between 6d. and 5s., depending on the size of the order.

The Thames and some history

From beer we turn to water.

All cities begin with water, and often they are born at the river crossing nearest to the open sea. London Bridge marks that place. It is the last bridge (except for the hinged Tower Bridge) before the Thames estuary broadens out and finally becomes the North Sea.

South of the river was too marshy and so the Romans chose the north bank for their city. They built a town and followed their normal military practice of situating their fort close against a wall, so that the inhabitants, turning nasty, couldn't cut the garrison off from aid. The city as defined by the original Roman walls is still known to Londoners as the 'City', and tiny pieces of Roman wall can still be seen. The City has its own regulations and its policemen wear slightly different uniforms (you will notice red-striped armbands instead of blue).

Kings like Charles I who opposed the City usually came off worst. Men who understood the City's commerce gained its powerful support. William of Orange had the brilliant commercial idea of founding the Bank of England and borrowing money from it, and although this made the King dependent upon the City, it made the City a fervent supporter of the House of Orange, for it knew that a restored Jacobite king would never acknowledge that debt. In the twentieth century the City retains its special powers. Certain sorts of advertising are banned and no tramway lines have ever marred its streets. Before the Queen enters the City she is still met at Temple Bar and given formal permission by the Lord Mayor.

South of London Bridge is Southwark, named from a Saxon

word meaning southern work or fortification. The Icelandic sagas speak of Sudvirki near to Lundunaborg. Here to the south bank in 1066 William the Conqueror's soldiers came after the battle of Hastings, looking at the city that they would soon capture. Once there William built himself a fortress – the Tower – and went to live in it. It was a powerful institution and the men stationed there took tolls from passing cargo ships (e.g. 2 flagons from a wine ship) and, living on the fat of the land, earned the nickname 'beefeaters'.

The City did not exactly spread outwards; other 'cities' came into being near by and they joined together. Westminster was the most important; William the Conqueror was crowned there, and it soon became the governmental centre, with the Royal Treasury and finally the Parliament there too.

Halfway between the City and Westminster was the Temple. At first it was the most important temple of the Knights Templars, until the King crushed them. From the thirteenth century the Temple became the legal centre of Britain – and it is still. Trevelyan in his *History of England* says that the Temple's geographical position reflected the English lawyers' 'true political function as mediator between Crown and people' although if searching for a geographical analogy I would lean more towards Mr Justice Mathew when he said: 'In this country justice is open to all – like the Ritz Hotel.'

The river too was open to everyone and until the seventeenth century carried the only form of public transport, which is why London expanded only very slowly northwards. Not only did the King's officials go on daily errands by boat from the Tower to Westminster and the Mayor travel graciously in his gilded barge, but lawyers' clerks going to work at the Temple from a house in the City found the water better than the badly mended Strand.

It was because the City merchants forbade bear baiting, brothels and theatres in the City that Southwark – just across the water – became famous for all three facilities. These areas outside the walls were, understandably, called Libertys. Southwark was divided into three Libertys; one – the Liberty of the Clink – was under the jurisdiction of the Bishop of Winchester. It was so thick with brothels that the whores were called 'Winchester Geese'. There was a special cemetery for them. Near by the local theatres were the Bear Garden, the Rose and the Globe. In the final lines of *Troilus and Cressida* Shakespeare referred to the Winchester Geese:

> Brethren, and sisters, of the hold-door trade,
> Some two months hence, my will shall here be made:
> It should be now, but that my fear is this:
> Some galled goose of Winchester would hiss:
> Till then, I'll sweat, and seek about for eases;
> And at that time bequeath you my diseases.

Shakespeare was a rich and famous resident of Southwark whose tax collector – Ferdinando Clutterbook – had failed to collect his payments, but in 1600 Will did a private tax deal with the Bishop. In 1607 Will lashed out one pound for a forenoon knell of the great bell of St Saviour's for his youngest brother Edmund's funeral, when the little bell would have cost only a shilling.

One third of the local residents were watermen and they had a vested interest in plugging the bawds, bears, and bards, for on a good day 4,000 people crossed the water. Watermen had to row people across for a penny but yelled abuse if they got less than a 2d. tip.

The first public transport on the London streets was in 1625; it was so popular that within nine years there were cab ranks in the Strand with four coaches awaiting custom. But the coaches in the narrow streets caused congestion and annoyance like a Cadillac going through an Indian bazaar. So the sedan chair was invented. There were angry protests about using Englishmen as pack animals but the sedan chair was smooth over the bad roads and weaved in and out of the crowded streets like a motor-scooter through a traffic jam.

London Bridge was the only bridge across London's river until 1749, when a stone bridge was built at Westminster. The old London Bridge was a strange construction crowded with shops, taverns and houses, as well as a church. (Still today there are buildings called No. 1 and No. 2 London Bridge.) There were many supports to carry the weight, and this caused the Thames to rush through so dangerously that many Londoners insisted on landing and getting another boat on the far side of the bridge. The closeness of the supports also meant that in winter the river sometimes clogged up and froze over. When it did ice fairs were held on the river. After 650 years' use the old bridge was demolished in 1831 and rebuilt without shops and houses and with supports far enough apart to preclude an ice fair no matter how cold the weather.

In Dickens's day travellers – like those in *A Tale of Two Cities* – crossed from France and took the coach along the Great Dover Road, entering the City through Southwark; or if they arrived after dark – when the City was closed – they spent the night at an inn like the George (77 Borough High Street, S E 1). It is London's last galleried inn.

In spite of its being a tourist attraction nothing has affected the George Inn. It is exactly right; Dickens obviously thought so too, for he gave it a plug in *Little Dorrit*. There is a restaurant at the George which will serve you a good dinner. On summer evenings the George is endlessly besieged by tourists. If you'd prefer to see it at a quieter time, go during lunch; even then there might be a crowd, but don't miss it – the George is one of London's most evocative sights.

Dickens had rooms just down the road from here in Lant Street. He chose this locality so that he'd be able to visit his father in the debtors' prison across the road. Not far south along Borough High Street from the George, on the same side of the street, there is a corner shop marked the Tabard. There is nothing to see here now, but upon that same corner stood the Tabard Inn, where Chaucer and his pilgrims set out upon their journey to Canterbury.

Close by the George is another pub, the Anchor, at No. 1 Bankside. Listen carefully to the directions when you ask how to find it, for there are a couple of twists and turns down the narrow winding riverside streets. This little pub that overlooks the river was built in the seventeenth century. Previously another pub occupied the same site, which is so near to the site of Shakespeare's Globe theatre that it's possible the old bard himself took a pint hereabouts. The present pub, however, certainly felt the weight of Doctor Johnson on its boards.

Not far along the waterfront, at 49 Bankside, is the little house where Christopher Wren lived while St Paul's Cathedral was being built, or so it is said. From here he certainly could have kept an eye on it, as you can too. What's that clerihew –

> Sir Christopher Wren
> Said 'I am going to dine with some men.
> If anybody calls
> Say I'm designing St Paul's.'

On the other side of the Anchor stood the Clink prison. In the Anchor they had a tiny vertical room for hiding escapees who could afford the going rate for a tiny hidden room within easy reach of the prison.

One unusual sight on the Thames is a good-looking 75-ton boat named 'John Ashley'. The flag at the mast is a flying angel with the words 'The Missions to Seamen' on it. It's a floating church that travels up and down the river calling upon merchant ships. As well as religious services they have film shows aboard, a television room and a library. 'Don't bring the books back,' the Reverend F. Laight says, 'pass them on.'

Given a sunny day many Londoners head towards a stretch of water. Traffic jams of terrifying dimensions form on the roads back from Brighton and Southend, which are two of London's coastal suburbs. Anglers climb over fences and waste ground to reach mysterious stretches of canal that only anglers know. Busloads of trippers lumber to the big reservoirs so that whole families can stare at the smooth blue water in contemplative silence of the kind with which T. E. Lawrence viewed the desert. Large boats steam between Tower Pier and Southend via Greenwich, their decks alive with dancing, drinking, swearing, eating, laughing Londoners who suddenly become quiet and subdued as their feet touch dry land at day's end.

London's riverside has had whole books devoted to it and there is certainly enough to keep a tourist happy for weeks, from H.M.S. *Discovery*, the ship in which Scott went to Antarctica in 1901 (visitors welcome, afternoons only), to the *Cutty Sark*, last of the tea clippers, at Greenwich. The National

Maritime Museum at Greenwich has enough in it for a week's tour at least and, even better for the boat fanatic, you can get there from Westminster by river. Dan Farson was such a fanatic about the London River that he decided to live right on it.

River

Daniel Farson

Daniel Farson is the son of American author Negley Farson. Educated on both sides of the Atlantic, joined the Central Press Agency, London, at seventeen and became Parliamentary and Lobby Correspondent in the House of Commons. Served with American army in Germany after the war and went to Cambridge university under the G.I. Bill of Rights; photographer for *Picture Post*; free-lance journalist for the *Evening Standard*, which published reports of his trip round the world as a steward in the Merchant Navy. Well-known interviewer on British television with such series as 'Farson's Guide to the British'.

It often seems as if London is unaware of the great river that runs through the middle of it. People crowd the banks at Putney and Hammersmith each spring to watch the boat race, but to walk along the river or live there is another matter altogether. I realized this when I tried to find a home beside the water. What struck me as a reasonable ambition proved surprisingly difficult.

The picturesque stretches of Richmond and Chiswick did not appeal to me, they are too picturesque. The gracious houses of Cheyne Walk, where Whistler painted his river scenes, were too expensive and there was the roar of traffic from the road outside.

There is a hauntingly attractive bend of the river at Battersea, with the great chimneys of the power station in the background. And below the bridge there is a cluster of houseboats, but they offered none of the solitude I was looking for.

Further out there is Henley, whose famous Royal Regatta in early July has been attracting amateur oarsmen since 1839; and the Versailles of England – Hampton Court Palace, presented to Henry VIII by Cardinal Wolsey in 1526 – the home and birthplace of kings and queens until the reign of George II, when the buildings were opened to the public. But as far as I was concerned, these were places to visit.

So I was drawn to the dark, dirty waters beyond Tower Bridge: the working part of the Thames. First I took a pleasure boat from Westminster Pier down to Greenwich, jotting down any place where I might be able to live.

I wonder how many of the thousands who fly to Majorca each year ever bother to take this journey, which costs no more than the bus to the airport? It's not 'pretty' in the conventional sense, though on a fine day the whole river springs to life, but for anyone with a taste for history it cannot fail to excite. The Thames is a river that has seen everything, from long Venetian galleys, rowed by Turkish slaves, to dark and silent submarines.

Years ago people used to fish here, but I doubt if it was ever clean, simply less polluted by modern chemicals. I have an old song-sheet, 'The Lamentation of Father Thames', which shows him in the water exclaiming 'Here's a mess I'm in', a dead cat caught in his trident, a sewer and a gas works belching behind him, and some of London's famous whitebait 'looking black' swimming around him. If a docker falls into the water today he's taken to hospital and has his stomach pumped out, though small children seem to paddle happily on the tiny beach below the Tower. Once I moored a boat at the famous pub, the Prospect of Whitby, and a stranger kindly tied the rope for me, or thought he did, for as I stepped on to the iron ladder the boat slipped away and, to the delight of the crowd, I disappeared under the water. After surfacing I managed to splutter that I always make a spectacular entrance – then I was sick. There is a great effort now to clear the Thames of pollution, and fish have been seen again at Greenwich. A school of porpoise came there at the end of 1965, and a circus owner tried to have them lassoed until he was stopped by officials of the Crown.

The Tower of London never fails to fascinate me. Nine centuries old, it started as a fortress and became both a palace and a prison. Today it is still a fortress, garrisoned with troops, but has a toy-town appearance as if it's made of papier mâché. Past the derelict cannon in front of it, and the small beach I mentioned, and under Tower Bridge which still opens to let the taller vessels through.

On to Execution Dock, where anyone sentenced for a crime committed on the water was hung at low-tide and kept there till three tides had washed over the corpse as a warning to potential villains on passing ships.

Towards Ratcliffe, named after the red cliffs that once lined the shore, whence Frobisher sailed 'for the search of the passage to China', and on to Limehouse, named after the lime kiln that once stood here, whence Raleigh sailed on his third voyage to Guyana.

Round the horseshoe of the Isle of Dogs to Greenwich, one of the splendid sights of Europe, unknown to most Londoners yet admired by such visitors as Canaletto, whose painting of the scene can be seen in the Queen's House on the hill above. The pleasure boat moors beside the *Cutty Sark*, once the fastest sailing ship of its day, now preserved in dry dock. To the other side is the great naval hospital designed by Wren, with its spacious Painted Hall, so named because of its magnificent painted ceiling. It was built as a hospital for disabled sailors. Age and infirmity did not subdue the ancient mariners – far from it, their drunken behaviour so scandalized the residents that they were removed to another part of Greenwich. Now Wren's building houses the Royal Naval College for the higher education of naval officers.

I find museums oppressive, but the National Maritime Museum at Greenwich is my exception. I return to it often – it is so large one has to. Immense, gaudy figureheads that decorated the bows of warships tower over models of ships. Rooms devoted to Nelson have his china and glass and his own uniform, that might have been a child's; it makes one wonder how so small a man coped with the fourteen and a half stone of Lady Hamilton.

Between the two wings of the museum is the Queen's House by Inigo Jones, a masterpiece of simple elegance, and behind it at the top of the hill the Observatory that gives the world Greenwich Mean Time and from which one has a fine view of this part of London.

Later I made the journey on foot, or rather many journeys, in search of my new home, for the riverside is a maze of streets that seem to go in no reasonable direction and alleys that stop abruptly at the water where a ferry used to carry the traveller to the other side.

They were hot summer evenings and the narrow streets, cut with black shadows from the warehouses, were strangely deserted. If only because of the solitude I felt I was in a different country and I remembered that when Jack London arrived, to make his journey into the abyss, and asked his smart friends exactly where the East End was, they waved vaguely in an easterly direction. It is still true that the moment one passes Tower Bridge one has entered another territory. Conversely, the East Enders feel the same when they cross into the West End.

There is a curved street beside the bridge that leads into The Highway that was once Ratcliffe Highway, the toughest street in London. Gustave Doré, among his astounding engravings of London in the 1870s, records a fight outside one of the 'dens' scattered along the road, and an account refers to 'chairs and tables screwed to the floor' to avoid their use in the free fights for which the place was noted. Men of sinister appearance were busy at the cooking ranges, preparing the evening meals. Mingled odours of frying food and vile tobacco permeated the atmosphere and when there was a cry of 'Murder', the policeman said, 'Stand still, gentlemen, this happens every five minutes in these parts.'

The Highway is now a wide, empty street, but parallel is Cable Street, recently called the 'wickedest street in London' after a man had been attacked there and lay dying in the gutter, ignored by the frightened passers-by. Cable Street is now in the process of being 'cleaned up', but on the drowsy evenings when I first saw it, the West Indians took their chairs outside on the pavements to catch the last touches of the sun and I might not have been in England at all.

For me, it was a new sort of exploration. I'd turn a corner, and stumble across a place I hadn't even noticed from the river, like the small pub, the Town of Ramsgate. Here Judge Jeffreys, the merciless 'Hanging Judge', was caught waiting for the ship that was to take him from his enemies. Beside it, at Wapping Old Stairs, they found the first part of the body in the 1966 'torso' murder mystery.

Exploration, but no success. My journeys were fruitless, for all the places I had noted were derelict, occupied by river police and their families, or wrong for some reason or other. The reaction to my inquiries confirmed what I'd suspected: the Londoner is so indifferent to his river that only a handful of people live beside it unless they have to. Our attitude – in contrast to that of the Parisians who take every advantage of the Seine – is all the more absurd when one considers that London has thrived because of the Thames and is one of the largest ports in the world; 30 per cent of Britain's exports go from London, compared to 3 per cent from Glasgow.

I gave up the search, and then, of course, it all happened at once. I heard of a flat that was being converted above a barge-repair yard at Limehouse. At the same time, Antony Armstrong-Jones, as he was then, told me he had found the place on the river he was looking for. I kept quiet and still don't know if we were after the same house, but I believe he changed his mind and in due course I was invited to the housewarming of The Little Midshipman at Rotherhithe, recently demolished after its last years of unexpected fame.

Meanwhile I tracked down the owners of the barge yard, invited them to an expensive lunch at Wheeler's, and in spite of all protests that the place would be unsuitable, persuaded them to let me move in.

At last I stood on my balcony and absorbed the view. The small Elizabethan house, with the original brick and timber, but no ground floor as this is part of the barge yard, lies on the bend of the river at Limehouse Reach with a five-mile curve towards Greenwich. Up river, the top of Tower Bridge appears in the distance. Opposite is a rather desolate stretch known as Cuckold's Point. Below lie the barges, much as they did in a drawing by Whistler in 1854. But they still tried to dissuade me, wondering why on earth I wished to exchange a house in Pelham Place, with Cecil Beaton as my neighbour, for the dirt of Limehouse and an old, retired boxer called Chalky in the upper flat next door.

My landlady proved to be a splendid octogenarian called Mrs Woodward Fisher, one of the true characters of the river. When he was a boy, her husband won the Doggett Coat and Badge race, a traditional event rowed by six young Watermen on 1 August. This was started in 1716 by an actor called Doggett to commemorate the accession of George I; he offered, as a prize, an orange coat of 'antique' cut with a silver badge on the right sleeve displaying the White Horse of Hanover. Today the winner receives money instead.

Starting with a single barge, the Fisher family soon became one of the biggest owners of river property, and Mrs Fisher still commands a fleet of tugs and barges from a radio room in her large house in Blackheath, rousing her men from their tea-breaks. On her radio or the phone she is often mistaken for a man, for she speaks in a gruff voice, and indeed her appearance, with monocle and stock, has a marked resemblance to George Arliss. At first I was scared of her, but now know the kindness that lies beneath the commanding appearance. She has just won her battle for a permanent home opposite Greenwich for one of her many 'causes' – the Blackwall rowing club.

Then, as I stood beside her, she pointed out all the disadvantages with scrupulous honesty – the excruciating noise of the electric scrapers removing rust from the old barges; the grime from the coal-loading wharf nearby covering the balcony with a layer of black dust; the smell at low tide. But I could hear no noise, see no dirt, smell no smell. This was what I had wanted all the time – for once the reality surpassed the dream.

All I saw were the two wild duck making their nest in the pilings of the coal-wharf; a flight of swans beating their way down the river in single file; a barge rowed upstream with the tide, the men with their long poles standing out in silhouette against the shimmering Thames.

With trees and tubs and window-boxes, I turned the balcony into a small garden, where we could eat outside. The locals, whose one ambition was to move out of the district, accused me of slumming; my friends also accused me of slumming and asked how on earth I could sleep at night while the barges thundered together in the wake of passing ships. I countered that it was better than the din of traffic, and indeed the trumpeting of ships as they waited to enter Regent's Canal Dock made me think of great animals approaching some water hole. I ignored the large rat upstairs and the fumes which rose so strongly from below that they lifted the carpet.

Of course, the particular magic was the constant parade before me of the London river. Tugs leading strings of barges (there are over 5,000 on the river altogether); dirty freighters with trees tied to their masts on Christmas Day; ships with names like *Velasquez* and *The Cyprian Shore*; coasters from France, family boats with lines of laundry and a dog scampering along the deck; liners from Poland, their passengers staring as they passed; naval frigates; the *Britannia* with Princess Margaret and Lord Snowdon leaving on their wedding day for the West Indies; a submarine; Hovercraft; motor boats and racing skiffs and home-made yachts; and a man on water-skis in a black rubber suit. All the flotsam and jetsam of the sea, arriving and leaving for destinations I could only guess at. A few years before, I had sailed around the world as a steward in the Merchant Navy – now I felt I had a link with the sea again.

I learnt the eccentricities of the river. There is no speed limit here and no one side of the river to keep to. Driftwood rightfully belongs to the Queen and if a boatman fishes up a dead body he gets 7s. 6d. if it's on the south side, and 6s. on the north – so naturally he rows it to the south. The river police, three men in a boat on eight-hour shifts, pick up an average of seventy dead bodies and forty live ones a year. The gravel below me is a well-known resting place and a body of an old woman was discovered there a few days after I moved in.

It was here that Charles Dickens set the opening of *Our Mutual Friend*, with Rogue Riderhood searching for floating corpses he could rob: 'It's a curious thing, but the River sweeps in here and the tide settles the bodies among the piles and craft. Rogue knew that.' Inevitably it's said that Dickens stayed in my house and the bow-windowed Bunch of Grapes to the right of me sports a 'Dickens Room', claiming that 'The Six Jolly Fellowship-Porters' in the book is based on it. However, an old print of The Two Brewers, which used to be on the other side of me, coincides far more exactly with Dickens's description of a tavern of dropsical appearance . . . with a crazy wooden verandah impending over the water; indeed the whole house, inclusive of the complaining flag-staff on the roof, impended over the water, but seemed to have got into the condition of a faint-hearted diver who has paused so long on the brink that he will never go in at all.

My house had been a pub, the Waterman's Arms, and I've seen an old print of the small room with a couple of benches and a bare table and a big fire. The waterfront was scattered with modest pubs like this where sailors and East Enders could shelter from the cold and where the beer, at 2d. a pint and twice as strong as it is today, offered real nourishment. The street names convey the past: Gin Alley; Cinnamon Street; Rope-makers Fields; Kidney Stairs. My own is Narrow Street, crowded and cobbled, and used to be called Fore Street and Limehouse Street before that, for this was Chinatown and I arrived at the end of an era.

Before the war there was a labyrinth of houses interlocked by secret passages, so if a Chinese ran into a house at one end of the street he'd more than likely run out the other end. A docker has told me how he went to school 'sitting side by side with Chinese and half-castes and thinking nothing about it except how clever they invariably were, how softly spoken and polite'. His father used to bring home the pukka-boo gambling papers, small sheets covered with Chinese lettering, and the family would help him fill them in, as they might do with the pools today.

I just caught the last moments of Chinatown, The Commercial pub, where you heard more Chinese spoken than English, at the foot of Penny Fields, a has-been of a street of façades with peeling Chinese lettering. Now they have gone and new blocks with pretentious mosaics have taken their place. All that is left of the Chinatown of 'Limehouse Blues' and Dorian Gray's opium dens are a few street names – Oriental Street, which still has a Chinese Club, the Chun-yee, where members play mahjong; Mandarin Street with the Old Friends restaurant soon to be demolished; and a handful of other first-class restaurants run by Mr Lo-Cheong – the New Friends, The Good Friends and the Young Friends.

Whenever I regret the changes, I am rightly pounced on –

'You didn't have to live here, it's all very well for you.' It's hard to realize the poverty of only a few years ago, the fact that people lived in a state near starvation, dependent on soup kitchens, surviving with bare feet and bare fists. The traditional cockney of the cloth cap and muffler can still be seen among the older people, but in the pubs at night it's easy to see who is East and who is West, for the tourists seem to dress down for the occasion in headscarves and sweaters, while the locals stand out in their immaculate elegance, the young men in dark suits cut to strict orders by Jewish tailors, the girls with hair styles as elaborate as pagodas.

One can see that this was once the great melting-pot of nationalities, especially of the 100,000 Jews who came from Russia and Poland. At one time it was unusual to hear someone speaking English around Spitalfields. The Commercial Road still has a Yiddish theatre and a kosher market, open on Sundays. Bloom's, at Aldgate, is famous for its kosher food. Ordering wine from the House of Frumkin, I am always offered a small glass of cherry brandy and a slice of cake; at a party for old people I met Russians who haven't learnt to speak English and probably never will.

At the end of Commercial Road, beside the tall Limehouse church designed by Wren's pupil, Hawksmoor, and the hideous Sailor's Rest, known as the 'Stack of Bricks', is the junction of the great West India and East India Dock Roads. Built to carry the produce of the Indies from the docks, they're as crowded today as when Joseph Conrad described them in *Chance*: 'Great vans carrying enormous piled-up loads advanced swaying like mountains. It was as if the whole world existed only for selling and buying and those who had nothing to do with the movement of merchandise were of no account.'

At the corner is the Eastern Hotel where Conrad's fictitious sea captains used to stay; now the rooms upstairs are empty and it is simply a large, usually deserted pub. But the flavour of the sea is redolent in West India Dock Road outside, with Scandinavian seamen in blue jeans bleached by the sun and sea, and Lascars with paper parcels, walking up from the Docks. There is a ship's chandler next to the East and West Restaurant, an immense storehouse of ropes and lamps and everything pertaining to ships; and there's an outfitters with boots and denims and shirts and socks, hanging beside the owner, Morris Senneft, who sits outside on a stool when the weather is good and whose wife was murdered inside the shop one Sunday morning a few years ago.

I was working for television, and riverside characters began to appear in my programmes, such as the rat-catcher who'd set one rat free because it was crippled, only to have it bite him in the finger. 'All right, I says, that's your bleedin' lot!' and snapping his teeth together he showed how he'd bitten the rat's head off.

'Aren't you afraid of getting poisoned?' I asked.

'Lord no,' he said. 'The rat that bites me will get poisoned hisself.'

When we actually saw him biting a rat later it proved a grisly sight. Either it was a very tough rat or his teeth were no longer his own; far from a clean bite he had to stretch it in half. Both this shot and the word 'bleedin'' were cut from the programme.

One of my most successful programmes was a direct result of my move to the East End and my visits at night to the local pubs. I was startled to find that many were vast music palaces offering entertainment ranging from female impersonators to modern jazz. They had a bizarre atmosphere that was immediately attractive. On Sunday mornings, at the Bridge House, there was striptease (genuinely female) before a crowd of dockers who then went home to lunch. I took Armstrong-Jones, who appreciated it and took a photo, and later, Colin Wilson, who was rather shocked.

Some pubs sported stars like Queenie Watts, a magnificent 'belter' of traditional jazz who ran her own pub, the Ironbridge, with her husband Slim. Ray Martine devastated hecklers at the Deuragon Arms and has never been funnier; the Rising Sun, the most famous of the music pubs at that time, abounded with such local talent as 'Tex' the Cowboy, Ron Shepard a taxi-driver who impersonated Al Jolson, and the compère Welsh George.

Music hall, which had started in pubs like the Canterbury Arms at Lambeth just over a hundred years ago, seemed to have returned to the pubs again with all its exuberance. This time there was the added zest of seeing the performer 'live' instead of on the television screen, and I thought it would be ironic justice to make a programme on the boom in pub entertainment, particularly as it seemed to have gone unnoticed.

While I was preparing the programme, I stumbled across the next chapter in my life, a pub called the Newcastle Arms.

It stood at the top of a slipway on the Isle of Dogs where I was launching a speedboat, and as I waited for the tide to come in and float it I noticed several children playing in the mud. Their father, the landlord, told me later that he had delivered the last child himself in a remote army barracks when the midwife failed to arrive and I included him in a documentary called 'Birth'. Later, after evenings racing down on the boat to Galleon's Reach at Woolwich, and Gravesend, I'd moor near the Newcastle Arms and was always surprised to find the pub deserted. When I had to knock to get in and the landlord had to go round the corner to another pub to buy the drinks I'd ordered, I asked what on earth was happening. He told me he'd lost all his savings and as the brewers would not allow him credit he wanted to get out as soon as he could. No one wanted 'the pub with no beer' as it was then called on the Island. I looked around, thought of the pub programme, my interest in music hall, the river and the East End. In a moment of madness, I thought it might be fun to run a pub and within a month I was.

The pub was on two levels, which I liked, and by knocking down a wall one could look on to the stage in the saloon bar as if it was a small theatre. I decorated the public bar simply with prints and pictures of the river and the saloon in lush music-hall style with posters and prints. I had discovered a number of performers for the programme and Kim Cordell, now famous, became our compère. Finally, and simply from sentiment, I changed the name to the pub that once existed in my own home – the Waterman's Arms.

Though the Isle of Dogs is just beyond Limehouse, I had seldom been there, for it's simply a U-shaped detour on the way to nowhere. Of course it isn't an island at all, unless you count the docks that lie at its base. After the turmoil of Commercial Road, it has extraordinary tranquillity. The roads are wider, there are parks and playing fields and a feeling of space. One enters over bridges, past high walls that are dwarfed by even higher ships, past groups of streets curiously named after girls – Sophia Street, Maria Street – or the Indies – Havannah Street, Cuba Street – or after ships, like Barque Street and Schooner Street. Millwall and Blackwall are named after the great walls that once kept back the floods, and the seven mills that once stood here. It is startling to realize that as late as 1800 the Chapel House was 'the only dwelling place upon the marsh'. A book recorded: 'The cold and swampy character of this tract of land would appear repulsive to all thoughts of human habitation.' The Isle of Dogs became populated with the building of the West India Docks which unearthed such strange remains as the tusks of an elephant and a petrified forest buried many feet below the watermark, possibly after an earthquake: 'a mass of decayed twigs, leaves and branches, encompassing huge trunks rotted through, yet perfect in every fibre'.

The West India Docks were opened in 1802, to ease the congestion of ships unloading in the middle of the river. Until then, mass plunder had been taken for granted: now, to the dismay of the locals, armed guards patrolled behind high walls. A special 'Free-Water Clause' allowed lightermen to take their barges into the docks without paying dues, and in 1900, when the West India Dock Company tried to revoke this, pleading a shortage of space, they were opposed so bitterly in Parliament that eight years later the Port of London Authority came into existence to settle such matters. Today the P.L.A. supervises the river. It was its launch, the *Havengore*, which carried the coffin of Sir Winston Churchill from the Tower to Waterloo.

The favourite explanation for the name of the 'Isle of Dogs' is that Charles II kept his kennels here when he lived across the water at Greenwich. One writer suggests it was originally the Isle of Ducks, and Pepys's reference – 'we were fain to stay there in the unlucky Isle of Dogs, in a chill place, the morning cool, the wind fresh, to our great discontent' – has led to the theory that it was named after the saying 'going to the dogs'. It strikes me as more likely that the saying grew from the place, for the bleak marshland and the felons hanging from gibbets along the shore cannot have been a welcoming sight for returning sailors. The version I like best is that of the faithful dog which stayed with the body of his master after he had been killed in a fight with another waterman. Driven by hunger, the dog would swim across to Greenwich and then return to guard the body until one visit when the dog attacked another waterman with such ferocity that the man confessed to the murder and was arrested.

By 1900 the Isle had improved so much that Walter Besant was able to describe it glowingly as

a place where one might deliberately choose to be born, because, apart from the general well-being of the people and the healthfulness of the air, there is a spirit of enterprise imbibed by every boy who grows up in this admirable island. There are no slums . . . I have never seen any hooligans . . . you will not see any drunken men nor beggars, nor any signs of misery.

As one of the docks was known as 'Drunken Dock' this must have been romanticism. The island had certainly relapsed by the time I arrived. But in those first months I never tired of turning round the corner to the small, well-cared-for 'Park of the Isle', right on the water's edge, with the magnificent view of Greenwich opposite. Next to the park is a glass dome which leads to the foot tunnel, coming up beside the Cutty Sark on the other side of the river. It had never occurred to me that one could walk under the Thames, and this became a regular journey with my dogs, up to the top of Greenwich Hill.

The television programme appeared as 'Time, Gentlemen, Please!' and a nightly invasion began to pour in from the West End. The Waterman's Arms became famous. An extraordinary range of celebrities came there: film stars like Groucho Marx and Claudette Colbert; impresarios such as Brian Epstein, David Merrick and Joan Littlewood; sportsmen like Billy Walker the boxer; Francis Bacon the painter; Bill Burroughs the author; singers like Tony Bennett and Sarah Vaughan. Shirley Bassey sang 'I Who Have Nothing' from the stage when she was unmistakably pregnant, and Judy Garland sang after midnight, with only the light coming from across the water and the lamp from the street outside. The evenings I remember with the most affection were on Christmas and New Year's Eve, with the crowded pub joining in the old songs.

Ironically, our success proved our undoing. In the two hectic hours before closing time, it was so crowded that people had to fight their way to the bar. It was painful to hear such remarks as: 'What fun! Let's watch and then we'll go for a drink to that empty pub nearby.' If the licensing laws were different and we had continued later or charged an entrance fee, there might have been a happy ending. But with virtually no day-time trade, the cost of our lavish entertainment could not be covered. I transferred The Waterman's at the beginning of 1966.

I was reminded that Pepys had called the Island 'unlucky'; perhaps he had a reason of his own. Certainly the immense iron paddle-ship the *Great Eastern*, designed by Isambard Brunel and built at Millwall, was ill-fated throughout its life. The largest vessel that had ever been constructed, it was partly submerged in the Thames at its first launching in 1857. A year later it was launched again, but Jules Verne in *A Floating City* writes that 'after twenty passages to England from America, one of which was marked by very serious disasters, the use of the *Great Eastern* was temporarily abandoned'. It was then used as a cable ship, bought by a French company, and even humiliated by a proposal that it should take coals from Newcastle to London. It was sold by auction in 1885, and when the 22,927 tons of metal were dismantled they revealed the skeletons of workmen who had been imprisoned within the iron walls.

It would be silly to mention any particular pub that is now 'the place' to visit, for it is the nature of the East End that it changes all the time. It is full of surprises, but beside it the river continues much as it has done for hundreds of years. I envy the person who now explores it for the first time, discovering the subtle beauty that lies beneath the grime, going, as Dickens did, 'in and out among vessels that seemed to have got afloat – among bowsprits staring into windows and windows staring into ships'. I know all too well that if I now see the dirt, and hear the noise, and smell the smells that once were pointed out to me – it is I who have changed.

A perfect Saturday, mostly books

My idea of a perfect London Saturday would begin with buying books. The place to start: Leicester Square Underground station. From here northwards, on both sides of Charing Cross Road, are many bookshops handling both new and second-hand books. I know of no other street in the world that can compare with it for the number and variety of books it offers. Some of the shops – e.g. Poole's at No. 86 – have gloomy great basements full of dusty books, each carefully ranged according to subject-matter, and ladders stand ready for you. Other shops specialize, one in encyclopedias, another in erotica. Zwemmer's is famous for books on art, architecture and design, Newman at No. 70 has a large number of military and gun books. A few doors away is a window full of publishers' remainders going for a song. Ascroft & Daw at No. 83 stock only paperback books and Collet's across the road have every Penguin in print. Farther along at No. 119 is Foyle's, the largest bookshop in the world, with four million volumes in thirty-two different departments. By the way, Dobell's shop at No. 77 specializes in jazz records with a separate department for folk records. On Saturday it is full of noisy enthusiasts.

If you still haven't seen enough books walk back south, past the Leicester Square Underground, passing on the way Solosy at No. 53 with many English and foreign newspapers and magazines. Turn left at Cecil Court. Here are more bookshops of many types. There's a greater chance of picking up a bargain, but a greater risk of finding nothing you want. Here too there are specialist shops, one of which is for motor-car maniacs. You are very near the Salisbury pub, so if you want to take a drink and a snack and unwrap your purchases, here's your chance. Incidentally, most of the Charing Cross Road bookshops are open on Saturday afternoon until about 5 p.m.

It's lunchtime. Just around the corner is Soho, a district packed with restaurants. Sheekey's, the Terrazza and Chez Solange (35 Cranbourn Street) are nearby. For a quick snack go to the Moka Bar (Greek Street at Shaftesbury Avenue end). All these places are near to Charing Cross Road.

After lunch walk right through Soho via Old Compton Street, Brewer Street and Golden Square to Carnaby Street for health food, pop music, camp junk and trousers that you can't sit down in. If you plan to buy something leave plenty of time: the shops are likely to be crowded (mostly with people just looking) and the service friendly and affable but as casual as the clothes.

After Carnaby Street walk through to Regent Street and take a taxi cab. If you haven't had enough models, mods and minis then take your cab to King's Road. When you see a *dense* crowd – and I do mean a *dense* crowd – tear your way through it to find the Guys n' Dolls coffee bar. From now on you are on your own, for my cab took me to Brown's Hotel, Albemarle Street, for afternoon tea. If you don't like English-style afternoon tea just take a grip on your thin cucumber sandwich and watch. The stage is set for 'There'll always be an England, Act One, Scene One: Afternoon Tea'. The fact that the cast are entirely American doesn't spoil the show one bit.

Saturday night. Perhaps you have already booked theatre seats weeks ahead. If not what about a concert? The Royal Festival Hall is the finest concert hall in London. There is an orchestral concert most nights of the year as well as special recitals in the smaller hall and some performances in the daytime. In the same building – which is on the south side of Waterloo Bridge – there is a bar and restaurant.

Next to the Festival Hall is the National Film Theatre, a cinema devoted entirely to the art of the film. Performances are at 6.15 p.m. and 8.30 p.m. and are likely to be anything from *Doctor Caligari* to Gary Cooper. Phone WAT 3232 to find out what's on. You'll need to become a member but the fee is quite small.

If your tastes are for recorded music then I would particularly recommend Discurio, 9 Shepherd Street, w 1, which specializes in records that other shops don't stock. For instance, it doesn't have singles or much interest in the top ten but you will find all manner of marches, church music and symphonic records from all countries there. For something a little more rare Collectors' Corner at 63 Monmouth Street, w c 2 (T E M 5614), has records dating back to the turn of the century and is particularly famous for producing rare vocal and operatic records. Naturally enough a real rarity can be expensive. Note that this is near the bookshops in Cecil Court.

Musica Rara at 2 Great Marlborough Street, w 1 (G E R 1576), sells ancient and exotic musical instruments from old English viols to extraordinary machines that I would rather were not pointed at me.

But back to Saturday evening and entertainment. On Saturday evenings throughout June and July a symphony orchestra plays by the lakeside at Kenwood. Even if it rains – and it rains every time I go – the orchestra continue to play (for they are under cover). The audience, too, given a chance to display true British staying power, stick it out defiantly. Seats can be booked by phoning T E M 5464. Take a ticket, take a chance and take an umbrella.

In those same grounds stands Kenwood House. There are £7 million worth of art treasures there, including paintings by Rembrandt, Gainsborough and Reynolds and some of the finest work of Robert Adam. It's open to the public until 7 p.m. in summer and the concerts don't start until 8 p.m. How you reconcile those two facts is up to you, but if you like doing nothing and the weather is dry this is just the place. To get to Kenwood take the single-decker bus (No. 210) parked to the left as you come out of Golders Green Underground station, or walk from Hampstead Underground. Anybody will tell you the direction. My suggestion: arrange for a mini-cab to be there when the concert ends.

One of the reasons I like to eat after a concert, theatre or film is that I enjoy talking about the show afterwards. If you feel the same way there are plenty of London restaurants happy to serve you at 11 p.m. but do yourself a favour and tell them you are coming late. If, when you get there, you don't have anything to say about the concert you'd better ask Spike Hughes to come along too.

Music

Spike Hughes

Born 1908 in London. Educated at Perse School, Cambridge; Vienna; Berlin; Florence. Composer, writer, broadcaster. Music: *High Yellow* (ballet, Savoy Theatre 1932, with Markova, Ashton); *Cinderella* (first opera specially written for television, B.B.C. 1938); pioneered jazz in Britain, recording about eighty of his compositions with his own band in London and New York, among them *Six Bells Stampede, Donegal Cradle Song* (1929–33); author and composer of *Frankie and Johnny* (TV musical for B.B.C. 1950); music for numerous documentary films 1929–61, and *Sailors Three*. Books: two volumes of autobiography, *Opening Bars, Second Movement*; studies of the operas of Mozart, Puccini and Verdi; *The Toscanini Legacy*; *Great Opera Houses*; *Glyndebourne: A History*; *The Art of Coarse Cricket*; *The Art of Coarse Travel*; *The Art of Coarse Gardening* (in preparation). In collaboration with his wife, Charmian, *Eating in France* and – in preparation – *Eating in Italy*. Music critic of the *Daily Herald* 1933–44; Mike of the *Melody Maker* 1931–45. Recreations: eating, drinking, motoring anywhere but in England, watching his wife gardening. Lives in a 1603 farmhouse in Ringmer, Sussex.

The world's first public concert hall was opened in London in 1672, in Whitefriars, a few yards south of Fleet Street. And for more than 250 years the city has attracted a constant stream of musicians of the highest class. But whereas most of the world has been well aware of this, Londoners themselves are inclined to forget it. So from time to time, they proclaim loudly, with the air of making a startling discovery, that London is not only a world musical centre, but indeed the centre of the world's music, no less. Although it is doubtful if any city has ever occupied this position – unless it was Berlin in the immediate pre-Hitler years, or New York in the immediate pre-war years

– in the 1960s Londoners have again been making loud claims to the world title.

It all began with Handel, who visited England in 1710 and liked it so much that he returned two years later and became an English citizen. He lived in London for forty-seven years and died at 25 Brook Street, Mayfair. After him came the 'London' Bach – Johann Christian, Johann Sebastian's youngest (eleventh) son, who wrote seven operas for London in the twenty years he lived there, and is buried in St Pancras churchyard. Mozart came as a boy of eight to live in Cecil Court, St Martin's Lane, then moved to 15 Frith Street, Soho, and finally to 180 Ebury Street, s w 1, where he wrote his first two symphonies. Haydn lived in London twice – the first time for eighteen months when he lodged at 45 Holborn and then at 18 Great Pulteney Street, where he wrote his first set of six 'London' symphonies; the second time, also for eighteen months, he lived at 1 Bury Street, St James's, where he wrote the second series of 'London' symphonies – the last six of his life's total of 104. When he wanted a rest from the turmoil of London, Haydn used to retire to the countryside quiet of Lisson Grove.

Cherubini wrote four operas for London in the 1780s, when he was Composer to the King for a year, and in 1815 he was here again – his fifth visit – to write a symphony for the newly founded Philharmonic Society of London. A little later in the nineteenth century Mendelssohn lived in Great Portland Street, and Weber died there when he was in London to conduct *Oberon* which he had written for Covent Garden. Rossini came to write an opera for the King's Theatre, but was swindled out of his advance by a bankrupt impresario and wrote nothing; instead he entertained the Prince Regent at Brighton Pavilion. Verdi wrote *I Masnadieri* for Jenny Lind at Her Majesty's in 1847, and a cantata for the International Exhibition of 1862, when he lived near 'St Regent's Park', as he put it.

Wagner stayed in Old Compton Street, Soho, when he was young and unknown, and at 12 Orme Square, Bayswater, when he was old and famous. Berlioz favoured St Marylebone: Harley Street, Queen Anne Street and Margaret Street were his addresses during five lengthy visits to London, where he worked as conductor of his own and other people's music (including a season at Drury Lane with an Italian opera company), and as a witty and observant correspondent for a Paris newspaper to which he reported:

In no country in the world is so much music consumed in a season as in London. Thanks to this immense consumption, all artists of genuine talent, after a few months spent in getting known, are sure to find work there. Once they have become known and been taken up, they are expected to come back every year; it is assumed they will reappear just like the pigeons in North America. And never, up to the end of their lives, are they known to deceive the expectations of the English public, that model of fidelity, which is always ready to welcome, applaud and admire them, 'without noting the irreparable ravages of the years'. One must have seen the rush, the turmoil of the musical life of favourite artists in London, to get a fair idea of it.

What Berlioz wrote in the 1850s still goes for London today. True, there were more concert halls and opera houses in the capital in those days than there are now, and it is doubtful whether modern London could match the time in June 1855, when Wagner was conducting a series of concerts for the old Philharmonic Society while Berlioz was conducting a series for the New Philharmonic Society. But the dog-like devotion of the London public to old favourites is still as characteristic of our metropolitan musical life as ever it was in Berlioz's day – more so, in fact, for in the past thirty years the annual musical 'season' has disappeared and the opportunities for the display of this loyalty and enthusiasm are now virtually non-stop.

With five full-sized symphony orchestras, as well as several smaller specialist ensembles all based on London and in need of as much work as they can get, it is hardly surprising that Christmas Eve and Christmas Day are now the only days in the year when there is not a public concert of some sort or other. And even those days are not entirely without music, of course, for the churches are open.

Each Saturday *The Times* lists the music to be heard in London's churches on the following day. At the top of the bill are St Paul's Cathedral, Westminster Abbey and Southwark Cathedral, where the English Choral Tradition, with its typical disembodied boy-soprano voices, known to musicians as 'the cathedral hoot', flourishes on a steady diet of familiar Victorian popular services – Stanford in C, Wood in D, Naylor in A, Wesley in F, Gray in E.

The best and most adventurous church music in London is heard in the Catholic churches, particularly at Westminster Cathedral and Brompton Oratory. Westminster in the first quarter of this century not only revolutionized the everyday Catholic musical repertoire in this country by performing the works of Palestrina, Lassus and Victoria in place of the sloppier nineteenth-century French and Italian composers so long suffered by English Catholics, but also reminded the Anglicans of the neglected glories of their own Tudor church music by singing Tallis, Byrd, Taverner, Morley, Weelkes and Gibbons, though never, of course, to the extent of persuading them to drop Stanford in C, any more than the Oratory can bear to be parted from César Franck.

The music at Catholic Westminster is also remarkable for the deliberately robust singing of the boys who are trained to avoid the 'cathedral hoot'; this gives the choir something of the natural, spontaneous quality of Italian church singing. This type of singing is considered a little too personal and emotional for Anglican taste, and the majority of London choir-masters still try to breed the 'pure' and deadly dull clinical voice that made Master Ernest Lough's famous record of Mendelssohn's 'O, for the wings of a dove' a million-copy seller.

London's churches play a great musical part in the working-day life of the Londoner, especially in the City, the West End and southern St Marylebone, where organ recitals and performances of recorded music are a regular and well-attended lunch-time feature in many of the smaller, more picturesque churches. And many of them serve as concert halls at night for the performance of entirely secular music by the numberless small orchestras and chamber ensembles dedicated to baroque music that have sprung up in the past decade.

Considering how much instrumental music is heard in London churches out of business hours, as it were, it is surprising that the accompaniment of Sunday services is not more ambitious than it is. However, the royal chapels of the Royal Hospital, Chelsea, the Military Chapel at Chelsea Barracks, and the Guards' Chapel at Wellington Barracks make up for this to a certain extent by regularly using a Guards' Band at their services to which the public is admitted. The musical repertoire is naturally a little limited – psalms, hymns, interludes – but at least it sounds different and it is unusual.

Whether or not it is because they have been brought up with so much church music going on around them, once they are in the concert hall Londoners observe a religious silence between the movements of concertos which one encounters nowhere else. It seems to be their belief that by coughing, stretching, stamping, sneezing, blowing their noses, squirming in their seats, muttering, whispering and rustling their programmes in 'silence' at the end of the first movement of the Beethoven violin concerto they are in some way showing deep respect for the composer and the integrity of his interpreter. Nearly every foreign virtuoso who encounters this peculiar behaviour for the first time finds it a disconcerting experience. Applause after the strain of performing that particular Beethoven first movement, for instance, breaks the tension and gives the soloist a desperately needed chance to relax for a moment and tune his instrument in comfort without feeling that a couple of thousand pairs of ears are listening to him doing it in an embarrassing silence. In all the fifty years he played in London Joseph Szigeti could never get used to this idiosyncrasy of the audiences; but he told me there was nothing he could do about it; he was a guest in London and had to accept local customs.

There is always consolation to be found in the applause at the end of the concerto, of course, which is rarely less than warm or lacking in the famous London 'fidelity' that Berlioz wrote about. This curious discipline is exercised even by the audience at the annual Promenade Concerts, held six nights a week for eight weeks from July to September in the Albert Hall. I say 'even' the Prom audiences because this nightly gathering of up to 8,000 people is in other respects the least inhibited musical audience in the world. Leaving aside its traditional exhibitionism on the first and last nights of the Prom season (when its antics with streamers and banners and funny hats have nothing to do with music but everything to do with the accident that it is all being televised), the Prom audience makes it a point of honour to applaud every work the very second it has finished – that is, before the famous Albert Hall echo of the last note has died down. There is not even a split moment of silent reflection at the end of a work that has ended quietly. It is a well-meaning audience, but not always very discriminating; and it invariably includes at least one fathead determined to get his solo 'Bravo!' in before the others, regardless of whether the performance deserves it or not.

The stranger to London may well be misled by the name of the Promenade Concerts; as he will soon discover if he goes to the Albert Hall, you are not encouraged to promenade during the music. You couldn't anyway. But even so – and this is the incomparable joy of the Proms – you are able to pick and choose, to come and go when you like – even during the music, if you are clever enough to station yourself near an exit. The best acoustics in the Hall are probably at the very back of the gallery – a belief confirmed when I found myself sitting on the floor there once, with Sir Adrian Boult next to me, listening to Bruno Walter and the Vienna Philharmonic. But the arena promenade is the most fun – a classless little world of its own. I have seen a Master of the King's Musick in a dirty old macintosh and a communist in tails on his way to a night club; I have seen composers sneak in to listen to their own music and sneak out again before they have to listen to anybody else's; I have shared scores with strangers and met critics taking a night off from work and actually enjoying what they heard.

The Proms are London's greatest musical achievement. Nowhere else in the world is there anything to compare with this series of concerts, whose policy since their foundation in 1895 by Sir Henry Wood (1869–1944) has been to offer an intense survey of the standard orchestral repertoire, to introduce new works and revive the unfamiliar or unfashionable ones. In the past few seasons the programmes have grown increasingly ambitious; where before Beethoven's Ninth Symphony was the only choral work regularly heard at these concerts, 'standard' works like the Brahms and Verdi Requiems, Walton's *Belshazzar's Feast*, Beethoven's Mass in D, Haydn's *Creation* have been included as well as less familiar things such as Berlioz's Requiem, *Childhood of Christ* and *Damnation of*

Faust, Beethoven's Choral Fantasia and Mass in C, several of Haydn's Masses and a performance of Walton's *Façade* in its original form as 'an entertainment' for small orchestra and two speakers of Edith Sitwell's poems (not strictly a choral work, of course, but typical of the unusual forms that find their way into the Prom programmes).

The most startling and successful innovation at the Proms, however, has been the introduction of concert performances of opera. This has brought the full Glyndebourne Festival Opera company to the Albert Hall in performances of Mozart's *Figaro*, *Don Giovanni*, *Così fan tutte*, *Idomeneo* and *The Magic Flute*, Monteverdi's *Incoronazione di Poppea* and Verdi's *Macbeth*, but presented in such a way (the invention of Glyndebourne's General Manager, Moran Caplat) that the singers are not chained to a row of chairs at the front of the platform but appear on a small raised platform behind the orchestra where they are free to come and go as their cues dictate. Glyndebourne's lead was followed by the Covent Garden company who have contributed successful concert versions at the Proms of their productions of Schönberg's *Moses and Aaron*, Verdi's *Otello* and as much of Wagner's *Walküre* as time would permit (Acts I and III).

With the wide repertoire it now offers, the few weeks of the modern Prom season have been known to involve twenty different conductors (not including visiting composer-conductors), nine orchestras (two of them from out of town), and no fewer than seventeen choirs. Except for help from composers and his orchestra leader for the last item of the evening, Sir Henry Wood managed all by himself with one orchestra for the first forty-four years of the Proms, in programmes relatively no less demanding than they are today. But there was only ever one Henry Wood and he perhaps more than any of his contemporaries kept London up to scratch as a world music centre, performing Schönberg's *Five Orchestral Pieces* as early as 1912 and in 1933 anticipating the present vogue for Mahler with a performance of the huge Eighth Symphony.

The Proms are strictly a summer phenomenon; they have never caught on in the winter – a situation which applies very much (and more understandably) to another unique musical activity in London: bands playing in the parks. From May to September military and brass bands play for an hour and a half or more on Sundays and Bank Holidays, morning and afternoon, in Hyde Park, Kensington Gardens, Regent's Park, and Greenwich Park. In St James's Park they play on Whit Monday and ordinary weekdays (never on Sundays), when there are two sessions daily – at lunch time (12.30–2) and after tea (5.30–7).

The Londoner's craving for open-air music with his lunchtime sandwich is generously satisfied in the summer months with bands on the steps of St Paul's Cathedral (Thursdays), in Finsbury Circus Gardens (Wednesdays), Lincoln's Inn Fields (Tuesdays and Thursdays) and every working day of the week in Victoria Embankment Gardens at Charing Cross. The Victoria Embankment Gardens bandstand is the busiest in London: from mid-May to mid-September there are two programmes every day, mid-day and evening.

There is never any question of a London park band playing only subject to 'weather permitting'. London bandsmen are born troupers and play conscientiously through the programme even if the rain is sloshing down and there is no audience to hear them.

Bands *are* to be heard in the winter months, but not in the parks. One or other of the five Guards Bands marches daily (often the wrong way down one-way streets and regardless of traffic lights) to Buckingham Palace for the Changing of the Guard and plays loudly on its way. Bands, too, are very much part of the pre-match and half-time periods of big Rugby games at Twickenham. Bands at Lord's Cricket Ground in the summer, on the other hand, seem to be extinct, but it is not so long ago that the annual match in August between the Royal Artillery and the Royal Engineers was shown in the fixture list with the words 'Band if possible' in parentheses. A band always did turn up and, what's more, seemed to play without pausing for breath all the time the game was in progress. It gave the match a pleasantly festive air and was as powerful a soporific for the spectator in the fierce sunlight of a London August as the cricket itself.

The cricket band, like all but the marching bands of London, had a rather undemanding kind of repertoire – selections from Gilbert and Sullivan, popular 'grand' opera, cornet and euphonium solos, Drury Lane musicals (not always the latest), waltzes by Strauss and Lehar, the *Peer Gynt* suites, potpourris of Noël Coward.

There is no shortage of music or of people to listen to it in London; there is only a frustrating shortage of places to perform it in. The destruction of the Queen's Hall by German bombs in 1941 deprived London of a beautiful hall with an unmistakable, sympathetic atmosphere, and the sort of acoustics that are born and not made (the headstone of its grave is the St George's Hotel). If, in spite of the construction of the Royal Festival Hall, the loss of Queen's Hall somehow still makes Londoners feel they are one concert hall short of the normal, this is because the production of music in London has increased almost beyond practical bounds. Two halls suitable for orchestral concerts are no longer enough, as they were before the war. In those days only the London Symphony Orchestra, the London Philharmonic and the B.B.C. Symphony Orchestra needed accommodation; today these three orchestras have to share two halls with the Royal Philharmonic Orchestra, the New Philharmonia, the London Mozart Players, as well as regular visiting orchestras from the provinces like the Hallé, the City of Birmingham and the Royal Liverpool Philharmonic.

As a result, buildings never intended for concerts are being used in desperation and with varying degrees of success; it has also meant that a great deal of London's musical life has become decentralized. Only Fairfield Hall at Croydon is an intentional concert hall; for the rest, cinemas at Swiss Cottage and Enfield, Town Halls at Kensington, Chelsea, Wimbledon, Hammersmith, Watford, Fulham, museums, institutes, schools, libraries, church halls, lecture rooms – almost anything with four walls and an improvised fire exit has to serve to appease the Londoner's gargantuan appetite for music.

Only one recital hall survives from pre-war London, the 540-seat Wigmore Hall where since 1901 recitals by international figures like Busoni, Ysaÿe, Schnabel, Cortot, Szigeti, Petri and Pachmann have alternated with first appearances by beginners who hire the hall, paper it with their friends, and hope that the money they spend will at least produce a quotable notice in *The Times* and the *Daily Telegraph*. Two new small concert halls, however, have recently opened on the South Bank, a few yards from the Festival Hall – a small auditorium seating 1,100 and a recital room seating 372. Some relief of the orchestral congestion has also been promised by the inclusion in the City of London's Barbican arts centre plan of a 2,000-seat concert hall which is to be leased to the London Symphony Orchestra as its permanent home. Presumably, unless the L.S.O. is to give seven concerts a week there, the hall will be sub-let to others, which also ought to help matters.

Meanwhile, London musical life follows an oddly Victorian pattern: the concert hall dominated by German music, the opera by Italian. London has two opera houses, each open for about ten months of the year. The Royal Opera House, Covent Garden, seats 2,114, averages about seven performances a fortnight and is expensive (lowest price is usually 7s. 6d. with a possible top of £7 17s. 6d.). Sadler's Wells seats 1,523, performs five nights a week and totals over 200 performances a season. Its prices are reasonable, ranging from 5s. to 25s. on weekdays and to 30s. on first nights and Saturdays.

At Sadler's Wells opera is sung in English, at Covent Garden nearly always in the language the opera was written in. Covent Garden's policy has made it easier for star foreign singers to join in when new productions of Verdi, Mozart, Wagner and Puccini are mounted. This is a commendable practice, but after the star singers have appeared in a limited number of performances the resident company fills all the major roles, the original production is 'rehearsed' by a staff producer and the result is very often a very tired repertory version of what may have originally been an outstanding experience. One effect of the constant international traffic in singers at Covent Garden has been to encourage the audience to applaud at the end of arias and so make the visiting artists feel at home by giving them the reception to which they are accustomed and which they sometimes deserve. Obviously opera is not considered such serious music as a Beethoven concerto.

Where two opera houses are sufficient to cope with the operatic demands of cities like Paris, Vienna and New York, and are one more than is considered necessary in Milan, Rome, Brussels, Naples and most other cities, London's two lyric theatres are not nearly enough to cope with the quite extraordinary amount of operatic activity that goes on in the city. The source of all this activity is a dozen or so organizations, some amateur, some semi-professional. One or two, based in the suburbs, style themselves Grand Opera Societies and no nonsense; but most of them call themselves self-consciously 'Groups'. For some reason to be an opera 'company' is now regarded as slipping back unforgivably into the bad old ways of Tory misrule.

These opera 'groups' produce opera in a form which I think is peculiar to London and which is best defined as 'Town Hall Opera'. They do not perform in theatres for there are none available; but except in the comparatively rare event of giving opera in a concert version, they use the stages of their local town halls and do the job as properly as the rather limited theatrical amenities of the hall permit.

The outstanding feature of London Town Hall Opera is the repertoire, which is sensibly as far removed from that of the two professional opera houses as possible. Even the Grand Opera Societies which have regularly performed Gounod's *Faust* since their formation half a century ago, when it was one of the most popular operas ever written, are now performing a rarity. The rest of the 'groups', on the other hand, concentrate mostly on operas that have never been particularly popular but which they believe are worth reviving, and which in an ideal world would be part of the everyday opera repertoire. This belief applies to almost anything from Monteverdi to Hans Werner Henze.

The busiest and most ambitious manifestation of opera-group activity is found at St Pancras, now renamed Camden, Arts Festival during February and March each year. The operatic policy of this festival since its foundation in 1955 has been the performance of typically unfamiliar operas presented by various 'groups' and sponsored by the Libraries and Arts Committee of the Borough. The principal singers in these productions are professional, although most of them are singing roles above their station, as it were, and which they would not normally be asked to sing at Covent Garden or Sadler's Wells; the orchestras are also usually professional, but the choruses are not. Perhaps the most worthwhile experience of the St Pancras festivals has been the performance of early, unfamiliar Verdi – of operas like *Ernani, Il Corsaro, I Masnadieri, Un Giorno di regno* or *Aroldo*, which in some cases had never been performed in England at all before.

The universal interest in Verdi developed in the past thirty years has brought with it a new international curiosity about the music of his immediate predecessors, Rossini, Donizetti and Bellini. St Pancras, both in and out of its festival periods, has contributed handsomely to satisfying this curiosity and has thrown in unfamiliar operas by Handel, Haydn, Cherubini, Auber and Gluck for good measure.

The one unsatisfactory feature of Town Hall Opera in London – when it is good, at any rate – is that it is so ephemeral. Town halls are solidly booked for a variety of functions throughout the year and it is almost impossible to put on any production for more than a couple of evenings. This is regretted by some of the critics, but it is a matter of opinion whether very many of the performances they praise so ecstatically are really all that good. The fact remains, however, that all this operatic activity is something peculiar to modern London; and typical, for it has a strong touch about it of the amateurism and improvisation which the English admire so much in music. What is most typical of all, of course, is that this new enthusiasm should be for the one form of music to which the English, having no operatic tradition of their own, are traditionally indifferent. But then that's just the sort of thing that has kept London the musical centre it is all these centuries.

London luxuries

Shopping in London can be a fruitful and educative business, but forget any idea that it will be an inexpensive one. No large cities provide merchandise cheaply, although London does offer bargains in services and atmosphere. I remember when I was a kid saving up my pocket money to buy a leather wallet from Swaine Adeney Brigg & Sons (185 Piccadilly) and even now I never pass the shop without remembering the feeling I had when I emerged with the best leather wallet I have ever owned. I lost it. Perhaps that's why I never persevered with luxury. I've never had a Savile Row suit nor a made-to-measure shirt, although I've looked into the shop window of Turnbull & Asser (71 Jermyn Street) enough times to feel I owe them rent. I've bought at least a dozen Eton College ties as gifts for visiting foreigners, but I've never had nerve enough to wear one myself (although I must admit buying them in my dirtiest clothes has not been unamusing). I once went into a very flash barber's but left immediately before the stage where they apply a hairnet.

But if you have a taste for luxury shopping then shop in style, hire a Rolls Royce Silver Cloud with driver from Patrick Barthropp Ltd, Colnbrook Court, Sloane Avenue, s w 3 (k e n 8292). It will cost you about £14 for fifty miles and about 10s. per mile thereafter. If you can convince them that you are a really superb driver they might let you have a Rolls for self-drive.

Perhaps your idea of luxury is rare stamps. The best-known dealer is Stanley Gibbons, 391 Strand, w c 2, which most collectors already know. Another is the London Stamp Exchange, 5 Buckingham Street, w c 2, which will show you some fantastic rarities. If you prefer the excitement of an auction there are regular stamp auctions at several London rooms, e.g. Harmer, 41 New Bond Street w 1 (MAY 0218), but don't scratch your nose at the wrong moment.

No visitor interested in British stamps should miss the philatelic sales counter in the King Edward Building, King Edward Street, E C 1 (opposite St Paul's). Recent issues are on sale – pictorial landscapes, British paintings, flora and discovery – as well as issues normally on sale only in Wales or Scotland. I bought hundreds of my favourite – British birds – and used them on all my mail for weeks. Here too there are first day covers and presentation packs.

Maggs Brothers live in a superb house at 50 Berkeley Square, w 1. They sell rare books, manuscripts and oriental miniature paintings. They are very long-suffering with customers who have only a couple of quid to spend, and when I couldn't afford a letter from Nelson – 120 guineas – let me have a signed, red wax-sealed envelope from Wellington for only 5s. I was so impressed with the bargain – Wellington it seems was such a compulsive signer that he's a buyer's market – that I have been back to gape at the goodies there many times since.

It's amazing to me how cheap ancient coins are. Of course there are rarities that can cost hundreds of pounds, but on the other hand I have a coin of Constantine the Great bought in a shop for less than 10s. B. A. Seaby at 65 Great Portland Street, w 1, is a very large outfit which buys, sells and assesses. It has patient experts anxious to talk, but please promise me you won't weld gadgets on the back of the coins and make them into cuff-links.

Once some foreign friends of mine were taken with a luxury tobacco shop, named Fribourg & Treyer, at 34 Haymarket, near Piccadilly Circus, which sells the cheapest luxury souvenir in London: fine Wedgwood ashtrays at less than £1 each. Having looked at the superb shopfront my friends entered the shop and probed, weighed, discussed, priced and photographed everything in the shop. They left at a leisurely pace while I smiled apologetically and felt obliged to purchase a small pack of snuff which I never did use. Really I'm not equipped to advise you about luxury. Now if you are interested in things dirty and slightly broken, that's my subject.

London luxuries

Londoners, unlike Europeans and Americans, do not disdain secondhand things. Personally I prefer a book that has already been read, especially if the previous readers have left neat annotations in the margin. The less salubrious parts of London are dotted with grubby little junk shops and the sight of one is enough to lose me for an hour. If you want a secondhand umbrella ask your cab driver. The ones left in taxis are seldom claimed and after a few years most drivers amass quite a collection. On Friday mornings the Bermondsey Market (sometimes called the Caledonian Market) is held not far from Tower Bridge. It's not cheap but providing the weather is kind it will provide certain entertainment and a possible treasure, if not a bargain. Unless your driver knows the way, the simplest – but probably slightly roundabout – route is to go south over Tower Bridge and keep going until you see an Esso station on your right. Adjacent to the station is the market. It's held only on Fridays: go as early as you can. Six a.m. is not too early to go and although the earliest I've made it is 8.30 a.m. I've seen large vans already loaded and driving away.

The items on sale range from Victorian dolls to modern silver (in fact it's very high on silverware lately), old pictures, odds and ends of porcelain, eighteenth century uniforms, antique jewellery, African carving, miners' lamps and tea services in monogrammed cases. It's more interesting than Portobello Road Market, which is held in the west part of London on Saturday morning, Friday morning's customers often being Portobello Road stall holders.

If you don't buy enough to weigh you down, this might be the morning to visit the Tower of London – it's just up the road. It opens at 10 a.m. Or if it stays fine, get on a boat at Tower Pier either to return to Westminster or travel to Greenwich, or places farther afield. From here merchant ships with luxury accommodation leave for all parts of the world.

Luxury is just a matter of taste and circumstances. For prisoners in the Tower it was a luxury to be beheaded on Tower Green, for the riff-raff were executed on Tower Hill with every Tom, Dick, and Harry standing by. No, I was never one for a lot of luxury. If you are, listen to my mate Godfrey.

Self-indulgence

Godfrey Smith

Born 1926. Read Philosophy, Politics and Economics at Worcester College, Oxford; President of the Oxford Union 1950. One wife, three daughters. Lives in 1840-type house a stone's throw from Lord's cricket ground. Novels – *The Flaw in the Crystal* (1954), *The Friends* (1959), *The Business of Loving* (1961), *The Network* (1964), *The Londoners* (1967). Editor of the *Sunday Times* Magazine since 1965. Consolations: Bolivar cigars, barbecues, Beethoven quartets. Clubs – M.C.C., Savile, Press. Played rugger for South of Thames public schools 1944. Weight – 17 stone.

Luxury starts at Trumper's in Curzon Street. Like most London luxuries, it is surprisingly cheap: a haircut costs 8s. 6d., a shampoo 3s. 6d. and there are hot towels too for another half-crown.

Though the original Mr Trumper passed on some twenty years ago, the shop is still run with Edwardian panache by his daughter. It's a magic place with its great hour-glass bottles of mysterious unguents, its fat sponges, its sporting prints, and its grave deferential barbers. Trumper's announces proudly on its window-pane that it was 'by appointment to Kings George V and VI' and all the men there look as if they've sheared royal locks personally. They date from the day when a boy had to put down £100 for his five-year apprenticeship, was paid nothing until his fourth year when he got 2s. 6d. a week, and practised shaving on an old pig's bladder for the first three years. Trumper's has twenty-three different hair dressings ranging from a fine mist to a rich oil; and six shampoos, of which my favourite is lemon, though you might prefer the egg or A.D. (polite shorthand for anti-dandruff). The main point about

Trumper's is that they do make you feel like a man, and that's a good start nowadays.

When I leave Trumper's on a Saturday morning (you can park the car outside on a meter quite easily before 11 a.m.), there are several agreeable possibilities. Curzon Street is studded with inviting doorways. A few yards up on the left opposite is the Mirabelle restaurant, still probably the most gracious place in the West End to spend £12 on lunch for two.

Then you can stroll eastwards past the Thoroughbred Breeders' Association and the Third Church of Christ Scientist to the Washington Hotel. I once peered through the curtains on a dark night and saw Ian Fleming entertaining a mysterious lady to dinner. It has always had an ambience of romantic decadence for me since then.

Cross over again and turn left into Shepherd Market. Though it's a tourist trap you can get one bargain there: the Express café is run by Italians and is one of the best places to get a good breakfast at 7 a.m. after an all-night outing; egg, bacon and chips cost only 3s. 3d. Even the most unsuspecting tourist can hardly help noticing the inviting little doorway with the chummy gold doorbells marked Colette, first floor, and Jacqueline, second floor. You should not, however, be misled by the advertisements for masseuses on cards outside the shops; a friend of mine tottering out of Shepherds, the smart boozer, at 3 p.m. one Saturday called on one and got half an hour's battering from an expert's palms. She said afterwards that she'd walloped him extra hard for thinking she was the other kind of masseuse. So watch it.

Up Shepherd Street lives Stirling Moss in his all-electronic house; opposite is Radio Luxembourg, London, and on the corner the refurbished Curzon Cinema, long renowned for the most comfortable snogging seats in London; now an inviting confection of black glass and Monica Vitti films.

You can head on eastwards towards Park Lane but it's too early usually to drift into the Tiberio in Queen Street, where Mario will not only provide the best Italian food in town, but convince the lady you are with that she's the most gorgeous thing he's ever seen. His compliments flow with natural grace. 'It makes me feel good,' an American girl commented once, 'it makes you feel good and it makes him feel good. So why not?'

However, at this time in the morning I like to potter down Half Moon Street and cross over to the Ritz, where amidst faded green-and-gold splendour they serve up the best champagne cocktails London can offer. They cost 11s. 0d. each but they're worth it. They're made with one lump of sugar, one *drop* of Angostura bitters, just a dash of brandy (too much would kill the taste of the champagne), filled with iced non-vintage bubbly, and topped up with one twist of orange peel. You can get cheaper champagne cocktails in London; in the Savoy's American Bar they are 8s. 6d. each and, like the Ritz, they throw in the olives, cashews, crisps, and cheese footballs for free. The Champagne Bar at the Connaught Rooms does champagne cocktails at 7s. 6d. but their cheapness frankly doesn't compensate for the ambience.

If you want a panoramic view of London you can't do better than the Rooftop Bar at the Hilton though it does seem to draw lone melancholics who've left their wives. The cocktails are average; that is, too yellow in colour, decorated with a huge slice of orange and a cherry speared with a plastic mini-sword. They're 10s. 6d. each. The barmen are informal, cosmopolitan, and chatty, but start to clear away rather too pointedly when closing time comes.

After that, you need a dry, intellectual pleasure. A taxi will swiftly carry you to the London Library at 14 St James's Square. This is undoubtedly one of the cheapest luxuries England has to offer. Imagine 750,000 volumes, virtually all on open shelves, from which you can remove ten at any one time for 14 gns. a year. You can keep them as long as you like; only when some other member happens to need one of the volumes you have will you receive a courteous invitation from the Librarian to return them. On the receipt of a postcard and a deposit to cover postage they will despatch books to you anywhere in the British Isles done up in stout brown paper and string.

From the Library it's only a few paces to Jermyn Street. This is a thoroughfare resonant with *luxe*. At Turnbull & Asser, for instance, they make shirts for the House of Lords and Mr Paul McCartney. They've been in the business for eighty-odd years and they have over five hundred materials to choose from. The speciality is shirts in silk and voile, though they will, at a pinch, run you up something in poplin for £5 10s. A magnificently ruffled red silk shirt for the evening costs 14 gns., and a brocade dressing-gown about 52 gns. (in cashmere it would be nearer 70 gns.). Smoking jackets, although not as fashionable as they once were, run out at 25 to 30 gns.

Harvie & Hudson's sell shirts too in Jermyn Street, and say they launched the striped-shirt style (heavy black on white) a few years back. Personally, I like the shirt department at Simpson's where they'll make you something wild in mauve or shocking pink for £5 10s. or £6 10s.

At 21 Jermyn Street, Codner, Coombs & Dobbie will make you a pair of handmade shoes in about eight weeks for £26. The cost of making the last for your first pair of shoes is included in the price but the last remains their property. Once they've made it they can go on supplying you for ever; it's really their capital. Their customers order from every part of the world – they see perhaps three customers a day in the actual flesh. Repairing the shoes costs about £5 but for this they are completely overhauled and, except for the uppers, more or less remade. They have one customer who brought a pair of shoes in for repair which he bought before the 1914–18 war, and it's not uncommon for them to get in shoes made more than thirty years ago. They also make slippers lined with glacé kid at 18 gns., monogrammed at 19 gns. (Cecil Bernstein wanted a pair like Alfred Hitchcock's when he saw them).

From here it's hard to resist Fortnum & Mason's which indeed backs on to Jermyn Street. It is of course renowned for its hampers ranging from the college tuck-box at £3 5s. through the celebration gift basket at £9, up to the fabulous hampers suitable for film stars to present to their directors. They cost 52 gns., for which you get petits fours, chocolates, crystallized fruits, Red Seal Scotch whisky, cigars, caviare, Grand Marnier peaches, crystallized ginger, turtle soup, royal blend India and Ceylon tea, terrine de foie gras truffée, six spices, a pot of marmalade, a tongue, nuts, fruit salad, and, rather inexplicably, Bronnley talc and soap, and Fortnum's own bath essence. Fortnum's will send you a pound of caviare in a ceramic pot with sturgeon etched round its middle in black for about £18.

I would add only one *caveat* about Fortnum's; it is superb, but the best game pies in London come from Selfridges. The form is to ring up two or three days before and get the chef to make it for you, then pick it up from their pie department on the morning of your party. Sizes range from £2 10s. downwards. The big one serves a dozen people comfortably, and is ideal for demolishing with a bottle of Krug in the car park before the Oxford and Cambridge game at Twickenham.

London is a good city for one of the great unsung luxuries: exercise. You can walk across six London parks (St James's, Green Park, Hyde Park, Regent's Park, Primrose Hill and Hampstead Heath) on an iridescent spring morning, traversing stone pavements only intermittently. You start at St James's Park and end up in Highgate Village where there is a place called The Village Cake Shop which will make you a well-earned poached egg on toast. However, if that sounds too much like hard work, you should go to the David Morgan Health Club at 3 Hanover Square. Members pay 40 gns. a year for the benefit of using its gleaming ingeniously designed stainless steel equipment. It has an air of assured opulence with its fitted carpets and Scandinavian timber, and when you emerge after your planned bout of exercise and a sauna bath you feel nineteen again. The only point is you must use it regularly; three times a week costs you a mere 5s. a visit; if you only call in once every six weeks it works out expensive.

The great sporting institution of London is the Marylebone Cricket Club at Lord's. It used to be said that you had to be put down at birth for this select côterie to stand any chance of getting in while you could enjoy it. This is no longer true, especially now they've introduced associate membership which gives you nearly all the advantages of the full treatment except voting. But it still takes a year or two to wear that noble orange-and-yellow striped tie (to wear it as of right that is – no one can stop you going into Neal's in Burlington Arcade and buying one for 22s. The difference in your status rating is immediate and dramatic; people cash your cheques without question and people in pubs earnestly solicit your views on the state of play).

However, if you are impatient, you can get most of the advantages of the M.C.C. by joining the *Middlesex* Cricket Club whose headquarters are also at Lord's. For 4 gns. a year, when Middlesex are playing there, you can drink in the Pavilion Bar, watch the cricket from the Long Room, one of the most gracious in England, and eat a solid club lunch in the members' dining-room. It's not so much the cricket as the Edwardian sense of spaciousness, timelessness, and peace that the place engenders.

From Lord's I like to walk up St John's Wood High Street to call on Mr Quirk, the grey-haired, scholarly cigar dealer. There are bigger and finer cigar shops in London, but none, I think, better. He will sell you anything from a slender Schimmelpenninck to a lordly Bolivar. If you really want to do the thing properly, ask Mr Quirk to get you a hundred Bolivars and store them in his humidor for you. It will cost you £37 or 7s. a cigar, but for this you are getting perfection. The box itself is a delight and inside it the cigars are not pressed flat as they are in ordinary batches of twenty-five, but firm, plump, fresh, and aromatic, tied together in two delicious bunches of fifty with wide ribbons. You just call and help yourself to a handful whenever you are passing by.

I am assuming in all this that you have plenty of cash – though increasingly London is following New York and Los Angeles in becoming a credit capital where ready money is almost a handicap. Credit cards greatly simplify life, provided you can stand the racket when the bills come in. American Express is the biggest credit system; it will cost you 4 gns. a year (you get a travelling alarm clock as a joining present to soften the blow). From then on you can quite simply travel the world on tick. The Diners' Club is another useful American-based credit system which will see you right not only at restaurants but at a host of stores, hotels, car hire firms, and garages.

A further type of credit of great convenience to the sporting man is an account at Ladbroke's. You can then always ring up and put a tenner on a horse or a big fight without question. Ladbroke's in fact will quote you odds on almost any big event and took £1,622,000 on the result of the 1966 General Election.

Credit at bookshops is another agreeable luxury. Blackwell's in Oxford has an especial charm for any old member of the university who can still walk in, sign his name and college and cart away armfuls of new novels. In London Foyle's is the biggest, but rather impersonal, while Bumpus excel at second-hand and antiquarian books. I recently sent an identical letter to Blackwell's, Foyle's and Bumpus, asking for a longish set of secondhand volumes. While the two big boys still had my letter in their in-trays, the man from Bumpus, a courteous and learned figure, had actually arrived in my office, bearing with him a complete set of Aldous Huxley first editions which he sold me there and then for 30s. each. The fact that we only then discovered that one of the set had been signed by Huxley himself, and so was probably worth a tenner alone, did not dismay him at all; he is now hard at work collecting other sets for me.

Record shops don't give credit nearly so readily; but here the important thing is to equip yourself with a copy of *The Stereo Record Guide* by Edward Greenfield, Ivan Marsh and Denis Stevens, which systematically lists not only the finest classical stereo recordings but also, by popular request, the best mono versions too.

Should the Amadeus Quartet be a little too far up the market for you, there are always home movies in which J. Arthur Rank is now doing a brisk business. You can hire a projector and operator for about £10 a show through a photographic dealer. A black-and-white feature film costs about £6, colour £9–£10, cartoons between 12s. 6d. and 25s. For this, though, you get an enormous range of possibilities, from film classics through Westerns like *Destry* and *Davy Crockett* to musicals like *The Glen Miller Story* or *Expresso Bongo*. Or you can try one of their sporting series like *Historic Heavyweight Fights, Ski Mania* or the Gaumont British Newsreel of Roger Bannister running the first-ever four-minute mile.

If, however, you prefer to make your own entertainment you will find that London harbours some of the world's best talkers. Among men I would rate Anthony Blond, the publisher, pretty high, and among women Dee Wells (otherwise Mrs A. J. Ayer) takes some stopping when she is in full flight. I once went on a two-strong delegation to Israel with her and, as we drove endlessly across the Negev desert, she regaled our hosts with a continuous stream of anecdotage which was all the more remarkable for being delivered from the depths of a fur coat. I remember asking her at one point what the good Israelis could make of us two. 'I guess,' she said, 'they think that you are Colonel Blimp and I am a gangster's moll.'

I suppose Jonathan Miller is an even better talker than Anthony Blond, but his intellectual equipment is so formidable that despite his evident sweetness he sometimes puts the wind up people. The laws of libel preclude me from warning you of the leading bores in London whom you would do well to run a mile to avoid. Actually London's champion bore died two years ago, but there are one or two up-and-coming young thrusters jockeying for the vacant title.

The best party-giver in London is still publisher George Weidenfeld.

The London Season carries on but no longer matters. However, should its archaic rituals appeal to you, you can buy your way into the lot; from the faded pink splendour of the Leander Blazers at Henley to the Moss-Bros-clad crowd at Ascot. *The Times* prints lists of deb dances and any young man with a reasonably good ear for Mayfair Cockney and a dinner jacket can still con his way in if he feels that desperate about it. A hard-up Harrovian of my acquaintance tells me you can actually get *paid* by the girl's father to take her out; however, he considers it ungentlemanly to keep the change and returns it at the end of the evening.

Should romance overtake you in the small hours, Doolittle's own Covent Garden Market is in action from 5 a.m. every morning except Sunday, and though nominally wholesale they can be talked into selling a couple of dozen dew-fresh blooms. To their great credit, two London hotels, the Hilton and the Royal Garden, have florists which will dispense flowers to all comers till 10 p.m. each night except Sunday.

The Oliver Messel suite at the Dorchester is probably the most sought-after hotel accommodation. It's on the seventh floor, has one very large sitting-room, two bedrooms, two bathrooms, and an entrance hall. And it costs 35 gns. a night. But you can go higher; their Terrace Suite is 40 gns. a night without meals and service, but is air-conditioned, fitted with radio and television and has a private garden facing Hyde Park.

The Westbury Hotel offers the Hartnell Suite, designed by the royal dress designer and costing a mere 25 gns. a night. The main bedroom is in apple-blossom pink and pale blue with lots of mirrors, while the single bedroom has a suede bedhead and a French linen picture. The sitting-room has light brackets in the form of white cockatoos and a cocktail cabinet and television set are concealed behind false book bindings either side of the fireplace.

If you want someone to share all this splendour with you I am not sure I can help. As Alfred Doolittle observed in *My Fair Lady*: 'There are drinks and girls all over London.' I've told you about the drinks; the rest is up to you.

Sunday

London on Sunday: just try saying those three words in any
language and the chances are the response will be sophisticated
groans. What do people do on a Sunday, they ask. Well, I don't
know what *they* do, but I stay in bed with a cup of tea and
read every Sunday newspaper I can lay my hands on. That's
quite a variety of human experience because the Sunday papers
can vary from the *News of the World* (criminal memoirs), to the
Sunday Times (generals' memoirs and coloured central-heating
advertisements), via the *People* ('Nudist tells all') and the
Observer (an inquiry into gas stoves).

But the real go-getter will be at Billingsgate Market, Lower
Thames Street, EC3, at 6 a.m. On Sundays it's a shellfish market
and you'll see winkles, whelks, cockles and shrimps and all
the things the Londoner likes for tea.

There is only a handful of men at Billingsgate on a Sunday
and if you feel like going, just between you and me, 7.30 a.m.
is quite early enough. It is cheap. Most of the sellers will let
you have small amounts at the wholesale rate whether they
think you are in the fish business or a tourist. A good-sized
crab can cost you 2s. 6d., but it's the shiny little black winkles
that the Londoner likes, pulled out of the shell with a pin, just
a sprinkle of vinegar, salt and pepper, and accompanied by
thin brown bread and butter.

Most of the buyers will be selling this seafood outside
pubs by 11 a.m. and what is then still unsold they will push
around the streets crying out 'winkles and shrimps' as they
go. Not in your posh part of town perhaps but they'll come
around my part.

Incidentally, theirs is one of the few London street cries

still heard. The others I hear are the coalman, the
milkman shouting 'milko' as he leaves milk on a doorstep and
sometimes the call of the knife-grinder with his wheelbarrow
that turns upside down to become a grindstone. Chair-menders
are other regular street criers. There is also the doleful cry of
'lumber' from the totters. These men, sometimes called rag
and bone men, collect old junk – ancient gas stoves, clothes,
broken book-shelves, or just rags and bottles – which they
will sort out and sell. Metal is their most profitable line. They
are among the last people using horses as working transport.
They are very good talkers and whatever value you put on
the items you give them it usually ends up with them getting
paid for taking it away.

The totters take their loads to rag and metal collecting
centres where they are bought by weight. When selling a
fireplace they will bury a fire brick inside it and will
spend happy hours arguing spiritedly about the thickness
of a copper lining. One old man used to tie small chunks
of lead into the sleeves of his bundles of rags. He evaded
detection for five years then one morning he realized that
the price per pound of lead was higher than the price of
rags.

Several of these collecting centres are in Cheshire Street
(behind Bishopsgate Goods Station, Shoreditch High Street).
On Sunday morning totters – and all sorts of other people – go
along to that same stretch of road to sell the treasures that they
have sorted out from the junk they've collected during the week.
There are lots of myths about how early markets start and
although this market is a dealers' source of supply they
themselves are sometimes waiting here at 5 a.m. for the totters
to arrive, so you'll have to look sharp to get a bargain. (I got
three Doulton cups and saucers and plates for 15s. and a
war-surplus bush jacket for 2s. at 8 a.m.) By 9 a.m. it's really
thin on the ground. One man's treasure is another man's debris
and you'll have to burrow through ancient T V sets, broken
ice skates, torn umbrellas and dog-eared books before you find
anything worth buying. This is not a tourist place yet, so wear
your shabby old clothes to go there. You haven't got any?
This could be your big chance to buy some. What about a bus

conductor's cap? The peak is bent but the badge is still good, solid brass.

The animal market in Sclater Street nearby is by no means amusing. Birds flutter around in tiny cages, puppies whine, and fish gasping for air at the surface of overcrowded tanks make it like visiting an Auschwitz for animals. One visitor asked me why a nation of animal lovers allowed it. I'm still trying to think of an answer.

If you like the idea of driving yourself for a day then make that day a Sunday. (Get your travel agent to book it before you come; one-day Sunday car hire at short notice is difficult, especially during summer.)

Buses tend to dry up on Sunday, but the normally horrendous parking situation relaxes. The meters aren't in operation, and the ticket stickers are at home sticking pins in effigies of motorists.

Think twice however before driving yourself *out* of London on a sunny Sunday or you might hit that one final jam they're always promising that they'll lay a new highway over.

Later in the morning in London, Petticoat Lane will start; there's not much for a tourist to buy, but if you go along on Sunday you'll see the noisiest and most crowded of the London markets. Aldgate is the nearest Underground station and it's quite close to the Cheshire Street market mentioned above. This market is in what was until quite recently the predominantly Jewish part of the city. Old Montague Street – known to its graduates as Old Montague Strasse – was one of the nearest things that London had to a ghetto district. Sunday being a working day here, the shops are open and all London comes to buy. There are several such markets close by, some of them so near that they virtually join up with this one. You'll be offered clothes new and secondhand, very cheap chinaware (some of it factory rejects), toys, vegetables, hair lotion and gramophone records all mixed up together, each vendor shouting as loud as possible and the record stalls playing the top ten simultaneously. Listen to the back and forth between vendors and buyers. Look out for the bloke who throws an entire china dinner service up in the air and catches it. He's bound to drop it one day. And yours could be the day. There's lots to eat here including

good Jewish bread, warm *beigels*, pickled cucumber, excellent
smoked salmon, buckling and pickled herrings. Often when
coping with Sunday guests I've rushed out to 'the lane'
half an hour before they arrived and served them with a big
spread of East End delicacies. You'll see all sorts of non-
Jewish specialities there too; jellied eels, candy floss, toffee-
apples, and that ancient ancestor of Coke – sarsaparilla.
Notice stalls of oriental perfume and silk scarves
with exotic Indian salesmen shouting their wares and the
photographer who'll put a monkey on your shoulder to pose
with you. The 'dips' and the coppers are regulars here too, so
keep your wallet buttoned down and don't buy any knocked-off
cameras or watches.

Jews have always tended to remain in large towns and most
of Britain's Jewish population are in London. Perhaps in
response to a history of persecution Jews prefer to be
self-employed. Around Whitechapel and near to Oxford Circus
small workshops are packed close together. The signs say
'Shoulder pads, buttons or C M T' (cut, make and trim) and
trolley-loads of garments swing and sway as they are pushed
into the high-topped vans that transport them.

The sons of the immigrants from Warsaw and Riga work
in the neighbourhoods where their fathers worked, but they do
not live there. Around Whitechapel the tiny houses have
Pakistani faces at the windows and the synagogues are silent
and empty.

A few years ago it was possible to stand in Old Lion Yard
or Lower Old Montague Street (adjacent to the market) and
imagine yourself in some Balkan village. There was still an
open-fronted shop with a tub of pickled herrings and once there
was an old woman selling *beigels* on the corner. The people
were all old, and one seldom saw a person under thirty. The
women wore black, with a scarf tied tight around their heads.
Old white-bearded men walked slowly towards the synagogue a
book held close against the face so that they would not gaze
upon a woman who was not their wife.

Now the ghetto has all but gone. Jewish communities are in
Hampstead and Golders Green and even Bloom's restaurant
has a branch there. Bloom's in Whitechapel (90 Whitechapel

High Street, nearby) is still popular of course. On weekdays businessmen go there to discuss buttons as once they did with a gown-trade goy (me in 1951!). Isow's – another Jewish restaurant – at 6 Brewer Street, w 1 in Soho is quite different in food and atmosphere. Gone is all trace of East Europe and one could all too easily be in the heart of Manhattan. For me it's more American than any other place in London and the food is as Jewish as Sammy Davis Jr.

But perhaps there is still time before lunch to go to church. Go to St Paul's or over London Bridge to Southwark Cathedral. Both are just under a mile away: you'd enjoy the walk. Or go to Westminister Abbey – but whichever or whenever you visit go when there is a service. Hear the organ and sing with the choir, for these places are alive and awe-inspiring as they have always been and shouldn't be visited when they are silent museums. If you don't feel like a cathedral that morning, worship in the Guards' Chapel in St James's Park. The chapel is in the military barracks near to Buckingham Palace. At the morning service at 10.30 a.m. there is a military band to provide the music. Evensong at 6.30 p.m. is also worth the journey.

An entrance at the side of Buckingham Palace admits you to a part of the Palace known as the Queen's Gallery. It is a small exhibition of paintings. On Sundays the gallery is open from 2 to 5 p.m. Most London museums are open only during the afternoon on Sunday.

At lunchtime in Soho the Terrazza and Young's Chinese Restaurant (13 West Street) are open. In Chelsea Alvaro's is open. Lyons Corner Houses are open too.

After lunch there's a chance to see more people. At that end of Hyde Park closest to Marble Arch (the Underground station is conveniently near) there is a small patch of ground called Speakers' Corner. Here anyone with the gab, guts or gumption to drag himself onto a box can hold forth on any subject short of treason, blasphemy or the advisability of riot. There are plenty of such gabby fellows and they each are attended by hecklers who deride, argue or just yell responses to each point made. Watch out for the tattooed man and the group around the Irish flags. Here on this spot during the eighteenth century public floggings were staged, with an occasional military

execution for variety. Out there where the traffic of Edgware
Road pours ceaselessly into the vortex of the great roundabout
a small stone slab marks the site of Tyburn Tree, the most
infamous site of public hangings in all London. It was a
slow, cruel death and sometimes a friend of the condemned
man broke through the crowd and dragged at his ankles to
make death come more quickly. Until 1783 there were public
executions here, now there is just traffic.

After listening to the speakers, walk across the park to the
Serpentine where there is swimming and boating. Near the
bridge over the water there is a modern glassed-in restaurant
and bar. It's a great place to be in a thunderstorm but on a fine
Sunday it is always overcrowded.

If you keep near to Park Lane on your walk through the park
you will reach Hyde Park Corner and Apsley House. It once
rejoiced in the address of No. 1 London. Now it is the
Wellington Museum and has fine works of art as well as
personal items that belonged to the Iron Duke. On Sundays it's
open from 2.30 until 6 p.m. and is one of the few London
museums that charge admission.

By sundown on the Sabbath you will have seen Londoners of
many shapes, sizes and sorts. And perhaps you will have
captured them on movie film and immortalized them on
recording tape. And perhaps you will understand why I spend
Sundays in bed. That's just a personal point of view; for an
entirely different one I asked John Marshall.

Mood

Austin John Marshall

Born 1937 in the Midlands. Schooled at Christ's Hospital, Sussex.
Joined the *Observer*'s editorial design team in 1961.

Started writing when the activities of his two small children sabo-
taged hopes of a studio at his home in Blackheath, South London.
'Design needs space and lots of vulnerable equipment but I find I
can write anywhere, on my knee, on a train, in bed, in the bath.' Has
written for the *Observer*, *Town* and other magazines.

Married to Sussex folksinger Shirley Collins. 'I now find myself
designing her L.P. sleeves *and* writing her notes.' In fact a script he
wrote for his wife to appear in has been produced by B.B.C.
television.

What would I like to keep in my mind's eye if I were leaving
London for twenty years? Trafalgar Square? Yes, but standing
on the worn steps of St-Martin-in-the-Fields when I first came
to London in the autumn of 1953, hearing the whole goddam
place exploding with church bells and the twittering of a million
starlings.

Walking round the yard of Victoria Station about a foot off
the ground after a Ray Charles concert.

Running with a girl across Waterloo Bridge under a towering thundercloud, still shaken with laughter from *Jour de Fête*
at the National Film Theatre.

Looking out of a bed-sitter window on a summer evening in
Westbourne Grove, and with a thrill of excitement, seeing
Spades for the first time: just lolling about in vivid shirts and
pork-pie hats, all relaxed and still.

Walking in the sodium-lit Kilburn High Road, in love, at
3 a.m. talking of Bach, while the all-night buses and eight-
wheel auto-tankers ground by unheeded.

Sitting through freezing February days to draw a Georgian terrace house in Church Row, Hampstead, discovering something special about proportion in buildings.

Coming out of the Tate Gallery seeing everything – the river, Millbank, Vauxhall Bridge Road – for a moment through the eyes of Turner, the Pre-Raphaelites, Manet, Whistler.

But however innocent I was, London is a bride with very grubby drawers on, her rejected suitors and cast-off bridegrooms all jammed up grumpily together like Chelsea Pensioners. Nash, Wren, Sir George Gilbert Scott, and a pageant of triers have each had a go at imposing their will on her. Latterly, a cheery, burly 'layman critic' of architecture, called Ian Nairn, has admitted that the character of London exists only in her extreme diversity. 'Long live the thousand villages' is his slogan.

And where the localities have been left alone by Hitler's bombs and the bulldozers of post-war development, London has, in Chelsea, Hampstead, Highgate, Blackheath, Islington, Soho, *quartiers* as colourful, diverse and vital as you could wish. But these are ornaments, fringe benefits which any city can stick on the wall. Has London a real heart? Well, it has got Piccadilly Circus, where there are so many neon signs that when painter Joe Tilson was commissioned to design one he was able to produce an effective competing sign (which was up for over a year) by the simple device of making it out of reflecting surfaces. No fewer than nineteen bus routes go past this paste jewel set in a noisy asphalt sea.

One of the best places to get above the sea in the centre of town is New Zealand House at the bottom of the Haymarket. To reach the roof terrace you must exercise some bare-faced cheek and just walk in as if on business, or approach their press office as a bona fide visitor to London, or come from New Zealand. They made these rules because there were so many tourists going up the tower that the lifts were never free. Assuming that you are either possessed of enough initiative or contacts to get to the top, pick a fine day and make the ascent. Buses crawl around like red bugs: the tops of domes glow bright green. It is a good place to see how the planning authorities have, until now, separated out all the new tower blocks so that they stick up like sore thumbs; there are no clusters to make even a mini-Manhattan.

Until fifteen years ago central London was almost all on one level, between four and eight storeys, with just the church steeples and other landmarks like Tower Bridge and the Houses of Parliament making their mark. But always the steeples could hold up a warning index finger to remind the builders not to overreach themselves. For me, this is illustrated by my favourite London buildings, all nineteenth century. The Gothic commercial buildings are the ones I love, like the Prudential Assurance Building in Holborn. I suppose there might conceivably be an element of hypocrisy in dressing up an insurance building in ecclesiastical gear, but what delight there is in this red-brick fantasy. Then there's St Pancras Station Hotel, sitting on the Euston Road, an enormous cathedral consecrated to the worship of the railways. See it soon, it might be demolished.

Another of my favourites is the Memorial Hall, with its spiky Gothic minarets looking over Farringdon Street. Then there's the Law Courts, like a bloody great bat in the Strand, ready to take off and swoop down on wrongdoers. Inside, the reception hall is really like a cathedral. And then the seat of the law-makers themselves, the Houses of Parliament: the basic classical shape is almost buried under a fantastic buzz of vertical strokes, stone encrustations, tracery, and general moody. If architecture is frozen music then these darlings are long, ornate ballads to an epoch when you felt that conscience hadn't quite given up the struggle. Any modern block, in the same idiom of frozen music, is just a single crash, one chord. Some chords may be more harmonious than others, but they give themselves away all at once. Big-band jazz in glass and Portland stone. No God *v.* Mammon stuff, for instance, about the Shell tower – crash! – on the South Bank site of Britain's last romantic fling, the 1951 Festival. Even Shell people call it Sing-Sing. Vickers tower, Millbank, more melodic, with a kinky kinda curve, but still one statement. State House, Holborn – clang! – with a spot of sculptural culture, Barbara Hepworth style, at its feet. Stag Place, Victoria – clomp! – as cheerless an enclosure as ever looked impressive on an architect's perspective drawing – you know, the kind where all the people have pointed spikes for legs.

The newest and nicest tower block is Centre Point – boing! – which owing to narrow pavements round its site at the junction of Oxford Street and Charing Cross Road had to be built without scaffolding. This meant that its forty-odd storeys had to be hauled up in pre-fabricated bits, and dictated its rather jolly kit-built look. It has been called the first 'pop' building, and sitting as it does at one end of Denmark Street, nerve centre of the pop music world, this is as it should be. A hit. Likewise the Post Office Tower, stacked like a pile of green cotton reels further up Tottenham Court Road.

We're still musing on top of New Zealand House, so let's get down and go somewhere memorable. How does frozen music sound down here? In the streets, which are all too narrow for their traffic, the noise grumbles and trundles with a particularly claustrophobic, solid sound. Walking in London can soon generate gloomy thoughts about its music. How about 'London is a massed choir and orchestra, singing an anthem to the triumph of money and power over town planning'? Or 'London is dogs-in-office, a fat ticket-collector slamming the gate in your face in the name of the smooth running machine – the individual suffering for the many'? But London is also Tower Bridge going up at 5.45 p.m. in the middle of the evening rush hour, thousands of cars on both sides of the river held up for one small white sail boat with a mast too tall to pass underneath. The many suffering for the individual.

London is wanton, careless with its surprises. For instance, if you come out of Blackfriars Station and turn and look at the place-names that are sculpted on the front, you'll see that you could once get a ticket direct to St Petersburg. Go up Queen Victoria Street and in a while you'll see a curious little building on the left – the College of Arms, where gentlemen with titles like Garter King of Arms and his experts in heraldry will knock you up a family escutcheon for a consideration. The courtyard is full of strange heraldic beasts, and colourful designs rather like a garden in *Alice in Wonderland*. You feel the whole place is about to come alive, in some great whimsical British anthropomorphism. But then, about ten paces further on, is a totally unexpected opening in the buildings, and you can see towering over you the wholly serious majesty of St Paul's. Walk up fourteen steps to a landing, nine more steps and along another longer level, then eight more steps and there you are. If you go up in the evening sometimes and walk across the west front, the bells echo around the new-built courtyard, and so you get ten peals for the price of one. The old Madam has just had a face-lift and her dome has been in curlers for about two years, but come up Ludgate Hill at night and carry the view of that floodlit west front to your grave. I will.

The City of London pays a lot of lip-service to regalia, livery, guilds and all that jazz. But it's a doomy, forbidding place to me, where nothing counts but profits, and the Financial Times Index, like a pop-chart, is the dominant life-force. Few people love it enough to live there (the Barbican development may change that) and the place is so empty on a Sunday that it seems to have been done over with nerve gas.

I've lived in London now for thirteen years, which makes me a newcomer I suppose. The first seven years I spent travelling up and down the Northern line from Hampstead, at first to design school, and then later hawking my work round.

Hampstead Heath meant the last of my sporting youth. Midnight swims in the ponds, autumn evening football on fields sloping down among the trees. Once, at a sports meeting the day after an all-night party, I remember I climbed Parliament Hill which looks over a sports field and half London, and lay down to sleep. I awoke just in time to sprint down to the track and win the discus.

More gracious evenings could be passed at the summer lakeside concerts at Kenwood. Hampstead is a stinking rich part of town, but one of the cheaper pleasures is two stops down the Northern Line at Chalk Farm where you can get the best ice cream in London at Marine Ices. You can stand licking a double Marsala cone looking across the road at the Round House, where Arnold Wesker's dream of culture for the masses, his Centre 42 project, is planned.

Down the road and round the corner in Regent's Park Road is that other attempt to build Jerusalem in England's totally ungrateful land; looking like a grammar school that needs a wash behind the ears, the English Folk Dance and Song Society's Cecil Sharp House.

Then I lived four years in Little Venice. If you take a number 15, 6 or 8 bus from the grumbling bowels of Oxford Street, and swing around the new Marble Arch roundabout, past Speakers' Corner, you head north-west up the Edgware Road. It is still just as straight and no wider than when it was built to let two columns of four-abreast Roman infantry pass comfortably. So, with not quite room for four lanes of slow-moving traffic, you've plenty of time to admire this shoddiest, grimmest mile of sheer visual bedlam. Then just as the world seems to be completely dissolving in a kaleidoscope of hi-fi shops, cheap furniture stores and nasty pubs, the road widens out into the bland reaches of Maida Vale. Get off here and walk back to where you half-saw railings sloping down in two leafy avenues beside a stretch of canal. Walk down either side, Maida Avenue on the left bank, Blomfield Road on the right, and immediately find yourself in as peaceful and enchanted a quarter-mile of townscape as it is possible to imagine. Two avenues, the canal between; trees lining both. Cross Warwick Avenue at the bottom and follow Blomfield Road around the basin. This is Little Venice proper, with a real island in the middle. Turn left, to where, if you're lucky, you'll see a blue and white barge pulled up – the Zoo bus. (Easter to September, 10 a.m.–6 p.m.) The barge, usually full of children going to the Zoo, will chug slowly round the basin and sweep you under the bridge you have just crossed. The pretty houses on the right tend to be obscure offices, while those on the left belong to well-off actors or playwrights, or stockbrokers making like actors or playwrights. Don't worry whether the barge will fit into the tiny-looking tunnel at the end of this section. It does. The old bargemen used to lie down and walk their barges through with their feet on the tunnel roof. Out into the sun again, past lush back gardens with low sweeping trees, Marylebone Goods Yards, under marvellous iron bridges, and suddenly all trees, solid on either bank, as you curve round the northern rim of

Regent's Park. Disembark and admire Lord Snowdon's beautiful aviary, shimmering like some vast crystal on its silver struts. Don't be side-tracked today into the caged and furry surprises of the Zoo itself, but skirting to the right of it set off across Regent's Park. A boating lake beckons, specked with little sailing dinghies. and terrace after noble Nash terrace gazes calmly between the trees, trees where Goldie, the Zoo's golden eagle, has twice kept the nation on tenterhooks by escaping and defying his keepers for days on end. And trees where, on an autumn afternoon, you might be lucky enough to see great wheeling battalions of starlings assembling. Cross over to the south-eastern corner of the park to let the sophisticated modern asymmetry of Denis Lasdun's design for the Royal College of Physicians act as an antidote to the classicism of Nash's elegant façades; then along the recently-restored Park Crescent and into Portland Place, the broad northern entrance to the West End. You pass the B.B.C. ('Nation shall speak peace unto Nation' is the inscription in the reception hall. Big deal.) Turn the corner to see All Souls, a beautiful Nash wedding-cake church with an absolutely symmetrical round tower and needle spire. On down the sweep of Regent Street – to the Mall and more greenery, as you cross to St James's Park. This joins on to the Horse Guards Parade, with the Admiralty one side and the Treasury the other. Turn your back on Whitehall's corridors of power and *not* pausing to glance at Buckingham Palace, stroll through Green Park, under the new Hyde Park underpass, into Knightsbridge, and along to Bowater House, finishing a long walk beside the extraordinary Epstein nude figures group, all straining to get into the Park.

This is the image to close on. The incongruous romanticism of these figures, hybrids of Hellenic and Egyptian styles, is wrong for London really, but nothing will ever be 'right' in such a polyglot soupmix of people, buildings, sights and moods. So my last twenty-year memory may just as well be Epstein's naïve, sinewy freak. The dusty committees and planning offices where the decisions will finally be taken to channel the traffic, design the fun palaces and appropriate the cash to make London worth living in are light years away from Epstein's embarrassing generosity of soul. But the reasons why they *will* take the decisions will have something to do with the indefatigable optimism of what Epstein and all his brother optimists, architects, designers, sculptors and other madmen, were trying to say.

Kids

Children have sixteen weeks' holiday a year, so why should they foul up your three? Having asked yourself that question and found no answer, you've got to find something to do with the little blackguards while they are in London.

There is a collection of torture instruments in the Tower of London. There are also in London a number of 'Adventure Playgrounds'. To an adult they look like an uncared-for battleground, but they are well supervised and the idea is that the children are encouraged to initiate, build and cooperate. One at St John's Wood Terrace, N W 8, has an old car, old clothes and some strange wooden structures. The last I heard of it the kids were making a film. Another similar playground is at Ampton Street, Gray's Inn Road, W C 2, right in the centre of town. Here they are, I believe, bonfire-prone but, again, the kids are supervised. Try T E R 4536.

Some day nurseries will take children for an hour or so. One of them is in Hampstead on the north side of town. It's called the House on the Hill (H A M 1662). The other is in the Knightsbridge shopping district (K N I 9847) and will cost about £1 for half a day. Cots, prams, high chairs etc. can be rented from Harrods (S L O 1234).

The London education authorities have many places which will look after children without charge. During the normal term-time there are 139 play-centres which are open from 4 p.m. until 6.30 p.m. and take children between 5 and 11 years old. There are another 66 Junior Clubs which look after 11 to 15-year-olds between 6.30 p.m. and 8.30 p.m. During school holidays they are all replaced by 75 play-centres which are designed to take a wide age-range of

children and are open from 9 a.m. until 5.30 p.m. All these
centres are under trained supervision and there is instruction
in drama, painting and games (including in some cases even
billiards). Meals will be provided for only 1s. Visitors may use
these centres for their children. There is no charge. For details
phone County Hall (W A T 5000). Local libraries often have
lectures, film shows and story-telling sessions in the children's
department. Call in and ask.

If your kid is as nutty as I think he might well be, try taking
him to Nathan's (12 Panton Street, w 1) or Berman's
(30 Rupert Street, w 1) and hiring a costume for him. They are
theatrical costumiers but will rent you clothes for a party. Let
him have a beard and moustache too, preferably of a style
that keeps his mouth closed.

If you don't care how much noise he makes Mr Tomasso at
P A L 4198 will let you have a genuine London barrel organ for
£4 15s. 0d. per day and I wouldn't mind having a go at that
myself. If your kid is big enough to push it round the streets
you might come out of the trip with a profit.

London has many highly skilled model makers. Beatties,
formerly Bassett-Lowke's, at 112 High Holborn, w c 1, has
trains, boats, yachts and cars. They are more for engineers than
for children but take him if he's quiet. Beatties has two other
shops: in the Broadway, Southgate, and a third called the
Southgate Hobby Shop at 3 Dennis Parade, Winchmore Hill
Road, N 14, which handles secondhand and part-exchange
deals on model railways; but that's not very central. A little
more central is a model-aircraft shop called Nicholls at
308 Holloway Road, N 7, which handles all kinds of aircraft
kits but specializes in radio-controlled models. This could be
quite interesting if you don't let the kids get near it.

At 59 Cadogan Street there is a shop called Steam Age which
handles all manner of toy trains etc., and near Leicester Square
at 10 Cecil Court there is a small shop just devoted to trains.
Very close to this shop is Pollock's Toy Museum and toy
theatre at 44 Monmouth Street, w c 2. The people who run it
are happy to show you over it without even mentioning, let
alone plugging, their own line in historic toy theatres, which
make unusual souvenirs and inexpensive gifts.

There is a doll shop at 15 Moscow Road, Queensway, w 2 (P A R 7880), run by Miss Hickman, who got started when she decided to sell off a few of her own collection and has been buying and selling them ever since. The shop opens and closes spasmodically and although we talked to her neighbours none of us researching ever did get to speak to Miss H.

Kids crazy about animals can spend a day on Foal Farm, Biggin Hill, Kent (Biggin Hill 2386). This is outside London but only commuters' distance away. The Farm is run by the Friends of Animals League and is a collecting centre for unwanted or ill-treated animals. Phone them up if you are interested in going along to see them.

If you are thinking of bringing pets into Britain there are strict regulations to observe. Dogs and cats – whether they have been inoculated or not – have to spend six months in approved kennels. What's more, you must have a licence from the Ministry of Agriculture, Hook Rise South, Tolworth, Surbiton, Surrey. They won't consider issuing one until you have arranged with the kennels to collect the animal from the port or airport.

So you see you are up against some pretty tough officialdom right from the start. If you still want to continue, then get a list of the kennels they approve (they will send you a list) and write direct. To keep a dog six months in quarantine will cost you between £54 and £90 according to how hungry it gets.

Remember that an animal that has been on a ship that has stopped in a foreign port is regarded as having been abroad, quite irrespective of whether it got off and looked around.

There is no restriction on the importation of amphibia, frogs or freshwater fish (although they'll want you to get a licence just to tell them you are coming), but the salmon family and trout are prohibited. Birds are O.K. unless they are parrots, and the latter will be let in if they are sure it's your pet (again get a licence first). Mice, reptiles and monkeys are allowed in and don't have to be inoculated.

So if you think the immigration boys are tough on humans, you want to do one trip as an animal and you'll find out.

Railway stations and airports may be your idea of hell but many children can't get enough of them. London Airport is

well equipped to handle visitors; there is a roof garden with a
playground and a public address system that identifies each
aeroplane and tells its destination. When you've had all that
you can take you can sit in the airport restaurant and watch
the aeroplanes while eating, although if you want a seat
anywhere near the window you'll have to wield a good deal
more influence than I have.

Look out for excellent books about buses, trains, aeroplanes
etc. published by Ian Allan – most large bookstalls sell them.
They are cleverly designed to appeal both to children and
fanatical grown-ups.

Some kids enjoy museums. If the weather's nice but unsettled
(as is often the case), you may not want to spend the whole
afternoon inside. Anyway, younger children usually get bored
after an hour or so and start using the place as an indoor
running track. Fortunately there are a number of museums that
are located in parks.

The London Museum, for instance, is in Kensington Gardens
at the west side of Hyde Park. Exhibits trace the development
of London from the Stone Age to Queen Victoria. When the
little people start to sag and drag, whip them out into the park.
There's a big playground with slides, swings, sandboxes and
so on, to one side of the museum. The Round Pond is
directly in front of it. Watch grown men sail beautifully
detailed scale-model boats, and little boys sail anything
that's handy. If it's breezy, there may be another group of
serious hobbyists flying kites near by. There's also a
bandstand.

After you've had your fill of all this you could do worse than
stroll to the restaurant (near the bridge over the Serpentine
lake) and have tea.

If your kids drive you to drink, remember that they are not
allowed inside pubs. Some pubs have gardens, courtyards or
tables and chairs outside and you'll have to find that sort of
pub unless you leave the youngsters outside the door with a
lemonade and a bag of potato crisps.

Between Chelsea Bridge and Albert Bridge on the south side
of the river there is the Battersea Fun Fair. Don't go along
expecting sophisticated Copenhagen Tivoli. This place is brash,

vulgar and strictly commercial. Prettier by far after dark but I don't suppose the children will notice the difference.

The Battersea Fun Fair can also be reached by water during the summer from various piers on the Thames. When you have had enough of the swings, roundabouts and tree-walk you can wander into two hundred acres of park that adjoin the fun fair. You can look at the outdoor sculpture exhibits, hire a boat or play tennis. Perhaps by now you just want to lie down on the grass and let the kids run out of steam. This is the place to do it. Battersea is the least used London park and Londoners, who like it that way, keep dark about it. If you still care, there is a bird sanctuary and many flowers.

Children

Drusilla Beyfus

Drusilla Beyfus works in Fleet Street, television and publishing. She is associate editor of the *Weekend Telegraph*, co-author of a work on modern etiquette, *Lady Behave*, and currently engaged on a book on marriage. Married to Milton Shulman, and has three children under nine. Lives in Eaton Square and during the holidays is generally out of touch in the Cotswolds. Enjoys cooking, walking and reflecting on the general problem of being a woman today.

Boredom and what-shall-we-do? blues afflict every child, but in London the cure is rarely far away. There is an extraordinary variety of things for young people of all ages to do and see.

Children always prefer to participate and London is fortunate in possessing tourist attractions where the action can be shared. My suggestions are largely based on trips, ideas and expeditions which make allowances for the incredible energy and curiosity of the young.

Perhaps London's special claim on the affections of all its visitors is that here history can be seen happening all over again. Monarchs and palaces, pageantry and military display, traditional uniforms and ancient ceremony, these are part of the established order of the day. Everyone knows about, and few children with the chance to go would dream of missing, the Changing of the Guard ceremony at Buckingham Palace. To see what has been described as Britain's secret weapon – royal panoply – in action, follow the Horse Guards on their daily route from Wellington Barracks, along the Mall to the Horse Guards in Whitehall. The Guard is changed at 11 a.m. daily and the Old Guard makes its way back to the barracks. An extension of this idea is to make a sortie to see Chelsea Barracks, which provides a more up-to-date concept of Britain's military equipment.

It is well worth while making the necessary arrangements to visit the Royal Mews to see the gilded state carriages, the coaching horses, liveries and stables. The Royal Mews is open to the public on Wednesday and Thursday from 2 p.m. to 4 p.m. Go to the turnstiles at Buckingham Palace. Entrance 2s. 6d. for adults, 1s. for children.

Take a steamer down the Thames to get to Greenwich and visit the famous tea-clipper, the *Cutty Sark*, which is preserved in dry dock. Visitors can go aboard and examine the cabins and gallery. There are also the Royal Barges to see and the National Maritime Museum.

Children with parents or keepers who have the energy to organize a dawn trip would not be disappointed in the spectacle of the big vegetable, fruit, and flower market, Covent Garden; the same goes for Billingsgate, the huge fish market. A hearty British breakfast afterwards tastes extremely good.

The major London museums are particularly in tune with the instinctive tastes and interests of young visitors. Perhaps because so much of this country's development has been advanced by boat, train, industrial machine, adventure and exploration, we have produced collectors and curators with a boyish delight in working models. The Science Museum, South Kensington, is good value, especially for the curious-minded who tend to ask 'What does it *do*?' when confronted by a plainly static exhibit. Here is a *Boy's Own* paradise of beautifully detailed models of famous steam-engines equipped with locomotive parts that can be set in motion by pressing a button. Wheels turn, pistons pump, shafts shift and the whole laborious complexity of the industrial revolution gears into action once again. Also, look out for the coal-mining equipment which can be worked, the illuminated models demonstrating industrial chemical processes (children need never be muddled again about the derivatives of coal tar), and early printing presses. Upstairs is the aircraft gallery with, among other marvellous exhibits, a life-size reconstruction of the Wright brothers' early frail flying machine, whilst the children's gallery presents a series of basic scientific exercises for visitors.

At the National History Museum, next door, there is a good scheme for eight- to fifteen-year-olds. Exhibits (regarded as the world's finest in zoology, entomology, geology, mineralogy and botany) can be painted or drawn and coloured with materials supplied by the authorities. Paper, pencil, crayons and stool provided, but not paints. Attractions include giant skeletons of prehistoric beasts, galleries of stuffed animals, and drawer upon drawer of trays of exquisite beetles which can be pulled out for close inspection.

The Victoria and Albert Musuem has a unique collection of fine and applied art. Children especially relish the gallery with model theatre sets which light up at the touch of a button; the series of rooms furnished in chronological style through the ages (note the gargantuan family beds in the first Elizabethan age); and bizarre oddities such as Tipu's Tiger, an Indian fantasy representing a tiger devouring a supine officer of the East India Company with sound effects – you turn a handle and the works inside emit four tigerish growls for each human shriek. The Javanese shadow puppets have an action value too – they move gracefully at the turn of a handle.

For girls, I wouldn't omit a trip to the Bethnal Green Museum. This collection is noted for antique dolls' houses (press a button and the lamps and lights in the interiors of the houses are switched on), toys and period costumes.

Madame Tussaud's should be visited for all the obvious reasons and also for the room of Dioramas. These small-scale 3-D tableaux are sometimes a compensation for younger members of the party who may be bored or overawed by vast galleries filled with effigies of public figures.

The Imperial War Museum, Lambeth Road, is a source of joy to the warlike with an inimitable collection of fierce weapons and splendid naval, military and aerial trophies.

Curiously enough the very centre of London is a good place for studying wildlife. St James's Park is a bird sanctuary and it must be said that the ducks are the best-fed in the world, so constantly are they tempted with morsels from admirers. Here there are pelicans, interesting water birds and geese. Holland Park has its peacocks strutting around on their lawns; Golders Hill Park, near Hampstead Heath, has angora rabbits, deer and some very pretty poultry; Battersea Park has water birds, black sheep and goats.

In Regent's Park there is the Zoo which offers a series of extra-curricular attractions. The Chimps' Tea Party is usually held out of doors and the celebrated feeding times for sea-lions, penguins, pelicans, lions and tigers, eagles and reptiles are worth attending. Zoo diet schedules should be checked up on in advance. For example, the lions, tigers and eagles do not get a bite to eat on a Wednesday. Children may also like to take advantage of a spin in a trap pulled by a llama, or a ride on a Shetland pony.

Working on the indisputable principle that the finest treat is one which is in fact a sequence of treats, I can advise in favour of these combined operations. Go to the Tower of London by the river-steamers which leave frequently from Charing Cross Pier and Westminster Pier. You get a splendid picture-postcard view of Big Ben and the Houses of Parliament, a curious cameo study of the newly cleaned St Paul's cathedral glimpsed through a frame of dockyard buildings. Then, gradually, the medieval grey Tower comes into view with battlements, fluttering stand-ards and iron gates. The nearby Tower Bridge deserves to be seen in action. This is in effect two drawbridges. A bell rings, the normal flow of traffic across the bridge is halted, and it opens up across the middle to let the big ships pass through.

At the Tower itself, a visit to the Crown Jewels is imperative, but remember that on a summer weekend a queue is inevitable. Least crowded times for visiting are mid-week working hours. The Beefeaters, for all their splendidly intimidating uniforms, are not as remote as their stance suggests. They will answer questions about the Tower. Make a point of seeing the Chapel of St John, unaltered in its structure since the time it was built in 1080. Silence is requested here, which prompted one five-year-old I took who was unfamiliar with a state of absolute hush, to pipe up with a loud 'Has anything happened?' The White Tower Armoury has a collection of bloodthirsty but beautifully designed antique guns, knives and swords as well as the presence of an original execution block in wood. For young children the endless flights of twisty stone stairs going up to the top of the Tower past arrow-narrow window-slits and down again are as much fun as anything. Note the ravens hopping about the daisy-faced lawns in summer, carrying their legend with them.

A matinée followed by a sticky tea is a combination of pleasures at which London excels. It is the home of classic children's entertainment. *Peter Pan* and the Pantomime, *Alice*, *Cinderella* and *Toad, Oliver Twist, Treasure Island* and *The Christmas Carol* are the evergreens of traditional show business. If I was making the reservations I should make a bee-line for any Shakespearian play produced by the National Theatre Company or the Royal Shakespeare Company. And I would try to arrange to see the Royal Ballet productions at the Royal Opera House of the *Sleeping Beauty, Swan Lake, Cinderella* or *Boutique Fantasque*.

I should hope that Billy Smart's Circus would be in town and that I could get my party to it. This circus is characterized by superlatives, the mostest in elephants, the spangliest of tights, the bravest in little galloping horses. Check in the advertisement columns of the daily press for the location and times. Theatre ticket agencies, of course, will have all the information required.

After an afternoon show it will probably be too late for tea in a shop, but all the West End hotels serve tuck-type teas. The Savoy, the Strand Palace, the Piccadilly, the Cavendish are all within easy reach of theatreland. If tea is scheduled for earlier in the afternoon, go to the roof garden at Derry & Toms, a big Kensington department store where there are huge trees on the skyline, gardens and a Spanish patio décor. Fortnum & Mason, Piccadilly, have a lively soda-fountain service and Searcy Tansley, Sloane Street, the well-known catering firm, provides very English-style teas.

A planned trip to the theatre is one thing, but what about the odd afternoon or evening which needs to be filled in with some spontaneous activity? Try the Studio One and Two cinemas which have a policy aimed at a 'family' audience. London has several news and cartoon cinemas which are particularly enjoyable both for young children and their parents. Because no item in the programme is longer than about ten minutes, the young person in question can be whipped out smartly when boredom strikes, without feeling that he or she is missing the

remainder of a big show. Cinerama with its 3-D colour programme is a reliable fill-in for a wet afternoon.

With bib-stage children eating out can be a problem. A
number of restaurants have not yet cottoned on to the fact that
babies and toddlers accompany their parents everywhere these
days, and provision for the nursery element is often inadequate.
But sometimes the sniffy look from the waiter is worse than the
service and a number of crusty old establishments have been
known to unbend when a toddler appears to be fed. The Savoy
restaurants and the Berkeley Grill are among the places where
the management is happy to include small children in the clientele. For older children, there are plenty of places. At the
Causerie at Claridge's there is a centre table piled with interesting *hors d'œuvres*. You take a plate and help yourself to
whatever takes your fancy. The Savoy Grill scores for those
who like to take their time deliberating over a long menu
studded with exotic dishes but which provides the chance of a
final choice of cold ham and chips (*pommes frites* to them).

At the Connaught Hotel, around adult drinks time, kindly
waiters can be seen bearing silver trays laden with Cokes,
lemonade and dishes of cocktail crispy things for junior guests.

On a less costly level there are two unrivalled guzzling treats
which should be rated as specialities of the region. First,
London ice-creams, which have improved out of all recog-
nition in the last few years (informed child opinion currently
recommends a Wall's Zoom ice, a pop art favourite on a stick
in three intermingled lurid colours, made in a combination of
water ice and cream ice). Second, sweets and chocolates. A
visit to a confectioner's in any side street will produce a bag of
tuck even for small change. The range of suckable sweets such
as barley sugar, butterscotch, humbugs, fudge, lemon drops,
pear drops and peppermints is only rivalled by the selection of
chewable trifles such as wine-gums and fruit pastilles, liquorice,
cream-lined toffees, chocolated-coated toffees and nougat-based
chews on sticks.

Whatever a child's hobby or interest, the chances are that
London has a densely variegated supply of items which bring
a sense of treasure tracked down. This is as true of stamps and
butterflies as of conjuring tricks, false noses, fireworks, camping

equipment, Batman gear, model soldiers, trains, cars and boats. British soft toys for babies and nursery use are imaginatively designed and made in long-lasting luxurious materials. Bicycles, scooters, tricycles and dolls' prams are usually good value. A recent improvement has been in the range and quality of cheap playthings. Hamley's of Regent Street and Selfridges of Oxford Street have a good stock of cheap toys that work. The games counters include the best from abroad and it is possible to see all the world's latest in diversions and distractions that come packed flat in a box.

Children rarely vote a spell at Harrods a waste of time. The store has a pet shop with a realistic choice of domestic pets including white mice, hamsters, singing birds, puppies, tortoises, parrots and the occasional reptile, together with appropriate equipment and foods. The children's book section is noted for its immensely varied stock – anything that's good and new is there. There are three restaurants, and the Health Bar downstairs serves delectable fresh fruit juices during shopping hours. You sit up on a stool to sip your drink. The toy department displays major items of equipment such as outdoor climbing frames besides smaller things on the tiddlywinks level. This is also a good place for dolls and dolls' clothes and cots. At Christmas, Santa Claus is in evidence listening to whispered confidences from young visitors and roping in the orders from hooked parents. In addition there is the extra-mural attraction of an escalator serving four floors up and down which can be enjoyed, I regret, in a totally unproductive manner, and a grandiose ladies' cloakroom with a penny-in-the-slot weighing machine.

A change from the inevitable restrictions and disciplines involved in sight-seeing or shopping may be needed. The answer is sport, and London has a lot to offer. Ice-skating goes on at Queen's Ice Skating Club, Bayswater (membership necessary, but this can usually be arranged immediately). Tennis and squash are also at Queen's (but references from members are expected), outdoor swimming pools exist in Hyde Park, at the Oasis in Holborn, or a little way out of town at Roehampton Club, where the pool is open to the public.

Riding can be had in the Rotten Row at Hyde Park or in the

wide open spaces of Richmond Park. The magazine *Horse and Hound* publishes advertisements of riding schools near the London parks. There is sailing on the Thames at Chiswick or on the Serpentine, fishing at Highgate Ponds, walking on Hampstead Heath, boating at Battersea Park. Dry ski-ing classes are held at the dry-ski school at Lillywhite's, Piccadilly. Lessons start after the store closes at 6 p.m.

A good run and freedom to play outdoors on green grass within a short distance of Piccadilly is one of the special advantages of the London parks. Apart from sheer space, some offer playgrounds with free merry-go-rounds, swings, slides, see-saws and maypoles. The best two, I think, are the playgrounds at Kensington Gardens with the Round Pond near by, and Regent's Park.

Most trips with numbers of children involved are in practice perfect for one age-group only, but the glorious exception to this rule is Battersea Fun Fair. Crowded, noisy, colourful and brash, this is a permanent fairground open during a long summer season. A visit to the fair is often the first choice of local London children when asked what they would best like to do with Saturday afternoon.

The technique of successful holiday-making in London, with children, is to lay, well ahead of time, a few plans for trips and treats. Children are so easily excited by and interested in projected new experiences. It would be a great pity if the promised treat never materialized for lack of parental foresight. London is no exception to the general rule that many of the nicest things to do, places to visit, entertainments, get booked up ahead. A tour round the Royal Mint, for example, would be a splendid excursion for children, but during the top tourist months the tours become heavily booked. The same applies to a meal in the restaurant at the top of the recently opened G.P.O. Tower. This is the tallest building in London and provides the city with its main Telephone Exchange. The restaurant floor slowly rotates so as to give diners an all-round aerial view of London.

So when travelling with children your motto should be: book early, tomorrow is sooner than you think.

The City

Like its Second World War, London's Great Fire broke out on
the first Sunday morning in September. By Thursday they were
blowing up sections of the City and even then were only able
to save about a fifth. Thirteen thousand houses were destroyed
and about 200,000 people were made homeless.

Within eleven days a new city had been planned and within
ten years the rebuilding was complete. Not as planned however,
for the homeless Londoners had returned to their gutted homes,
and with wood, tile and plaster fashioned shelter, and foiled
the planners who wanted London slashed with avenues and
stabbed with vistas. If only it was as simple to foil today's
planners. They seem unable to accept the fact that the City's
attraction is its secrets; the alley that conceals a leafy
churchyard and the winding street that surprises you with a
close-up façade.

Yet again in the first days of September – this time in 1940 –
the City of London suffered from terrible fire. The *Luftwaffe*
rained incendiaries down. The City burned and this time the
planners had their way. They dropped a million tons of
concrete upon the city and fashioned it into malformed cubes.
Pale grey neon-eyed bastions of commerce kick slyly at the
few remaining nooks and crannies of the city before trampling
them under.

If I could show you only one small part of my town I would
begin at lunchtime when the City taverns tucked away in
narrow alleys are busy. Next door to them elegant Wren
churches brim over with music. Start at St Stephen Walbrook,
which is literally next door to the massive Mansion House.
Wren built this to try out his ideas before doing St Paul's. It

has an interior that I guarantee will delight you even if you
are not interested in church interiors. There are frequent piano
recitals here at lunchtimes. Ask the City Information Office
(MON 3131 – far the best information service we found,
although it only operates 9 a.m.–5 p.m.) and make sure there's
one the day you go. Just around the corner at 38¼ Cornhill
is the famous Simpson's Tavern (quite different from
Simpson in the Strand). Have a drink there, then pop around
the corner to the George and Vulture and the Jamaica Wine
House, side by side in St Michael's Alley, and have two more.

If you liked that – and I'm certain you did or you'd never
be reading this kind of book – take a look at a quite different
type of church. St Bartholomew-the-Great is at West Smithfield
(just over half a mile away). On this large open space – once
just outside the city wall – tournaments were held, peasants
revolted and martyrs were hanged, burned or sometimes boiled
alive. 'Passing by Smithfield I saw a miserable creature burning
who had murdered her husband', wrote John Evelyn in his
diary on 10 May 1652 and, without even pausing for a new
paragraph, went on to talk about the art show he was going
to see.

In the east corner of this great space you'll notice an ancient
half-timbered building over a gateway. Go through it and into
the tiny church. The original parts of the church were built in
1140. For some time the church was used as a factory, printing
works and stables. One printing employee who worked here
was Benjamin Franklin. If St Stephen Walbrook reflected the
cool, well-bred, scientific elegance of Wren, then this place is
more like Quasimodo. Very often the organ plays at lunchtime
and it's easy to imagine that, just across the square, they are
boiling the martyrs again.

Across the other side of the open place is Smithfield meat
market. Until 1868 herds of cattle were driven through this
part of town to Newgate just down the road. They passed the
Magpie and Stump (18 Old Bailey) – which used to sell fine
seats for the spectacle of public executions, but which now
sells pints to detectives and lawyers from the Criminal Court
across the road – and then were slaughtered. In 1868 both cattle
and men were granted a more private demise.

That should be enough churches and pubs for one lunch hour but another fine Wren church is St Mary-le-Bow, Cheapside (not far east of St Paul's). A cockney is said to be a person born within earshot of Bow bells; at one time this must have meant anyone born in London. A 'cheap' by the way means a marketplace and in fourteenth-century celebrations a conduit in Cheapside flowed with red wine. St Mary-le-Bow has a fine rebuilt interior with stereo gramophone concerts at certain lunchtimes. From here go for a quick one at Ye Olde Watling Inn and another at Williamson's Tavern, both very close in Bow Lane. (Ask for Williamson's, it's rather tucked away.) Ye Olde Watling Inn was reputed to be the first place rebuilt by Wren after the fire so that his workmen could have a drink. Um.

You are now near Guildhall but I'll assume that your tourist bus trip has already shown you that. If not remember that on alternate Thursdays there is a small procession of bewigged councillors with maces and swords. On Wednesdays at 12.30 p.m. there is a handbell practice. Failing either of those events make sure you see if there's an exhibition in the Art Gallery there; some of them are super. See also the Clock Museum. It has historic clocks and watches from Mary Queen of Scots' skeleton watch to Nelson's pearl and diamond timepiece.

When I reach a city I don't know, I follow a well-tried course of action. I buy a large map and a guide book. I take a sight-seeing bus trip and then I study the photo shops. Not in order to look at equipment or purchase film, but to see their selection of coloured photo slides. I never buy one. I look for parts of the town I feel are worth investigating, I study a street plan and get a rough idea of the shape of the town. Then I make contact with people who live there, for by then I am in a position to understand the descriptions and directions they give me. Residents refer to major railway stations even if they never enter them so it's as well to know where they are.

Because my first object – when researching – is to collect information, I keep a notebook and a sketchbook and use the camera to supplement my notes and drawings. A colour photo of a street can save a great deal of note taking and there, in an instant, is filed the exact colouring of buildings, clothing styles, vehicles, etc. I use an 8 mm. movie camera and sometimes I use it on single frame or very short bursts for viewing frame by frame on an editing machine. This type of photo is best made in good light in the most banal way possible.

But your friends will not thank *you* for a couple of hours of colour slides taken in the most banal way. Your motive isn't to prove you went to London but rather to show what you liked about it. Very high speed colour films – High Speed Ektachrome is the one I'm using until I hear of a better and faster one – make atmospheric pictures simple, even in very poor light.

The river Thames early in the morning can be very beautiful. The river is at is most active then and if the sky is overcast, what does it matter? The Houses of Parliament seen from Lambeth Bridge is a bit of a change from the usual view. Twilight in London sometimes brings a frail misty light and from shadowy trees in the park the traffic at Marble Arch and Hyde Park Corner will make long golden glow-worms of light if the exposure is long enough.

The grey narrow city streets with monotone bowler-hatted men can give you endless delicate pastel tones. I'm something of a nut about shop fronts and I photograph them endlessly. A little tobacconist's shop plastered with adverts for Sunday papers, chocolate bars and cigarettes, with the door leaning dangerously and milk bottles lined up by the milkman, makes me grab my half-frame camera.

For a bird's-eye view photo of London try the Shell Building (south side of Waterloo Bridge) or New Zealand House on the Haymarket, just south-east of Piccadilly Circus. There's also the Vickers Tower on the south bank of the Thames, the Fire Monument just opposite the Temple Underground station (you'll have to walk up a spiral staircase) and the gallery on top of the dome of St Paul's Cathedral. The highest building in London is the G.P.O. tower. It is 620 feet tall which is pretty impressive until you remember that medieval London's Old St Paul's spire was over 500 feet.

You can't get up to see Big Ben unless you're a horologist. And you can't get up Nelson's Column unless you're a pigeon. From a high building at night you'll notice the varying colours of each neighbourhood's street lights. Near Parliament and the Palace they have retained the gentle green-coloured gas lamps, although some lamp-posts have been adapted to the white electric bulb. Lucky Palace not to have the ugly orange-coloured sodium arc lamps that, being cheaper than the blue-white ones, demark the poorer districts of London.

With high-speed colour film I am surprised that more tourists don't shoot interiors. Photographed through the window, a quaint city restaurant with all the hats piled in the entrance hall, or the table at the George set for dinner, can be a memorable souvenir, even if other people find it dark and blurry.

Crowded places, like Speakers' Corner and the street markets, are a natural for coloured movies, and if it's pouring with rain so much the better as long as you protect the camera. I use a polythene bag with a small hole for the lens.

If you want portraits in crowded places then a reflex camera can be the very tool to use, but it's surprising what you can do by pointing the camera one way while taking an intense interest in something the other way.

I know of nowhere as atmospheric as Westminster School (Dean's Yard). Take a camera there just as the light is failing. From there walk into Westminster Abbey Cloisters and see the Chapter House.

Usually a couple of hours before high water (details from the current A.A. handbook) Tower Bridge will open. It opens on an average five or six times per day. Take a movie camera and get an unusual piece of footage from the grounds of the Tower of London.

London is no place to buy a camera even if you take advantage of the purchase tax concessions. Visitors from the U.S.A. might be well advised to bring film too. At present it's more expensive in Britain.

Bowens at 9 Gerrard Street, W 1 (GER 6419) has handled camera repairs for me, with care – and, even more important, speed. Meanwhile Photovision, 29 Palmer Street, SW1 (VIC 4197) will rent you a camera, a Polaroid Land Camera if you wish. Or you can rent a projector to see your results. Prices are from 2s. 6d. per day for a simple camera, the other two items being 5s. and 15s. a day respectively.

Photography

Adrian Flowers

Born in the general depression, is still recovering. A typical can-
cerian who moves sideways out of trouble. His main occupation is
advertising and editorial photography. He has taken food pictures
for the *Observer* and took the cover picture of Twiggy for this book.
His studio in Tite Street, Chelsea, is crammed full of equipment,
all of which he insists is absolutely necessary. His home is in
Kentish Town, where he keeps his wife, three sons, one daughter,
a dog and a cat, and an au pair girl. He owns four old cars, which
are shared by his assistants, and a launch for touring the Thames.
Keeps fit by playing football every day with his faithful bitch, Sarah.
His aim in life, apart from keeping his wife happy, is to take the
picture of all time.

If you already have a camera when you arrive in London,
the first thing to do is to call at James Smith & Sons, 53
New Oxford Street, where you can acquire an umbrella. Get
a large one and on leaving take a picture of this changeless
shop.

An umbrella will help you to feel part of the scene; may prevent rain if you're superstitious; could protect you from rain
while you record London at its most remarkable; can be leaned
on nonchalantly while waiting for right moments; makes you
look less like a photographer and may well become your most
cherished souvenir.

If you haven't a camera, then you need to borrow, hire or
buy one. To borrow you need a friend. To hire you need to
leave a full deposit. London is not the best place to buy equipment because of high purchase tax but, if you have the money,
buying is the easiest, and there are many shops to help you.

There are the Piccadilly Photo Centre Ltd, at 16 Piccadilly

Arcade; Dixons, at 88 Oxford Street; Wallace Heaton, at 93 Fleet Street; and Paul Fraser, at 24 Oxford Street: all but the first have other branches. Pelling & Cross is at 104 Baker Street, whilst further up, at 234, is Kafetz Cameras, small but with the most personal approach.

There are people who enjoy taking pictures and sticking colour prints into albums but do not want to know anything technical about photography. For these wise folk I thoroughly recommend any of the Kodak instamatic cameras or the Voigt-lander Bessy K which takes the same instamatic film packs. Kodacolor (colour negative) film should be used if colour prints are desired.

Those who wish to have the ultimate (within the 35mm. range of cameras) might agree that the Nikkormat together with a few lenses (say 28, 50 and 105 mm.) provides the answer. But I would seriously suggest that anyone wanting to see London in all its aspects without getting tired out by the weight of their camera apparatus should buy one of the half-frame cameras such as the Olympus Pen D2 or the Canon Dial. Excellent pictures can be taken with these small cameras especially on such fine resolution film as Kodachrome. There is more depth of field with the Pen D2, and there is hardly any noise when firing or winding on. When you return home, really you will be amazed at how many successful pictures you have taken so casually.

Many people think of London as mainly grey and sombre and, if you want to concentrate on these aspects and turn your camera away from the bright red buses and the evergreen parks, you can do so most effectively, without colour bias in the shadows, by using Agfa C T 18 film.

Sooner or later though you will be forced to give in to the incessant reds: the telephone booths, the pillar boxes – some doubly fat with two slots – and the road warning signs, to say nothing of the Guards' red tunics. Red and green are every-where at all times, and in the spring blue bursts from the sky and you notice that some lamp posts and many signs are blue too.

But don't forget to punctuate some pictures with black – policemen and taxis will do.

In St James's Park, in April, the foreground of your picture can be swamped with yellow daffodils and then you have got the lot in one picture: the three primaries and the most powerful complementary! Green grass, yellow daffs, red soldiers, blue sky and Buckingham Palace as centre piece. Kodak film is the answer.

While you're in St James's Park remember there are colourful birds on the pond. To concentrate on the pelicans go to the keeper's hut at 3 p.m., when each bird gets given five pounds of whiting or herring.

The most remarkable view of London is probably the one painted by Canaletto, from the top of Lambeth Palace. It includes the Palace in the foreground and Westminster Abbey and St Paul's in the distance. It is unlikely that you will get permission to enter the Palace but it is worth recording something from the Decca Radar landing stage by Lambeth Bridge. This viewpoint will include the Houses of Parliament.

At the Tower of London ask a Beefeater if you can see the ravens. There is a legend concerning these birds: when the ravens leave the Tower, England will be defeated! But their wings are clipped to make sure they stay. Try a close-up of a Beefeater with a raven.

For the Tower itself try from the other side of the river or from the top of the Port of London Authority building. And don't forget Tower Bridge, an extraordinary structure which opens up to big ships many times a day. You may be as lucky as the photographer who saw and shot the bus that got caught in the middle as the bridge was opening.

Within walking distance of the Tower is a quarter mile of sordidness for the sinister-seeking. No one knows for certain who Jack the Ripper was, but his victims were self-evident. Not long after the last murder, new buildings were erected all over this area and streets were renamed. In spite of changes, there are still aspects which conjure up the foreboding which people must have suffered when Jack the Ripper was at large. The atmosphere of 'the evil quarter of a mile' can be captured on film if you are interested in doing so.

Christchurch is the church in the centre of it all. You can see old men sitting and leaning against the railings where they used to sleep when they could not afford fourpence for a doss house.

Ripper's Corner in Mitre Square has only one wall remaining. This is where the body of Catherine Eddowes, his fourth victim, was found. I suppose it is rather like collecting pregnant silences on tape, but even so, if you are interested in Jack the Ripper and have read all about the rippings, the experience of photographing this bit of wall will have a strange effect on you. The wall is in the southerly corner and should be taken in the gloom of dusk with the aid of the gas lamps that are still there.

In spite of the rebuilding, there is definitely something about this particular area of the East End. Have a look at Thrawl Street, Flower and Dean Street (Flowery Dean). After the church (Christchurch), going up Commercial Road just past Fournier Street, you will find Puma Court with bollards at the entrance. Further up turn right into Hanbury Street then left into Wilkes Street on the corner of which you will see the Gilead Medical Mission. After recording this and remembering that the old slaughter house was the inspiration and setting for the Ripper, you should take a look at the brown-tiled Jolly Butchers pub in Cabbage Court (Brick Lane). To round off the visit, not forgetting to inspect some dark and sinister alleyways, wend your way to the Cosy Café in Cheshire Street.

Some foreigners are most struck by the effect of twilight. Certainly some of London's special moments are at this time, as the artificial lights slowly take over. This is best felt near the river. All along the embankment is good for night shooting, especially the Victoria Embankment and the promenade between Westminster and Lambeth Bridges on the south side.

Trafalgar Square is worth taking at dusk. Nelson's column, the fountains and the National Gallery are all lit up. They are best viewed from Whitehall.

During the day Nelson can still look admirable without his column, apparently standing on a wooden box when viewed from Carlton House Terrace. At the end of this terrace is an unusually well-preserved example of bomb damage, contrasting strangely with the surroundings.

Soho is a square mile full of interest for photographers, both by day and by night. It boasts every kind of cosmopolitan activity with people of all races and classes rubbing shoulders against a complex background of small shops and restaurants, coffee bars, clubs and offices.

Start your shooting in Compton Street. Perhaps on this occasion it would be as well to look like a tourist to avoid being lynched. If you really want to remain incognito, hire a taxi to take you round in circles, up and down the one-way streets. You won't have to ask the driver to go slowly! With the window down, using a pre-set automatic camera you can get many fascinating shots this way. A taxi for half an hour of such cruising will cost about fifteen shillings, probably less than the cost of the film you will expose.

There is a lot of light knocking about at night in this area, and I would say that night-time shooting was more fun than day-time. There are also many strip clubs, if that is your interest, but don't let your camera be seen or heard.

If bright lights at night appeal to you, Leicester Square is not far away. Its best aspect is from Cranbourn Street. And then there is Piccadilly Circus, best taken from the corner of Lower Regent Street. It was at this spot that a tourist saw a professional photographer with a heavy tripod and intense expression apparently giving a long exposure. 'What exposure?' he asked. 'Fortnight at f8,' came the disconcerting reply. In fact of course, with fast colour film, one can get impressive results wide open at 1/30th. Even so you would only get some of the neon lights in at the same time. To get them all you can give one, two or more seconds at about f16. A tripod would be a help!

Remember, the more exposure time you give, the less rich in colour but the more you see in the shadows and on the black road.

Other lights at night can be seen in the fairground in Battersea Park. There's more to shoot in the pleasure gardens adjacent and on the pier, from where you can see the prettiest of bridges – Albert Bridge, lit up with a string of pearl-like white bulbs.

During the day at Battersea Park there is the Henry Moore sculpture permanently displayed, and a special sculpture exhibition each summer. Take brown bread to feed the ducks. With the birds on the lake in the foreground you can purposely get the chimneys of the Battersea Power Station in the background and perhaps a little of the gasometer to make quite sure you remember where you took the picture.

Back on the other side of the river it is worth visiting the Royal Hospital, Chelsea, for its Wren buildings and the old soldiers there. Two hundred of these pensioners parade in full dress uniform on 29 May – Oak Apple Day.

Also in May the Chelsea Flower Show is staged in the hospital grounds by the Royal Horticultural Society. The first day is the best for perfect flowers, but the last afternoon at about 4 p.m. is an extraordinary moment to capture with a movie camera. Suddenly, all the plants disappear. Everything is sold cheaply in an incredibly short time. People become locusts and the show is over. If you could get a hundred viewpoints at once, you would have the film of the year.

On a Friday morning walk through Leather Market Street, to look at the skins. Then go on to Bermondsey Street, where the Caledonian Market is probably the most charming of all to photograph.

Every Saturday morning the Portobello Road market presents a long mile of subject matter laid out for your inspection. There are humorous objects from the old homes of England and an excess of whatever is popular at the moment. It's a good idea to be with a companion who looks a likely customer. Look out for Tubby Isaacs' jellied eel stand.

On a Sunday morning Petticoat Lane (as the market in Middlesex Street is called) is full of happy material.

If wild monstrosities are your passion start with the Albert Memorial. Looking south you can include something of another monstrosity, the Albert Hall. Keep a constant look-out for other suitable subjects. You might care to inspect the neon-lit cinemas called Studios One and Two, in Oxford Street. By day or night they certainly look strange. Great Portland Street is the best viewpoint.

You've heard of the nightingale that sang in Berkeley Square? Well don't expect to see one when you go there; but you can discover the rather ugly tree (another monstrosity?) that the famous nightingale, some think, perched in while it sang.

The swinging variety of bird is to be found concentrated in the King's Road, Chelsea, on a Saturday afternoon. They are

perfect subject matter for the casual observer, suitably stationary because of the traffic jam both in the road and on the
pavement. Flocks of these creatures occur welded to the folded
hoods of vintage and modern open cars. The lone variety drive
their own smaller versions. Three-thirty p.m. is the peak display
time on a sunny occasion. Everyone is there to see or be seen.

Apart from the girls, there are many extraordinary and interesting people who find it necessary to be somewhere in the
King's Road. If you want to see and not be seen, a good tip is
to grab a window table in the pub called the Chelsea Potter
about midday. With your camera ready on your lap, protected
and encouraged by the pint of beer on the table, you can sit and
stare for three hours and shoot when it suits you.

Horse-riding takes place early every morning in Hyde Park's
Rotten Row. Mist will help. Cart horses with their drays are
picturesque and are still used by some breweries. Twenty-eight
horses leave Whitbread's in Chiswell Street during the course
of any day. They travel over a five-mile radius.

If you want Watney's you can have sixteen horses in three
teams. They leave Mortlake brewery between 9 and 10 every
morning.

While touring London, make sure you see it from some high
points. This will help you to get the place in perspective. The
most beautiful and outstanding high point still is St Paul's
Cathedral and I think you should climb to the Golden Gallery.
Take pictures westwards towards other high points you will
visit later, when you can return the gesture eastwards.

You will never tire of taking pictures of St Paul's. There is
a marvellous one you can get with a long-focus lens (500 mm.)
almost isolating the cathedral, with a red double-decker bus
for the base of the picture. You take this from the footpath of
Hungerford Bridge. Other views of St Paul's are from the far
end of Watling Street, in the early evening just after the Cathedral becomes floodlit (include details of the buildings in Watling
Street), and from half-way down Fleet Street when, with a very
long lens, you get the black spire of St Martin's (Ludgate Hill)
plus one of the two west towers of St Paul's in direct line with
the main tower, giving three different heights.

The Shell Building has a viewing terrace which you can visit for 2s. 6d. It is ideal for pictures of the river and the Houses of Parliament and is particularly good in dusky conditions with a long-focus lens when the street lights have just been turned on. Unfortunately it closes at 4 p.m., so one can only get this effect in mid-winter.

The G.P.O. Tower is a little disappointing. Take the lift to the viewing platform. You then walk down to the platform just below, which has no glass, and the wind blows through the bars (be careful your clip-on lens hood isn't wrenched off!). The longer focus the better. There is likely to be a lot of haze. Use fast black and white and red filter or infra-red film and filter.

The Monument was built by Wren to commemorate the Fire of London. It provides a good view of Tower Bridge. At 9 a.m. you can see porters still moving around Billingsgate Market below. The best time to take striking pictures is late afternoon. Point your long lens into the sun and hope for a special effect. You can use the balustrade for support or shoot through it including it in the foreground with a shorter lens.

A good example of what little remains from before the Fire is the row of Tudor houses (now shops) in Holborn near Chancery Lane Underground station. Shoot them from the other side of the road. You will probably include tops of taxis which will practically obscure the shop fronts. Using a long lens you can concentrate on details – the lettering, gas lamps, the dragon.

From Chancery Lane, walk through Lincoln's Inn Old Buildings into the New Square and then towards Carey Street and the Law Courts. On the way, there are shots to be taken through wrought-iron gates of tiny sculptures on elegant green lawns and if you are lucky there may be some passing barristers in full regalia (between 12.30 and 1.30 p.m.). Near by, in Portsmouth Street, you will find what claims to be the Old Curiosity Shop, immortalized by Charles Dickens, which you might like to snap.

A phenomenon of the City is the bowler hat. Swarms of these peculiar black objects pour forth over London Bridge at 8.30 a.m. every weekday. There are shots from all directions. From the north end of the bridge, with a long lens, you can compose a sea of bowlers, which if it rains suddenly will be transformed into a sea of umbrellas. This is good cine material as well. Between 5 and 5.30 p.m. these city gentlemen come from both directions in Cornhill converging on a small passage called Change Alley and out across Lombard Street to the Bank Underground station entrance where they pause to buy papers. Follow them into the tube and compose the bowler, brolly and news scene!

Take the 214 bus that goes up Tottenham Court Road to the end of its run – the bottom of Highgate West Hill. Just there, by the zebra crossing, is one of the entrances to Hampstead Heath (Parliament Hill at that point). Walk a few hundred yards to the top of the grassy hill. As you near the top you will have, looking southwards on a clear day, a fabulous view of London. Using infra-red filter and film you could probably photograph the Sussex Downs in the far distance.

From the same place you can see Highgate rising up to the north-east, St Michael's Church as the pinnacle (its spire is the highest point around London). At the bottom of this view are the Highgate Ponds. North-west from the same position you can see quite a bit of Hampstead. Between the two, the beautifully landscaped Hampstead Heath lies before you, rivalling any country landscape. On weekdays there are not many people, but at weekends the Heath is teeming with all and sundry including keen kite fliers, and the whole place is a riot of subject matter. Over the Bank Holiday weekends three fairs are put up on the edge of the Heath. So if you abhor this sort of thing, beware! At other times the Heath is really well worth exploring. Walk northwards until you come to Kenwood. Have a look inside the house and see the scene from the windows; it's perfect because of the phoney bridge. If it's pub time, visit the Spaniards near by, then take the single-deck 210 bus back to Highgate Village and walk down Swain's Lane to the cemetery. The whole place is really decadent, weird and peculiarly visual. If you don't get good pictures the experience might help you decide about cremation! The tomb of Karl Marx is there but, more important, so is that of Friese Greene! If you're exhausted, Waterlow Park is only a few yards away and there you can rest and look at the birds.

Obviously, there is a lot to take in at Regent's Park Zoo. I recommend observing the public as 'behind bars' material if you are there at a popular time. Imagine furless Humans looking out hungrily as the snooty Lama (keeper) walks by, casting a cursory glance. Dolphins are good fun for the quick snapper, and the chimps' tea-party at 4 p.m. is excellent cine.

The London Policeman is a must. You will find him anywhere or everywhere easily noticed in his strange tall helmet and still proudly not carrying a gun. The type that you want to photograph looks well fed, wears heavy boots, is obviously hot in the summer but doesn't show it and is ready to smile. You will notice a difference, especially in helmet design, between the Metropolitan and the City variety. The change takes place where the Strand meets Fleet Street. It may be possible to get both kinds in the same picture! Peak-capped, straight-faced policemen ride beautiful horses or drive Z-cars. There is another radio-controlled, helmeted, 1984, motor-bike breed.

The first thing many visitors to London notice if they come via Tilbury Docks is endless chimneys. I have not discovered the best viewpoint for the most chimneys, but I am sure this would make an impresssive opening shot to your slide show. The incessant coal consuming habit of the Victorian era is at last being cured, but not entirely.

Battersea Power Station continues to belch forth smoke which can look quite picturesque, especially at night as it is floodlit.

To understand the growth of London you need to know the river. I suggest you look at as many bridges as possible. They are all incredibly different right down to the last bit of filigree. Contrast Tower Bridge with Hammersmith. Albert is the prettiest but, surprisingly, Waterloo, even though designed in 1930, is probably the most beautiful.

Some visitors may not realize how confined was the original city. Remains of the Roman Wall have been exposed as a result of the bombing and the authorities have sensibly kept them that way at Midland House in Cooper's Row, off Trinity Square. You can record it best when the sun is at a critical angle and where the wall interweaves with the modern building.

Thinking historically, why not take a look at the monstrous early creatures of this planet? There are wonderful specimens at the Natural History Museum and you are allowed to take pictures. (Fast film needed unless you use flash.)

I mentioned the Fire of London. This reminds me of the even bigger fires in the last war and the fact that London survived. Was this due to the Spitfires in the Battle of Britain, or the gallant fire services? Both are worth photographing.

You can see a Spitfire in the Science Museum. There are many other things to photograph there. (Use fast colour.)

All the Fire Stations have Open Days, usually the second Saturday in September. The station at Lambeth is biggest, and sometimes it puts on impressive demonstrations. You will need long lenses and colour film for the fabulous red engines.

What I like about London is its infinite variety, complexity and subtlety. Everything everywhere is different. Take railings for example. Although many were melted down during the war, there are still hundreds of different designs. Railings, balustrades, street lamps, gates, can play an important part in your silhouette of London.

Look out for sculptures of all kinds. There are *avant garde* new ones appearing all the time.

There are many things I haven't mentioned – mods in Carnaby Street; the doorman at Fortnum's; the snuff shop in Charing Cross Road; Speakers' Corner; the Round Pond in Kensington Gardens and Spike Milligan's gnome-covered tree near by; cricket and football; sailing in Regent's Park; changing the Guard at Buckingham Palace; Eros in Piccadilly Circus taken from the top of a double-decker bus – London is full of photographic delights, but I would make one final suggestion.

That is, to follow up *My Fair Lady* in Covent Garden. I suggest you go to the theatre, Drury Lane for example, after which you can drink into the early hours in the specially licensed pubs. Then, at 4 or 5 in the morning use stamina to judge, with an unjaundiced eye, the picture-making possibilities of the famous flower and fruit markets.

Soho

The mood of London changes dramatically from hour to hour. The City district at weekday lunchtimes is crowded with bank messengers, brokers and office workers, the pubs are packed, churches full of music, and quiet gardens and churchyards are full of typists enjoying thirty minutes of sandwiches and sunshine. That same evening the whole place will be silent, and people from the raucous West End will be visiting the few restaurants that are still open because parking is so easy.

In Soho the changes are even more rapid; the residents rise early and depart to their jobs in all parts of the town just as the shopkeepers arrive, for it's rare to find a London shopkeeper who lives anywhere near his shop. The district has that strident, dusty feeling that Paris has at breakfast time. On the pavements gleaming blocks of ice dribble, and dustbin lids clang as the garbage men move through the streets keeping close to the walls like skilled house-to-house infantry. Then come the waiters. The restaurant doors open and garlic fries. Pubs start pouring and the first tourists arrive, huddled together for safety and staring hard at every passer-by.

As the evening begins there is a new invasion; buyers from Birmingham and advertising executives from Kensington come looking for luxury, lechery, love and laughter. In the barbers' shops men in nylon coats are leaning close to the mirrors and shaving themselves, for like many southern Europeans they see no reason to waste their pristine chins on a morning of work. Back home have come the residents; weary from semi-skilled jobs that don't require fluent English or good handwriting they sit down to a big plate of tagliatelle or lasagne al forno, relieved to speak their native tongue again.

Soho

Soho is London's most foreign quarter. Here is the greatest concentration of foreign food shops, restaurants and theatres. Here too are the striptease shows, as well as the confidence tricksters and petty criminals. Watch out for the signs: 'They're naked and they dance' says one, and another in a fish shop, 'We have nets but we never catch our customers.' A fruit-barrow boy has written 'Do not squeeze me until I'm yours' not only in English but in German, French and Italian. Another large sign says 'Take Cover downstairs' but proves to be a shop selling gramophone records. Eat the continental-style cream-cakes, and watch the chef cracking eggs, buy some pâté and ogle the photos of backsides. Smell the fresh bread and sip the fresh coffee. Argue with the barrow boys and buy a flower for your buttonhole. Read *Private Eye* and take a drink in the York Minster. Whistle at the girls and listen to the street musicians, for this is Soho where anything goes, and just make sure it's not your wallet.

There are patches of Soho pavement that have a social significance – the corner of Old Compton Street and Frith Street being one such patch – and you might see groups of men standing around there reading newspapers, smoking and what the police courts call loitering. These are unofficial labour exchanges. The men are seeking employment and denote their trade by where they stand. The corner of Frith and Compton was for waiters and the adjacent corner was for catering workers. Employers needing staff chatted them up and hired on the spot. With the present labour shortage these little silent crowds have almost gone but band leaders putting together a combo for a night or two still sift through the men standing in Archer Street on Mondays. So don't hang around gawping or you might find yourself playing second trombone with the London Philharmonic, or even soup-bashing in a local greasy-spoon.

There are all types of strip clubs. Most of them are dirty little basements where the walls are peeling at a faster rate than the dollies. Such places are usually rented to a strip-club operator because the end of the lease is so near that no normal business man is interested in such a short-term venture. The décor is likely to be a forty watt orange bulb and some slightly broken kitchen chairs. Sometimes there is not even a raised

part of the floor to suggest a stage. The girls will mostly be
either young teenagers who have run away from a home in the
Midlands or rather tough ladies. The clubs keep up a
continuous show by using the same girls who trot through Soho
at a fast clip seldom pausing for a cup of coffee. They are
recognized by rather passé hair-styles, mustard-coloured stage
make-up and a small case containing costume and cosmetics.
At least one place operates a communications system whereby
the doorman presses a warning bell when admitting customers
so that the girl downstairs can put on a record and go into a
finale routine all on her own as the customers are seated. She
then announces a twenty-minute intermission before rushing
down the street to find a couple of strippers with ten minutes to
spare. Meanwhile the customers are sitting staring at a curtain
and consuming rather a lot of terribly expensive drink.

It's not illegal to be a prostitute in London. A girl who wants
to go into business can, and does, sometimes, put up illuminated
signs with her name. Decorum forbids them adding the nature
of the services purveyed. Throughout Soho you'll notice
above the bell pushes large nameplates of girls who seem to be
without a patronym. None of them in any case can compete
with 'a common bawd', whose promising name was Joan
Jolybody, entered in the Calendar Rolls of 1420.

'No single woman to take money to lie with any man but she
lie with him all night till the morrow' said a law of 1162.
Nowadays, a recent investigation found, many prostitutes do
business with thirty clients each night.

Never has London shown a scarcity of prostitutes. Boswell
described his adventures with them; '... only seventeen, very
well looked', and refused to pay more than sixpence a time.
As early as 1669 there were London clubs where apprentices
could sing and meet their doxies. In the eighteenth century
there were 'cock and hen' clubs where young men could sing,
drink and meet whores. They gradually dropped in status until
in 1824 a writer comments that they were '... attended mostly
by young thieves'. Which perhaps accounts for the success of
'Henry's List of Covent Garden Ladies', an eighteenth-century
publication which named and described the courtesans of
the town.

In 1960 a Soho business man published a similar list called the *Ladies Directory*. It enjoyed a brief but spectacular success. A controversial legal battle ended with its being ruled an obscene magazine, and the publisher was sentenced to nine months in prison.

Nowadays some girls, forbidden to solicit custom on the pavement, place ads in the shop windows of local newsagents. Looking at the personal adverts outside certain newsagents' shops is a popular London pastime, not only in Soho but in many other parts of London too. Some are genuine ones from people selling secondhand prams or needing help with the housework, but some are thinly veiled offers of a more personal kind. 'Miss Wyplash phone 0 0 0 0' or 'Corrective treatment' from 'strict' ladies are often what the underworld calls fladge – flagellation. 'French lessons' is a popular euphemism, while language lessons from Swedish or German girls give a suggestion of flagellation. A friend of mine who owns a newsagent's declined to display an advert for 'Swedish lessons, phone 0 0 0 0' and had the following conversation with the indignant would-be advertiser.

W.B.A.: ... and I say you owe me some sort of explanation for refusing to take the advertisement.

NEWSAGENT: Possibly, miss, but I am permitted to decline any advert I don't like.

W.B.A.: But it's very unpleasant – and ungentlemanly – of you to give me no explanation.

NEWSAGENT: I'm truly sorry miss but I can't take it.

W.B.A.: Look, I give lessons in the Swedish language. If you want to re-word the advert by all means do so, but please don't just refuse it without telling me what's wrong.

NEWSAGENT: I'm sorry, miss.

W.B.A: What is it you think the advert implies?

NEWSAGENT: I wouldn't like to tell you, miss.

W.B.A.: It's the only way I can continue to live here. [*confidentially*] You see this is my only way of earning a living. What can be wrong with giving language lessons? Do you hate Swedish people?

NEWSAGENT: No miss, on the contrary I like them.

W.B.A.: Well please take my advert.

NEWSAGENT: I'm sorry, miss [*almost changing his mind*], but I really cannot.

W.B.A.: Look luv, take my ad and you can come round once a week and have a bit for free.

It is, as you may have already remarked, very hypocritical of the British to use foreign names to imply flagellation, for throughout the world for countless years flagellation has been known as the 'English vice', but then so has hypocrisy.

London prostitutes find that most of their clients seek flagellation and for this reason you will find that this perversion is catered for to a greater extent than any other. Strange antics in rubber clothing seem like favourite number two.

The adverts go in cycles, with someone thinking of some new idea and everyone copying it. It began with just the word 'model' followed by a phone number. One of the most recent is 'Young girl looking for new position' with copyists changing it to 'Young girl seeks unusual position' and then 'Beautiful young girl seeks exciting new position'. The classic perhaps will remain 'Beautiful young girl gives stimulating and relaxing exercises.'

Soho because of its character is subject to more rapid changes than any other part of the town. Because of that anyone who has lived there can drop all too easily into a parochial nostalgia that can be entertaining only to a very small number of people. The residents of the quarter have their own understanding, and the first people to recognize that you are not a visitor are the 'girls' who no longer greet you. Perhaps it's the only neighbourhood in the world where to be ignored is neighbourliness.

I remember a strange little club, near to the Casino, which catered to flower-girls (and whatever happened to flower-girls I'd like to know?) and ladies of ill-fame. After drinking all the afternoon they would emerge on to the pavement clutching their baskets, blooms somewhat withered by the warm alcohol-laden air and engage in arguments that sometimes came to blows. Snatches of conversation come back to me as I walk through the district. An unshaven man to a man and girl at four o'clock on a sunny afternoon, 'Well all I can say is thank you for a lovely party.' A prostitute with a bunch of flowers saying to her colleagues: 'Well all my clients have done too many hours solo and not enough dual.'

Soho is easily the most publicized part of London and publicity being what it is, the accent is always upon the 'square mile of vice' aspect. It should be stressed that, while I am not underwriting your health insurance, the chances of encountering violence or robbery are very low indeed. You may be overcharged, bored half to death, or contract ptomaine poisoning in a restaurant, but your person will be safe.

No matter what blandishments you succumb to from what dark doorway it's only your money they are after, and very few operators in Soho would resort to violence because this would be bad for business, and what's bad for business is bad for Soho. There is violence here between criminals, but that is discreet and unreported. Some ten minutes after the pubs close there is the slim possibility that you will see a couple of drunks trying to fight and stay upright and probably managing to do neither. For a moment it's easy to think that all the sensation-alist journalism is true, but I have won a reputation for soothsaying by betting that both such pugilists will prove to have the same out of town accent. So far I have always been right. Visitors come here with their friends, drink with their friends, argue with their friends, fight with their friends, get thrown out of pubs with their friends, get arrested with their friends, appear in court with their friends and return home with their friends, having had a real night out in London.

Another sight to watch out for very late at night in Soho is well-dressed gentlemen alighting from Ferrari or Humber cars to prod the garbage outside a restaurant. Proprietors of restaurants can read a rival's garbage, like a gypsy reads a hand, or a cobbler reads a pair of shoes. From the garbage they can tell the proportions of different types of food sold – frozen, tinned or fresh – which companies the restaurant is dealing with, what the state of business is, and a whole lot more. Some time I will start a garbage newsletter that, for a small fee, will enable restaurant proprietors to go straight home at night, but then they will no longer be able to tell their wives 'Sorry I'm late, *chérie*, I had a heavy night with the garbage.'

Underworld

Eric Clark

Eric Clark, twenty-nine, has been a reporter since leaving school thirteen years ago. After the *Daily Mail* and the *Guardian*, joined the *Observer*, where he specializes in specializing in nothing. Started a love-hate relationship with crime from his first job, working up from teenage gangs to train robbers and American gangsters. Lived in Soho until driven out by burglaries and blood in the communal lift. Loves: malt whisky, exercising first thing in the morning – and his wife, who has been known to write his stories for him. Hates: dogs, people who find crime glamorous, and English hypocrisy. Now working on a novel in which people actually get hurt when they are hit on the head.

It took London to give the world Rachmann, the vicious postwar property exploiter; the Messinas, operators of a vast vice ring, and the Great Train Robbery. Today London can boast the best and biggest pornography, some of the fastest-grabbing clip-joints on the European scene, a prostitution industry geared for every taste, and as vicious (and prosperous) gangland bosses as can be found anywhere outside of Mickey Spillane.

Crime in London is a major growth industry: more fire-arms, better weapons (ammonia squirted in the face is just as effective as a pickaxe handle and not half as crude), more woundings and assaults, lots more drug-taking, bigger and better robberies – all coupled with less and less chance of getting caught. The final acknowledgement of British leadership was made only recently when American syndicate bosses decided to invest their capital and experience in Britain's gilt-edged crime shares. 'It is,' said one, 'like having Prohibition or Las Vegas open up all over again.'

London, in short, is the great disprover of the old fairy story about crime not paying. Even criminals who fail can earn a near-guaranteed bonus by writing their memoirs or acting as advisers. The only real casualty of recent years is poor Jack Spot, once a London underworld king, and now in semi-seclusion in a furnished flat where he lives under an assumed name.

But for the tourist, fired by the living legend of London's criminality, the city still holds a reluctance about placing too much on show. Seeing – and admiring – one of London's law-breakings is something that still depends on chance. The London criminal, despite his obvious joy in contributing to the image of swinging London, still has to work with some secrecy. London is not like Las Vegas where one of the thrills is having the gangsters pointed out, although two of London's gang-land leaders make a point of turning up at the occasional film première or charity performance.

One of the tourist advantages of London's underworld is that the chances of becoming unpleasantly involved are fairly small. It is, as any gangster would tell you, a cause of lasting regret when a stray bullet hits a visitor. Gangsters, unless they are carrying out a pay raid, generally make a point of shooting only each other. London's public face of criminality is Soho. Its basic lawbreaking industries depend on consumer participation. Because of this it has to put many of its goods on show. The most basic of its industries is selling sex.

The best disreputable enterprise to examine in disreputable Soho is probably a pornographic bookshop. Soho currently has over a dozen of them – number growing fast – specializing in catering for tastes which W. H. Smith's do not satisfy. They are easy to find; just look for windows full of girlie magazines and pseudo textbooks. Inside there are more pin-up magazines and copies of *A History of Orgies*. Disregard them: the real stocks are to be found in a small room at the back, door marked 'Private'.

One man has to be convinced if you want to enter that inner sanctum: the manager, who stands inside the small back room and communicates with the front shop through a hatch. This man takes his books from a wholesaler and, in return for up to

£100 a week, shoulders the risks in the event of a raid by the Vice Squad. As a hazard it is not a very worrying one for the industry. The actual value of the material on the premises is low even if its sale or loan value is high, and books and photographs confiscated in a raid can be replaced quickly from further along the pipeline.

Like a barber or a tailor, the dirt-bookshop manager has his regular customers and he knows them (watch them walk straight through the door marked 'Private'). If you could get him talking he would tell you that the majority are businessmen, middle-aged and respectable-looking: the kind of men you can see on a commuter train any morning. 'A business run by businessmen for businessmen,' one manager enthuses. 'That's how I like to see it.'

As a potential viewer of the inner room you have one thing in your favour: the manager genuinely wants to take your money. The fear is whether you might be a plain-clothes detective making a pre-raid sortie. What to do? Try wearing spectacles; managers do not expect to see policemen in glasses. Whatever you wear you will have to wait for a quiet moment and then utter the magic 'Haven't you anything better?' At this stage be prepared to continue the conversation:

'What d'you mean, better?'

'Well, you know: more ... ahum ... better.'

It is not wise to extend the conversation beyond that: there is an inbuilt prejudice against talkers. It should be enough to earn a nod towards the door marked 'Private'. The room inside will certainly be tiny, with books grouped along two or three of the walls, divided into two main sections, straight 'porn' and sadism.

A fair price for unillustrated books (sample titles *Keep it in the family* and *The sexual life of Robinson Crusoe*) would be £3–£5 and for illustrated material between £6 and £9. Photographs, usually in sets of five, are filed. Inquirers, you will note, are specific: women, duos, lesbians, groups. Price: not more than £1 a set.

Books, but not photographs, will be sold on a half-price-back on return basis; the pencil-note on the cover is to show the manager the shop at which the book was originally bought. It is a business which, at first glance, seems to hurt no one. You might explain that in a few years' time to the ten-year-old runaway picked up in Soho and photographed with a collection of men before being rescued by the Police. Postcards of her will still be going around when she is married with a family.

Porn is not only for the consumer. There is a trade side to the industry. There are few prostitutes who do not keep a few photographs around as a stimulant for 'difficult' clients.

As everyone from Alice Springs to Little Rock knows, the last thing that the 1959 Street Offences Act did was to get rid of prostitution. It just swept the women who used to mob tourists off the main streets. Today their approach is a little more subtle, but not much.

In Soho they still operate on the streets, but not straying far from the doorways that lead to workrooms. Failing that, just look for the signs inside hallways: 'Lesley, second floor' or 'Model, up the stairs, turn right'. Two business-girls even fixed up a rudimentary neon sign at the foot of the stairs. Another tried shooting peas at passers-by, but abandoned the practice for reasons that probably owed more to the lack of need than the increased overheads. Boards outside some of the smaller shops display some interesting messages: 'Governess teaches French. Strict disciplinarian', as good a comment on one side of the English character as you will get.

Outside of Soho, Paddington, Notting Hill and Stepney have more than their share of girls. The Bayswater–Notting Hill section of London has 40–50 girls operating on an average weekday evening.

Queensway is a good street for studying display cards placed outside newsagents' shops. Current samples range from the simplicity of 'Doll for Sale' or 'Gentlemen – all facilities' to the more sophisticated 'Lady offers interesting accommodation for gentlemen in picturesque setting' or 'Lady owner-driver offers fast sports job with attractive pink upholstery'. Bedford Hill, Balham, is an area where the business has been enjoying a continuous growth. And, further out, to admire more sophisticated techniques, villages around Epping Forest see regular clients changing from their own cars into call-girls' vehicles.

Beware, though, of getting your car number listed: local police collect them.

As in most major cities, cab drivers and hotel porters are expert advisers. But the top rank, at the top prices, are a little like exclusive clubs: admission on personal recommendation.

Broadly speaking, prices depend on the area. In Bayswater–Notting Hill they range between £3 and £5. In Soho, where visitors and tourists provide the main custom, £5 is usual. In 'higher class' areas such as Shepherd Market the charge increases to around £10.

At this stage we recommend some caution. As in buying a shirt or a record-player, the trade slogan is 'Let the buyer beware'. Tracy, operating around Meard Street in Soho, for example, is an attractive blonde – until he removes his wig.

Beware too the pseudo-prostitute luring you into a clip-joint where the aim is simply to extract the maximum money (spent on foul, non-alcoholic drinks) in return for promises. Do not fall for it. You can buy £20 worth of orange juice, hear all the sweet words, and still find yourself out on the street with nothing more than added Vitamin C. If you are silly enough to get into the situation, do not argue. The bar-girl may look fragile; the bouncers in the back are not.

Not all clubs are clip-joints. Apart from the well-known nightclubs, which are as expensive and dull as nightclubs anywhere, there are drinking clubs which are amusing and safe provided only that you do not show large bundles of notes or mention nasty words like 'protection'. As most club owners will tell you, protection does not exist. That some then go into a back room to pay out is nothing to do with you. The simple rule for dividing clip-joints from drinking clubs is to beware of all places that send out girls to invite you inside.

Erotic films are easy game and, though highly illegal, run fairly straight. There is little point in looking for them. Let them find you. Hang around outside one of the girlie-cinemas. It should not be long before a tout suggests you make a short trip. The destination may surprise you. It may be a flat in a luxury block in Marylebone, but the show, even if the film flickers, will be genuine. The price depends on how rich you look, but a fiver may do it. Your greatest worry is the slender chance that the man sitting next to you, picked up in the same way, may be a detective. The film show might end with your having to give a statement, something hardly calculated to make the boss back home regard you as a pillar of the community.

Blue-film operators may also offer 'live' shows. Again you get what you pay for, something that cannot be said of many of the strip-clubs which are often as yawn-producing as you can get.

Because of this, it is always wisest to visit the better known strip-clubs rather than the places you have never heard of. Wherever you go, the show will be pretty disappointing (by the standards we are using here), so you might as well buy the prettiest girls and the most luxurious surroundings.

The gambling scene is likely to change because of the Government's plans to tighten the law. The intention is that gaming houses will no longer be able to make a profit out of participating in the play – the main source of their revenue. 'It will mean the end of high-class gaming,' said one operator when the plans were announced. Whether it will or not depends on how carefully Parliament drafts its new law and how smart the lawyers are. Chemin-de-fer, where the house acts only as referee, should continue. But be warned, this is the one game where stakes can most easily get out of hand. Roulette may be driven underground. If it is, better not play at all. Remember that even in a straight game the bank's advantage on single number bets is 2·7 per cent – enough to ensure that you are the loser in the long run. Think of what it could be like in an illegal game where the wheel might have been 'rigged'.

Some time around early evening in Soho you may feel in need of a fire-arm. It is not something we recommend under any circumstances, particularly in view of the fact that the laws about carrying a gun are pretty stringent. You will *not* get a fire-arm by applying for a licence. They are only given to members of recognized shooting clubs. The underworld, though, is geared to overcoming the problem. Getting a gun is possible although risky. The thing to do is ask around. No one will actually look very interested, but stay around and later that night a car may well draw up alongside and the offer will be made. There is no recommended selling price (remember this is not a dishwasher), but £25 would be fair. It could be, though, that the car that draws up beside you may contain a detective. A few people, including some criminals, still do not like guns. The man who nodded when you made your approach may have phoned the police about someone 'trying to buy a shooter'. Apart from straight sales, there is a lending library in guns. A Beretta, for example, used to work out at a £2 loaning fee. This, however, is a service run only among friends.

At the level of porn and prostitution, of blue films and clip-joints, it is easy to view London's underworld as an illegal but amusing place: Damon Runyon not Raymond Chandler. One thing, though, is worth remembering: this side of London is divided into sellers and suckers. And, however nice anyone may be, *you* are the sucker. Why not try the philosophy at its most simple: the three-card trick (good area, Charing Cross Road near Foyle's). First look at the game from across the road. Note the lookouts. Now note the men planted in the crowd by the operators. When they play, they win. Now you play. You will lose. There is one way of winning, although I am not sure I recommend it to anyone other than a four-minute miler spending his last day in Britain before emigrating.

First, wait until a good crowd gathers. Now put down your money on the first hand of the game. In your left hand hold a few notes so that it looks as though you will continue to play. Above all look earnest. You become the sucker who is going to be allowed to win a couple of times, firstly to urge you to bet heavier sums and secondly to encourage the rest of the crowd to participate. You are allowed to win. Now you are expected to bet again. Don't. Run like hell. As I said, it is not really recommended. Tightrope walking is safer.

Men like the three-card trick exponents are amusing only in fiction and musicals. London's criminal and near-criminal fraternity is not amusing, witty or beguiling. It is a group of people dedicated to earning the maximum money for the minimum effort and some of the racketeers would move into coshing old ladies without qualms if it were as safe and profitable. To get the message we suggest a look inside a Soho betting shop.

Not all the customers are playing with money taken from suckers, but enough are for you to see how lucrative it all is.

The most basic London crime is protection, the racket that involves a gangleader 'persuading' club owners to pay an agreed amount each week in return for not being bothered with 'trouble'. It is the rule of the shotgun and razor. As a racket it has taken London's two biggest gang bosses to the top, allowing them to branch out into legitimate enterprises and into sophisticated frauds.

The tentacles of these gangsters reach far – even into prison. The families of gang members serving prison sentences get help. The aim is not charity: it is just good business. A club owner talks with affection of one gangster who loaned money to help the club over a bad patch. It was a nice gesture; but the club still had to pay protection.

At this level people disappear without trace or die. It is an area of criminality best avoided. But the growth of gambling in Britain has made it possible to see some of these 'top' gangsters; many visit the clubs regularly.

London has not in the past been known as a drug centre. Believers in British supremacy may be glad to know that times are changing. The number of known narcotic addicts is still fairly small (753 at the time of the Brain Committee report on the problem in 1965), but it is fast growing and the addicts are getting younger. The main source of illicit drugs has been over-prescribing by doctors to registered addicts. It is proposed that in future narcotics will be available to addicts only at special treatment centres. It may work, but it will just as likely encourage the growth of the professional 'pusher'. One non-registered addict already claims to know nineteen places where he can buy narcotics in London. With morphine worth around £100 an ounce, inducements are great. In America gambling and drugs are the backbone of the syndicates.

London, not to be left behind, legalized gambling without enforcing controls and may now give the narcotics trafficker a boost. Until doctors are prevented from prescribing narcotics to addicts, Boots in Piccadilly Circus will be worth a visit at midnight, the hour when addicts can obtain their next day's dose.

Follow one (I don't recommend it) and you may see the needle go in. As a sight it is second only to seeing an addict being withdrawn from drugs at around the time when insects are crawling under his skin.

Looking at London through a criminal's eyes is a great game for a quiet day. Try the art galleries. Forget the pictures and try spotting the alarms. Is that hole near the radiator an infrared ray alarm? Best preparation for this kind of tour is to collect the literature which the alarm companies issue or buy the monthly *Security Gazette*.

Try a few brain-teasers too. What is an easy way of transferring large sums in a small space? Answer: take a look at the best stamp shops. Stamps, like diamonds or drugs, are good currency anywhere. Thieves have certainly thought so in the last few years.

Surrounded by so much crime it is worth turning your thoughts to the police. Scotland Yard is worth a peep inside the main door to see what a really courteous policeman can be like.

The Metropolitan Police has twenty-four Divisions, including the Thames Police. The best-known Yard Department is its Criminal Investigation, embracing among other things the Murder Squad, the Criminal Records Office, the Flying Squad (the 'heavy mob' to the underworld) and the Intelligence Squad which operates under cover, mingling with criminals, gathering material.

From outside, the new Metropolitan Police Headquarters in Broadway, Westminster, looks like any other office building. Inside it is equally disappointing, but a change from the cramped gloomy Victorian keep that was the police nerve centre until March 1967.

The Yard's Forensic Science Laboratory, where work may include anything from classifying blood to comparing the paint on a jemmy with that on a window, is now housed in a new police building in Lamb's Conduit Street, off Theobald's Road, in Holborn. The pathologists whose names keep cropping up during big murder inquiries are to be found at the forensic departments of the London, Guy's and St George's hospitals.

The Special Branch, responsible for internal security, make a point of keeping out of sight. You may spot them if you attend enough demonstrations organized by what the branch regard as extremist groups. A word of advice: attend too many gatherings looking for them and yours may join the two million files in their records office.

For criminal-type shopping, baby alarms linked with walkie-talkie outfits make a good, cheap way of 'bugging' a room; flick knives (illegal) can be found near some of the main railway stations; shotguns are still easy to obtain, and there is a firm at Watford which markets a ·45 Colt imitation as realistic as anyone could wish.

If you need a detective who gets results there is Barrie Quartermain at Kingston, Surrey; a more conservative choice would be the highly reputable John Walsh, an ex-C.I.D. man at Putney (both in the telephone book).

The Forensic Science Society at 107 Fenchurch Street, E C 3, will suggest where you can get a private ballistics test on a bullet or check a car for fingerprints.

For almost guaranteed blackmailing try answering wife-swapping ads in a number of easily obtained but rapidly changing small magazines. To prove sin is moving out from the centre get an invitation to a party in a dormitory suburb.

To be fully prepared for anything, try karate at Clapham or write Pat Butler (c/o Faber & Faber, 24 Russell Square, W C 1) to persuade him to teach his system of self-defence. And remember his ultimate advice for those in trouble: 'If you can't run and you can't fight, faint. With luck they'll think you have had a heart attack and run away.'

All through the night

London isn't an all-night city, not yet at any rate, although the restaurants here will serve a five-course meal at an hour when New York and Paris restaurateurs have long since got the chairs up on the tables. Wimpy bars – anglicized hamburger establishments – have several branches operating all round the clock. Try the Wimpy at 7 Edgware Road if you are near Marble Arch or, if you are in the Earls Court area, either 1 Earls Court Road or 250 Earls Court Road. The Golden Egg at 175 in the same road is another all-nighter, for this is kangaroo valley, where the tight-knit community of Australians, New Zealanders and South Africans have revolutionized London shop hours. I know that cooked food, bread, eggs and corn-flakes are also on sale here in Earls Court Road, for I've shopped for my breakfast groceries on my way home from London Airport in the early hours.

For the really hungry insomniac there are slot machines in Piccadilly Circus, King's Road and many other busy streets. Strange foods glitter behind their glassy navels and for a florin they will disgorge crimson drinks, spongy sandwiches and blunt pies; don't drop them on your toes.

For sit-down eating in the West End, try the Steak House (93 Shaftesbury Avenue) or Steak Encore at 20 Leicester Square. The newest all-nighter I know is the Maze in the basement of the Royal Garden Hotel, Kensington High Street, W 8.

Godfrey Davis runs a 24-hour car-hire service (V I C 8484) for self-drive or chauffeur-driven cars. I tried it at 2 a.m. between Sunday and August Bank Holiday Monday and got an instant offer of a car. I can't think of a better test than that.

Minor car repairs can be handled by Moon's Garage, 79 Davies Street, W 1 (H Y D 1441), and their break-down branch at 25 Taunton Place, N W 1 (P A D 7227) will come out four miles to assist. If you are a member the A.A. or R.A.C. will send out a patrol to you if you phone W H I 1200 or W H I 4343 respectively. There is no charge, but they will quiz you about your membership number before they call the patrol on the radio. Should you not be a member, they will offer you assistance provided you join.

If it's only petrol you need there are several all-night petrol pumps. There's one in the Savoy Adelphi Garage, Savoy Place (river side of the Savoy Hotel), and another one in Bruton Lane, if you go around Berkeley Square you'll spot it next to Berkeley Square House.

The only all-night post office is in King William IV Street, just off Trafalgar Square. Even during the day-time this is the best place from which to send a telegram. Nearby post offices have to phone your message to this office in any case; from here it's transmitted immediately.

Problem Ltd (T A T 8181) is a subscription service but if you phone them in an emergency they will probably help you out. Their switchboard – manned 24 hours – will find you plumbers, electricians, get your babysitters or plane tickets for you. I've been a member some time and recommend them.

The Excel Tenpin Bowl, 30 Shaftesbury Avenue, is open all night on Fridays and Saturdays but is liable to chicken out at 4 a.m. other nights. The snack bar keeps going as long as there are customers.

Barclays Bank in the B.O.A.C. terminal, Victoria, is open until 10 p.m. and will cash any Barclays cheque if you carry identification (or any other cheque by prior arrangement). In this same building there is a first-class medical service for yellow fever jabs, dental work and any other traveller's wear and tear. It's good, clean, polite and painless and highly recommended, but be there by 4 p.m. and if possible make an appointment. No need to be a bona fide traveller.

Boots the Chemist, right in Piccadilly Circus, is open 24 hours but will handle only prescriptions during the night. John Bell & Croyden, at 50 Wigmore Street, W 1, make up prescriptions after dark but will also sell certain items including contraceptives. Write it on a piece of paper if you don't like being overheard by the rather static group of blank-eyed men waiting for their prescriptions to be filled.

Perhaps by this time you are tired enough to want to go to bed. If you are short of money the cheapest large hotel is the Mount Pleasant Hotel, 53 Calthorpe Street, w c 1 (t e r 9781), which until recently was a Rowton House hostel for down-and-outs. Now it has been given a thorough face-lift. It will cost you 29s. 6d. for bed and breakfast, 15s. for dinner, plus 10 per cent service charge on everything. If you think that's too expensive for a place that used to be a hostel for down-and-outs then I think I agree with you. What about some unconverted hostels? There are still five Rowton Houses which now prefer to be called Rowton Hotels. At one time the men there were housed in dormitories but now they are separated into cubicles. There are also some real rooms. The charge varies from 6s. 6d. to 12s. 6d. a night. They are grim places, echoing with the cries and coughs of defeated men. Only one Rowton House will take one-night transients; Parkview House, 1 Churchyard Row, s e 11.

If you want a cheaper place than that, you can ask a policeman who will direct you to a charity organization. There are many of them, some very small and mostly confined to poor districts. A man who is on the run from the law can find somewhere to sleep by going to a large railway station after midnight. Easily picked out from the real travellers are derelict men on the benches hoping to sleep there. The men who doss regularly on the station benches put newspaper under them to quell the draught that comes through the slats. Most of them know somewhere a man can sleep for a few shillings with no questions asked. These places – always near large rail termini – used to shelter deserters, but now that there is no conscription in Britain there are virtually no deserters either.

The waiting-room is no good for a night's sleep because the police check railway tickets about midnight and watch the place afterwards. The best bet if all else fails is a train. First-class carriages are warmer than second. Carriages nearer the front are warmer than those near the back. Some trains are cleaned on arrival, some before morning departure. Some people who doss on trains prefer an uncleaned train, because that means they will be discovered by the cleaners who will probably make no fuss, instead of a railway official who might. It's no use checking the movements of trains against the indicator because the mail trains, which leave about 3 a.m., are not put up on the indicator.

If the police do pick you up as a vagrant they will almost never hold you for vagrancy, unless your clothes and cleanliness suggest that you are not a vagrant at all but some other category of law-breaker. What's more they won't ask you for your papers because a British citizen has no papers, which is perhaps the epitome of freedom. Since your clothes and accent will give you away, your best bet is to say your wife locked you out of the house and you have no money. Apparently this is a situation quite frequently met with by policemen who will be very understanding.

And now if you want to say that London policemen are wonderful I will agree without reservations.

Perhaps you would like a steam bath before retiring. Go into the Savoy Turkish bath (91 Jermyn Street, w 1) any time you like (men only, I'm afraid). The all-night fee (30s.) only lasts till 9.30 a.m. Beds are available to sleep off your sweat bath and in the morning they will fix you eggs and bacon.

You can get a hangover, have a Turkish bath and be back drinking again by 5 a.m. if you go to the Nag's Head opposite Covent Garden Opera House. Try to look like a local; the licensing laws are supposed to apply only to the market porters. To play it really cool, trot across the road to the market and buy a huge bunch of flowers wholesale, to help explain where you were all night. If she's right there with you, show her St Paul's church in the market (there's probably a tea van parked there) where Henry Higgins discovered Liza Doolittle, worried about, and later sang about, cockney diction.

All through the night heavy lorries have been clattering into town, down the centre of the deserted streets at speeds well over the limit, so that the drivers can sleep before the market really starts. Smithfield is the meat market, Billingsgate is for fish and Covent Garden for fruit, vegetables and flowers. The natives

of most cities tell the visitor to get up early and visit the market
although the natives do not themselves go. Nor do the more
astute tourists, for markets are markets and a crate of peaches
in Rome, Boston or Paris is the same crate of peaches. If you
are already up, then Covent Garden is the best market to see;
there's something gruesome about carcasses in the morning, and
dead fish are macabre. So go to Covent Garden and see the
fruit. See the down-and-outs – also nuns – picking up the
spilled items. It's a recognized thing that the needy can do so.
Don't expect it to be as interesting as Les Halles in Paris nor
to find anything available to match the onion soup and other
meals I have devoured there. The best you'll get at Covent
Garden is the beer and the rather powerful tea. While you're
drinking it, look back across the market from the church
portico. Imagine this piazza – as it was fashionably called – in
1631. It will need quite a feat of the imagination to picture it
as one of the most fashionable and genteel strolling places
in all Europe. The arcades echoed with the gossip of the
Coffee-house jet-set, and people lucky enough to live in one
of the grand houses that were part of Inigo Jones's plan
were the envy of London. But not for long.

In 1671 the Duke of Bedford got Charles II's permission to
hold a vegetable market here, and soon it became a notorious
haunt of thugs and robbers. Its fashionable days were over, but
the fashion for squares was only beginning. Within four years
of Covent Garden, Leicester Square was built, then Bloomsbury,
Soho, Grosvenor, St James's and Berkeley Squares followed.
Now London is a city of squares. A Dane, Steen Eiler Rasmussen in his *London: The Unique City*, says it better than I can:

On a summer day when the sun is shining you can walk for hours
from one square to another under fresh green trees and see
thousands of little circular spots cast by the sun on the green lawns.
But in the dark season the old squares are no less attractive. In the
afternoon, when lights begin to appear in the houses, when the tea is
served – a rite so sacred to the English – when London is being
swallowed up in the moisture and fog of the same yellowish colour
as the tea, the London square appears to be at the bottom of the sea
under branches whose indistinct outlines form a pattern like
seaweed floating overhead.

All through the night

No primitive man gained more comfort and delight from his open fire than does the Londoner. He'll do anything to enjoy one, including breaking the clean air laws.

A coal fire is the accompaniment to a foggy autumn afternoon. It heats the kettle for tea and provides hot toast. The English pay close attention to the design of their fireplaces. Brass implements shine there, dogs sleep there, slippers warm there. English ladies warm their hands and Englishmen their behinds there.

No coal fire will burn without a draught and if the sash windows don't provide it people will cut a slice off the bottom of the door. Englishmen don't tolerate draughts, they insist upon them. In the unmoving warm air of central heating the Englishman will feel unhappy and stifled. Watch him.

Tea is also available at a stall on the river side of Charing Cross Underground. You may see the same people that you saw picking up spilled vegetables in the market, for this is a favourite hangout of destitute men. They are quiet and polite and will offer you no harm. They might be waiting for the Silver Lady – a free canteen for the destitute – for this is its route.

Another place for a nocturnal cup of tea and snack is the West London Air Terminal. If by now you need a shave go into a toilet there and use the 6d.-in-the-slot electric shaver.

Some launderettes are open all night for people who like to do their laundry in the small hours. Social groups develop around the rotating washing and then disappear. Look in at 92 Crawford Street (off Baker Street), or Kenway Road, s w 5, off Earls Court Road, to check on the chat.

To pass yourself off as a Londoner say 'thank you' as often as possible and renounce 'farewell' in favour of 'bye-bye'. Frank Norman will help you decipher some more local idiom. This piece – the only reprint in the book – was the seed of *Fings Ain't Wot They Used T' Be* and I think it is quite a classic.

Slang

Frank Norman

Born 1930 in Bristol. He has lived in London almost all of his life. He has written five books including *Bang to Rights*, an autobiographical account of prison life, and *The Monkey Pulled His Hair*. He also wrote the play *Fings Ain't Wot They Used T' Be*, which was a great West End success. Works as a film and television scriptwriter and journalist. Lists his chief hobby as 'being against all ball games with the exception of snooker'.

When I thought about writing this piece about slang I wondered where would be the best place to start; it is a very difficult subject to write about when you have been talking it for the best part of your life as I have; you see, to someone like me, there is nothing whatever strange about it, in fact it is really like the man in the street trying to explain the English language. He, like me, would very likely have quite a job on his hands. For instance, there are quite a few words which are different yet which mean the same thing and there are quite a few words that are the same but which have different meanings. Take a word like *bird*. I think it is fairly well known that this word means 'girl' or 'woman', but perhaps it is not so well known that *bird* also means 'time'; this comes from rhyming slang (*bird-lime*) and this also has two meanings. 'I've only got another two months *bird* to do.' And 'Do you know what the *bird* is, John?' Then there is also *dicky-bird*, which is rhyming slang for 'word'. See what I mean? Some words seem obscure and do not look as though they have anything to do with the thing that they mean. One of the best examples of this is the word *geezer*; the predecessor of this word was *mug*, this was rhymed with 'steam-tug', so for a while the word *steamer* took its place; but not for long because it wasn't all that long before it was changed again, this time it became descriptive of what a steamer is, hence *geezer,* which gives off hot water and quite a lot of steam!

Some slang is very old and I think I am right in saying that most of these are words and phrases that are used in the *nick* (prisons). I wouldn't mind betting that a cell was called a *peter* before it was called a cell; if you follow me! Another one with whiskers on is *screw*; this goes back before there were locks on prison cells, instead they were s*crewed* up. There are quite a few more which I expect we will come across as we go along.

Cockney or *lags'* (convicts') slang is not the only slang that is used in this country; there is also drug addicts', queers' and lezs', and back slang, although the last one is no longer used to any great extent. Slang which is used by drug addicts is very closely linked with that which is used by musicians, and the queers' and lezs' is very closely linked with prostitutes' (*brasses*) slang. I will deal with each of these a little later. Let us first have a closer look at Cockney slang. I think the best way is to use some of it in a conversation between two *geezers,* one called Bill and the other called Cecil. They are laying about in a *kayf* (café) up *west* (the West End). The night before they have had it off on a *screwer* (burglary) for a nice little *tickle* (lot of money).

BILL: What do yer *reckon* (think of) that *bogey* (policeman) who came *sticking his hooter* (putting his nose) round the *gaff* (house) when we were in there last night?

CECIL: To tell yer the truth I thought he *sused* (suspected) there was something *buzzing* (going on). And I expected him to get on the *blower* (phone) to the *nick* (police station) and ask them to send the *hurry up* (police car).

BILL: No, I don't think he *sused* anything, because he was only a youngster just starting up in the game. But even if he had tumbled to us we would have had plenty of chances of having it away a bit on the hurry up because we had the motor out the back.

CECIL: I can't afford to get captured because I've already got six *cons* (convictions) and the last time I went *up the steps* (the sessions) the judge *stuck me in promise land for a neves* (told me I would get seven years next time).

BILL: Well, I don't know what you're screaming about, because I'm a dead cert to get *P.D.* (preventive detention) the next time I go up. And I've already heard a *whisper* (word) that there's a *W* (warrant) out for me up North.

CECIL: Do leave off.

BILL: It's all right for you, you're *laughing* (all right). You haven't got a *W* out for you. If you had I bet your *bottle would fall out* (you would be scared).

CECIL: Any old how I didn't know you had as many *cons* as that, what did you get them for?

BILL: Well, if you must know, I got my first one for a *jump up* (stealing a lorry), and one for a *blag* (wages snatch), and another for *tooling some flash tearaway* (cutting a *geezer* with a razor). Then I got a capture down to *larking* (nothing) when some *grass* (informer) told the law I had *blown a peter* (robbed a safe; blown open, with explosives), when it wasn't me at all. And the other two I got for *smashes* (smash and grabs).

CECIL: Versatile, ain't yer!

You can hear conversations like this anywhere, that is, if you ever go anywhere. I know some geezers who talk like that the whole time, and the truth is they just don't know any other way to talk, and as a matter of fact I myself have only just started to talk 'proper' and the only reason for this is because the people I talk to most these days wouldn't understand what I was talking about. I could if I had the room write pages and pages of conversations like that without hardly ever repeating myself, but that would be writing a book and I am not doing that, and I think it would get a bit boring after a while. Another thing I am trying very hard not to do is write a dictionary but I think that occasionally I will have to do something of the kind because it is the only way to explain meanings. For example, 'money' has a slang name; *gelt* is one, and there are many others; also most amounts of money have slang terms; some are rhyming, some racing, and some I do not have a clue about even though I have used them for years. As I have said, I think the only thing to do is have a short dictionary so that I can get them all in.

penny – *Clod*

sixpence – *Tanner* (you all know)
shilling – *Chip*
one and six – *Ky-bosh*
two and six – *Tosheroon*
five shillings – *Caser*
ten shillings – *Cows* (rhyming: cow's calf)
pound – *Nicker*, *once'r*, or *quid*
two pounds – *Duce* or *bice*
three pounds – *Tray* (but not used much)
four pounds – *Rouf*
five pounds – *Jack* (Jacks-Alive)
seven pounds – *Neves*
ten pounds – *Cockle* (rhyming: cock and hen)
twenty pounds – *Score*
twenty-five pounds – *Pony*
fifty pounds – *Half a ton*
one hundred – *Ton*, or a *one'r*
two hundred – *Twoer*
And so on up to five hundred which is a *Monkey*.

So there you are, now you know as much as I do about it.
There are a few alternatives to the above but as they would only
confuse you, and me too if it comes to that, I think the best
thing is to leave them out. These slang terms for money are also
used in connexion with prison sentences, etc., although most of
the terms for *bird* are entirely different. I think, while I am
about it, I might as well give you them as well, in the form of
another dictionary.

three months – *A carpet*
six months – *Half a stretch*
one year – *A stretch*
eighteen months – *Eighteen moon*
twenty-one months – *Pontoon*
two years – *Two stretch*
three or over – *Lagging*
four – *Rouf*
five – *Handful*
seven – *Neves*
ten – *Cockle*

Slang that is used in the nick is to a very large extent the same as that which is used by the Cockneys, but there is also a lot more that belongs to the nick alone. Quote: 'I was doing three days *chokey* (bread and water), which I got for passing a *stiff* (note) to some *schmock* (prick) who owed me a quarter of an ounce of *snout* (tobacco). Some *dodgey* (no good) *twirl* (warder) *clocked* (saw) me, and stuck me on the *carpet* (report). I didn't have no chance because it was a case of *bang to rights* (being captured red-handed). I tried to *chat* (talk) my way out of it but the old man didn't want to *know* (hear any explanations I had to give). I don't reckon him nothing because you can't give him any of the *old moody* (fool him). But I don't care because I can do this *standing* (on my head) *easily*, I've only got another *moon* (month) and then I'll be laughing, in fact to tell you the truth I am feeling a bit *gatey* (jumpy) already.

'I had a *fair bird* (good girl) when I got *nicked* (caught) but after I had done a *carpet* (three months), she *gave me the belt* (finished with me) and went off with some *schfatzer* (Negro), and the last I heard was he had *stuck her up the spout* (made her pregnant). I hope it drives her *bonkers* (mad) when she gets a *spook chavey* (Negro child), that'll teach her not to go around *charvering* (having sex) all over the place.'

This, like the conversation between Bill and Cecil, is the type of thing that is spoken every day in some quarters. *Moody*, like so many other words, does not only mean what it says above. It can also mean that you are trying to persuade someone that something is when it isn't, if you get me.

I think it might be a good idea to give a few other terms that are used in the nick, for instance: *darbes* (handcuffs), *P.O.* (principal officer), *piss hole* (lavatory), *meat wagon* (black maria), *half a sheet* (punishment that screws get, usually a fine).

Back slang is probably the most simple form of slang and yet one of the hardest to understand. I have already said that this is not used so much these days; when it was used the place to hear it would have been around the race-tracks. It works like this: you take the first letter off each word and add it on the end (e.g. *langs*). When you have done that, all you do is add an 'a' (*langsa*). As a rule you don't do this with short words, but, on the other hand, you do sometimes. 'I saw ouya the theroa ightna up the hpeilersa.' What helps to make this so difficult is the fact that a lot of ordinary slang words are used, *shpeiler* (*hpeilersa*); see what I mean?

I would like to have now a little *rabbit* (talk) about slang which is used by drug addicts; most of this comes to us from America where it is known as 'ziph' or 'jive'. This, as I have mentioned, is very closely linked with that which is used by jazz musicians and it is in fact very closely linked with jazz itself, because it is very rhythmical and jazzy. Words like *cool* and *hot, charge, dope,* and *crazy* are good examples. A conversation between a *hop head* (cocaine or morphine addict) and a *shit smoker* (marijuana addict) goes a bit like this. We will call them the *junky* and the *viper*.

JUNKY: I wish I was still on the *shit*, man; I get my *kicks* from a *pop* in the main, but this *H* is givin' me the itch.

VIPER: I dig, man, my *chick's* real tuned in to that *kick*, every time I see her she's doing a *flip*, but she's never got enough *bread* to give the *pusher*. She's real *gone,* dad; and she's never coming back. She thinks I'm a real sad *square*, 'cause I ain't got the habit yet.

JUNKY: Don't let it get you, man, just never be a *mainliner*, like me. I don't even *dig* them sounds no more; and *chicks* are just a *drag*.

VIPER: Yeah, *man*!

JUNKY: I'll see you, man. I'm going to get myself a *fix*.

I don't think this needs very much explanation. This slang is not used very much over here as yet, but in my opinion, it will be very soon, not necessarily by drug addicts but by the beat generation when it arrives. There are few drug addicts in this country and I expect that this is another reason why this slang is not so widely known but, even so, I think it is of particular interest because of the difference between it and Cockney slang. In my opinion this slang is on a very much higher level than the Cockney; while the Cockney or lag's slang has a certain amount of humour, this has none, this is a desperate language which is used by desperate people.

As drug addicts' slang is to musicians, so queers' and lezs' slang is to *brasses* (prostitutes). The best thing, once again, I think, will be to have a little *bunny* between a *queer* (homosexual) and a *lez* (lesbian) and a *brass*, which I think should be interesting considering that from my experience they don't talk to each other very much unless it's to *slag* one another (run each other down). (*Slag* also means someone who is no good.) We will call the queer *Tangerine* (who is an old queen), and the brass *Chechee*, and the lez we will call *Butch*, which is just another way of saying *lez*.

Chechee starts talking to Tangerine. 'Get you, darling, all done up in a *drag*, anyone would think you were a *palone*. I don't care what you do as long as you don't get on my beat, because I've only had three *short times* tonight, and one of them was a flage merchant.'

TANGERINE: Don't you have a go at me, dear, otherwise I'll get Butch to have a go at you.

BUTCH: You're very bold, darling, but it won't do you any good to *camp* around here. Why don't you go and get yourself a *fare*, and leave us alone.

TANGERINE: Do me one small favour, darling. I couldn't get a *fare* if I tried, you don't get any *bent* clients along here these days.

CHECHEE: I haven't got time to listen to you two talking about the *bona homeys* that you'd like to have; I've got to get the rent for my *lumber gaff* by the morning, otherwise my ponce will give me the *slingers*.

TANGERINE: Never mind, you can always find yourself another *Johnson*, darling, there's always plenty around.

BUTCH: What I need is a nice kinky little *mystery* who hasn't lost her *cherry* yet; if I could find one, I'd go straight.

You will, I think, notice the difference between this slang and any other and I think you will agree with me about it being slightly unpleasant, but even so, I think it is very expressive. For the benefit of the uninformed, a *palone* is a girl and *drag* is women's clothes, a *short time* means exactly what it says, 'the time it takes a brass to have sex with a client', and last but not least, a *mystery* is a young girl who no one knows anything about.

There you have four different types of slang, all of which are used to a greater or smaller extent in this country. There are, I am told, other slangs that are used up North and in Scotland, but as I have never been to either of these places, I am in no position to talk about them. The main one, of course, is the Cockney, and it is this one that I know most about, but even I cannot keep up with the changes that keep on occurring, almost daily. For instance, I was once having a rabbit with a geezer, about another geezer, when all of a sudden he said: 'I don't want to know nothing about that grass, I tumbled to him and gave him the *Lonsdale*.' Well, I've always reckoned myself pretty well up in what's buzzing, but *Lonsdale* really stumped me, in fact, I didn't have the first sus of what he was bunnying about. Any old how, after a load of uming and aring, I asked him what this word meant, and it turned out that it was our old friend *belt*; if you know anything about the punching world, you will know that the Lonsdale Belt is a prize that is given to the winner of a boxing match, if that is what they happen to be fighting for. Although my friend had not actually given him the Belt, if you see what I mean.

Things like this are happening all the time and as I say they are very hard to keep pace with. I have not yet said very much about names that are given to crimes of one kind and another, and what is more I am not going to, at least not in any big way because that would be getting back to the dictionary that I don't want. But there are one or two that I think are worth mentioning: *Jar up* is one of these, because I think it conveys quite a bit of humour. A jar is a piece of imitation jewellery (*tomfoolery*) that has been so well made that it appears to anyone who isn't in the know as the real thing; and to do a jar up is to sell some burk a piece. The jar comes when the person who has bought it, finds out that it's a fake. *Turn-over* also has a certain amount of humour (but it does depend quite a lot on what you consider funny). It means that you have robbed someone who you have just done a job with of their share (although I don't know if this is considered a crime in the eyes of the law). It also has other meanings that I will not go into just at the moment.

One of the main things about slang which I like very much is the bond between one person who speaks it and another. It is like a club and if you are a member, you are one of the 'chaps', and if you are not, you are a mug, but please don't get the idea that it is easy to be one of the 'chaps' because that is by no means the case, there are a few people who rather like the idea of using a little slang in their conversation just to make it a little 'flowery', but these geezers, even if they become proficient, are still not accepted by the 'chaps'; because you have to know the whole language backwards.

Dirge

Nitto, nark it, stoppo.
That's wot the whizz mob are saying,
Take yer fork from his outer, he's piping.
If yer banged then yer in fer a stripeing.

The fourpenny snore & the sweeny.
Dwell in the box for you.
So nitto, nark it, stoppo.
Or a carpets a lay-down for you.

Spending money

Shopping. Some West End shops remain open until 7 p.m. one evening a week – usually Thursday or Friday – but most close about 5.30 each evening. West End shops close at lunchtime on Saturday and don't reopen until Monday morning.

Small local shops stay open on Saturday afternoon, as do street markets, but close one afternoon, usually Wednesday or Thursday. Some small grocery shops stay open in the evenings and some open on Sundays too. They are only lawfully able to sell things that might perish if they were kept (i.e. not tinned goods, etc.). Most Londoners can direct you to a little man around the corner who is always open, so ask a local resident.

Banks close at 3 p.m. Monday to Friday and are open only briefly on Saturday morning. An exception to this is the Mayfair London Bank, 70 Park Lane, which is open 9 a.m. to 10 p.m. every day except Sunday. They will cash foreign money or travellers' cheques. They will also cash personal cheques for low amounts if you contact them during normal banking hours first, so that they can confirm with your bank that you really do have money there. Barclays Bank in the B.O.A.C. terminal is also open until 10 p.m. and will cash cheques from well-known banks if you carry good identification. There isn't a free market in foreign money so that after the banks close it can be difficult to get money changed. Very few London shops will take foreign money although some will take dollars. Travellers' cheques are easier to cash and quite a lot of places will take well-known credit cards. As a rule hotels – and some West End restaurants, e.g. the Caprice – will not take credit cards except Eurocards. (Eurocards do not take a fee from the establishment that honours them.)

In my experience most visitors like the big stores; C. & A., British Home Stores, Woolworth and – most popular of all – Marks & Spencer, known to Londoners as Marks and Sparks.

Vests and underpants sold at Marks & Spencer carry a St Michael label which has given rise to countless permutations of a story about a travelling salesman and an innocent Irish colleen that ends '. . . but bigorrah the good saint's name was on his vest'.

These stores are particularly good for visitors who don't speak English because the prices are clearly marked and all goods are on display. Londoners particularly favour the Marks at the Marble Arch end of Oxford Street because this is where experimental lines are tried out. Don't be disappointed therefore if you come back for another of the same and don't get it. The garments on sale are slightly pre-seasonal, so before autumn arrives all the summer clothes disappear. Remember this if you are taking a late holiday and want to buy something to wear.

Many tourists have a pilgrimage to the grave of Karl Marx high on their list of London sights. The founder of Marxism and the author of *Das Kapital* lies in the overgrown and dream-sequence-like Highgate Cemetery (entrance in Swain's Lane). The nearest Underground is Archway and the whole place is so fantastic that you might want to see it even if you oppose the surplus value theory. When you get there please note that the next grave along from Marx is that of a Mr Spenser; no one will believe me when I tell them.

Talking of economics, if the tax-free value of the goods you are buying is £5 or more, then you may take advantage of the Personal Export Scheme. This means that the goods will be delivered to the airport or seaport by which you intend to leave, and in this case you won't be charged purchase tax. This can be a considerable saving on certain goods. The same exemption applies if you have the goods sent direct to a foreign address. Ask at the shop for details bearing in mind that they will need a couple of days to get them to the airport, so don't try to do it the day you leave the country. You will see notices about this scheme in some shops. You will need your passport when you make the purchase.

Even if you don't wish to buy anything you might enjoy a trip to a large luxury store. Harrods (Knightsbridge Underground station) is the biggest and poshest. Look in at the animal department, food halls and book department. Best bargains here are the used books; they are near the library.

Fortnum & Mason's: exquisite packaged food, drink, smokes. Little fresh food. There is a restaurant, sherry bar and Soda Fountain. The latter is run like an anglicized American drug store and is a good place to meet. Avoid meeting there at the lunch hour as it's crowded with hostile natives.

Robert Jackson: practically next door to Fortnum's and very similar in style. Across the street is the covered Burlington Arcade full of discreet, elegant shops. This is also a good place to meet (someone you already know, I mean).

Along Piccadilly from Fortnum's in the other direction is Simpson's, which is one of the most popular shops for good quality ready-made men's clothes, if you know any ready-made men.

Selfridges – near Marble Arch – is a huge department store. It has a notably good food department in a separate building.

Sporting goods – tennis rackets, underwater apparatus, cricket bats, etc., plus winter-sports equipment from skis to woolly hats with bobbles on, can be supplied at Lillywhite's, Piccadilly Circus.

Moss Bros., Covent Garden (c o v 4567) is where you go to hire any sort of clothes. Harold Macmillan got his white fur hat there when he went to Moscow.

No matter that they have become something of an interior decorator's cliché, historical theatrical posters, playbills and programmes have a certain compulsive nostalgia attaching to them. Hall's at 17 Harrington Road, s w7, has a vast collection, most of them costing under £1. In fact if you will settle for historic postcards they'll be only a couple of bob.

Not expensive enough? Go sift through Mr Sunley's shop full of musical machines. As well as musical boxes there are mechanical canaries, clocks and dolls. The shop is right in the centre of town at 81 George Street, w 1.

More expensive? What about Sac Frères, 45 Old Bond Street, w 1, which specializes in antique amber artifacts from cigarette holders to necklaces. Or less expensive, according to your tastes, what about a miniature tree? Although it's a Japanese art – Mr Kusumoto works from his private address at 35 Camrose Avenue, Edgware – the trees can be either Japanese or terribly terribly British. Since Edgware is the last stop on the Underground you might prefer to discuss the matter with Mr Kusumoto at E D G 5969.

Some feminine ideas about spending are exemplified by this extract from a letter on the subject:

I'd empty out all of Aspreys and Fortnum's – adore everything they have. And Jaeger!

If I wanted clothes in London I think I'd stick to the kinky style – Carnaby Street, King's Road. For the dressier type of clothes I'd prefer the Parish fashion houses but if I had to get them in London the fashion houses do have nice things. Wouldn't be my choice though. Would get loads of sporty tweedy type of things for country life – sweaters, cardigans and matching twinsets in all different colours imaginable and matching skirts in tweeds and tartans.

Jay Kaye at 92 Piccadilly has adorable cashmere and lambs-wool but first I'd just go wandering down Bond Street trying to find little shops that no one else knows about.

I would definitely get a saddle and bridle at Moss Bros., and a made-to-measure riding outfit. Oh and also a wig and hairpieces from Vidal Sassoon at 171 New Bond Street (M A Y 9665) and Grosvenor House, Park Lane (M A Y 2463).

If it was Saturday I would go to Camden Passage with at least £50 in my pocket and buy the things I haven't been able to afford previous times and I'd have a mini-cab with me at all times not caring how long I made him wait – especially at Camden Passage because I'd be buying so much.

If you want to make your own way to Camden Passage, which is a street market selling everything from scratched gramophone records to Georgian silver, the nearest Underground station is Angel. It is very close. At one end of the passage is a Victorian fortress type of pub – Camden Head – and if the dealers have a good day it can become rather lively.

The easiest time to get into a hairdresser's without an appointment is when it opens (about 9 a.m. usually). Most West End ladies' hairdressers will provide eggs, bacon, coffee and orange juice for the customers and with a bit of sweet talking a man calling there to collect – and pay – can have his too. If you don't mind breakfasting among the lotions and ladies then this might help you to start the day on schedule.

Tipping. A waiter or waitress expects between ten and twelve per cent of the bill unless service is included. A taxi driver expects anything from 6d. to 2s. 6d. Anything above that and he will think you are a nut. Legally there is no need to give him a tip. A hotel or railway porter who gets you a cab and helps with the baggage would expect at least 2s. and more if there is a lot of luggage or he has been extra helpful. Most hotels include service on your bill. When you leave a hotel after a week or so you may wish to give an extra tip to the room maid, waiter, doorkeeper, etc. If so give it to them in person. Again it should be solely for service beyond what would normally be expected. Don't tip people who give you bad, rude or grudging service and then complain to your friends about how bad the service was. You are responsible for keeping it that way.

The only other people who will expect a tip will be hairdressers. A shilling for a man's hairdresser and 2s. 6d. for a woman's hairdresser. A posh woman's hairdresser in the West End will expect double that.

Shops

Drusilla Beyfus

I doubt if there is a better place in the world than London to buy a diamond necklace, a coach-built Mini car, a castle, a Renoir. London shops and showrooms specialize in the unbeatable luxury of quality goods, and always have done. In London there is an immense reserve of merchandise for customers who appreciate fine craftsmanship, real value for money and possessions designed to last for a lifetime.

Looking at the whole shopping scene from a woman's standpoint I think it is hard to resist the impression that the men win on fine points. Once this is admitted however, it must be said that women do splendidly. A woman's incurable taste for personal luxury is given gloriously free rein.

The first geographical fact for newcomers to the city to understand is that there are three major shopping areas in the heart of town.

First, Mayfair. To many, Mayfair symbolizes the West End because the neighbourhood contains so many shops, services and showrooms which are known all over the world. I take the Mayfair beat to extend down Regent Street, along Piccadilly, and up Bond Street with all the sidestreets in between. Oxford Street, which completes the square, is a vast thoroughfare flanked by huge merchandising emporiums, chain stores, department stores and fashion shops. There the emphasis is less on exclusivity than on popular appeal – a technique which is Oxford Street's own – but the street includes several dignified department stores. It is worth adding that Oxford Street has regained its pre-war reputation as a place to go to look for things to wear.

Second, Knightsbridge and its continuation through Sloane

Street and Sloane Square is a rewarding blend of the traditional and new departures with a marked emphasis on furnishing, antiques and clothes.

And third, although it is much smaller in size, I think I should include the King's Road as an area worth a special visit. It is now the home-stretch hunting ground for clothes for members of the swinging London set. Boutiques, small shops intermingled with antique shops and grocery stores for local residents give the King's Road a special neighbourhood flavour.

Everyone has their own reasons for enjoying London shopping but few people would disagree with the excuse of looking for antique jewellery. The supply is delightfully inexhaustible. The Burlington Arcade, off Piccadilly, is lined with the windows of jewellers offering the prettiest of antique rings, necklaces, cuff-links, brooches, bracelets. Bond Street undoubtedly offers one of the best opportunities ever of finding a diamond as big as the Ritz with Cartier, Asprey, Boucheron, Benson, competing with each other in diamond and gold studded allurement. The name of S. J. Phillips, 139 New Bond Street, is mentioned with affection by customers who say that there they find pieces that are both valuable and chic, a combination of virtues which is rarer than might be supposed.

Modern jewellery is a lively art in London. Pieces designed by well-known craftsmen and by experimental young designers can be found at a number of established antique jewellery businesses. Recently some shops have opened specializing in contemporary jewellery design; Hooper Bolton, 154 Walton Street, s w 1, and Andrew Grima, 80 Jermyn Street, w 1.

Despite gloomy forebodings about the drying up of the supply of antique furniture and *objets d'art* for sale, the stock in the shops and sale-rooms suggests a happier story. It is, sadly, true that it is much harder than it was to pick up an unrecognized bargain for a song. Customers in search of top-quality pieces however should not be disappointed, nor is there any serious shortage of pretty antiques at realistic prices. For top-quality pieces, two houses to try are Frank Partridge, 144 New Bond Street, and Mallet, 40 New Bond Street. This firm has a branch nearby in Davies Street where the furniture for sale is arranged informally in the manner of a private house and a small garden displays classical statuary and garden ornaments.

London has an astonishing number of antique shops outside the familiar Bond Street beat. Three of the many dealers widely acknowledged as being of the first rank are: Jeremy, 255 King's Road; Hamish, 335 Fulham Road, where the stock frequently includes pieces made in *bois clair*, a pale honey-coloured richly grained wood; and the Portmeirion Shop, 7 Pont Street, specializing in the odd exceptionally decorative piece of furniture.

What is particularly gratifying about hunting for collector's items in these small speciality shops is that the management are experts who have given the better part of their lives to knowing their subject. A cross-section of interests might include: for porcelain birds, Solti & Modiano, 43 Davies Street; for preserved butterflies and beetles, Janson, 44 Great Russell Street; for eighteenth-century chimney pieces, door fittings, fireplaces, T. Crowther, 282 North End Road, s w 6; sixteenth- and seventeenth-century European furniture, Ciancimino, 309 King's Road; for domestic silver of the early eighteenth century, Spink, 5 King Street, s w 1 (its classical and Middle Eastern antiquities, antique coins and medallions, and jade make this shop as good as a museum); for decorative minerals, the Jewel House, 35 Sloane Street, and Gregory Bottley, 30 Old Church Street; for Victorian stuffed and china birds, Balclutha, 10 Sloane Street.

Half the enjoyment of buying antiques lies in the search for them. The golden rule in London is that where there is one good little shop, others follow. Scout round Pimlico, the full length of the King's Road covering Chelsea and beyond, go to the Fulham Road, canvass Kensington Church Street, Islington and Hampstead.

Heal's, the pioneer modern furniture shop which was established at the turn of the century at 196 Tottenham Court Road, has at last been challenged. Vasa, 31 Lowndes Street, has positively sumptuous pieces of modern furniture made in sculpted hand-turned woods and fine leathers, from abroad. The stock also includes glass, *objets trouvés* and clothes to go with a modern setting. Habitat, 77 Fulham Road, has interior furnishings to meet modern needs, pieces ingeniously designed to combat most people's lack of space at home. Its clientele is young and professional. Habitat has another branch near Heal's at 156 Tottenham Court Road. For chairs from the Bauhaus, including pieces by Mies van der Rohe, and good craftsmanlike modern storage furniture, go to Aram, 57 King's Road.

Looking round fine art galleries and sales-rooms is an integral part of enjoying shopping in the West End, but in London all tastes have their dealer. Two of the many galleries dealing in old masters are Wildenstein, 147 New Bond Street, and Colnaghi, 14 Old Bond Street. Very few important modern painters and sculptors have not had their work exhibited in London and the galleries show the complete spectrum of modern art including the furthest-out *avant garde*. Among the liveliest galleries to visit are: Marlborough Fine Art, 39 Old Bond Street; Kasmin, 118 New Bond Street; Hanover Gallery, 32a St George Street; Arthur Tooth, 31 Bruton Street; Gimpel Fils, 50 South Molton Street; McRoberts & Tunnard, 34 Curzon Street; Robert Fraser Gallery, 69 Duke Street.

Places to go to for presents for men abound in St James's and Mayfair. These areas are hunting grounds for those small personal indulgences which craftsmen have often spent centuries in perfecting. Look out for the thinnest of gold cigarette cases and cigarette lighters and dress watches. Initialled velvet house slippers are at Peal, bootmakers, 48 Wigmore Street; embroidered braces and weightless silk underwear are at Turnbull & Asser, 71 Jermyn Street; sportive hats (and for women too) at Herbert Johnson, 38 New Bond Street; masculine scents and smells at Hermes, 52 Jermyn Street. In traditional British lairs of masculine peacockry the presence of women is tolerated but decisiveness is called for. Male shop assistants, and particularly elderly ones who have been in the business for years, are unfamiliar with requests from a havering girl for a raspberry pink shirt 'in about your size'.

British sports equipment is first class. Lillywhite's, Piccadilly and at 196 Sloane Street, deals in general sports equipment, and the sports departments at Harrods, Knightsbridge, and at Selfridges, Oxford Street, carry a wide range of goods. For fishing tackle, go to Hardy, 61 Pall Mall; for guns, go to Purdey,

57 South Audley Street; both world-famous speciality firms where they really know their stuff. For tailored sports clothes and especially for well-cut riding kit, the place is Bernard Wetherill, 55 Conduit Street.

What singles out London department stores from others of their kind is the comprehensive nature of the stock and the fact that each store has its own unique character. Shopping at Harrods is more a way of life than a process of acquiring mere goods. Harrods supplies theatre tickets, pets, French cheeses, classical records, haberdashery, bicycles, camping equipment, dress and furnishing fabrics, hire cars, cigars, vintage claret, modern silver, toothpaste, iced and decorated birthday cakes, carpets. And that's only the merest fraction of goods available without mentioning the services on tap. My favourite departments there are: the food and delicatessen (which to my mind is only rivalled by Paxton & Whitfield, 93 Jermyn Street) the children's clothes and toys, the haberdashery, and stationery departments.

Selfridges has a marvellous food section, good inexpensive children's clothes and linen. Fortnum & Mason, Piccadilly, ties with a speciality shop, the White House, 51 New Bond Street, for offering irresistible personal luxury in the form of finest softest gloves, hand-stitched silk nightdresses, chiffon and lacy wool bedjackets, small cushions shaped like an hour glass for the bed or car and made in organdie over silk and scores of things like that which are the nicest of their kind. Both Fortnum's and the White House sell line for line copies of Paris couture clothes, the softest filmiest baby shawls and other presents for new babies. A silk dressing gown from the White House folds up into pocket handkerchief size in a suitcase, rarely crushes and practically never wears out. The merchandise at Peter Jones, Sloane Square, reflects the taste of a group of informed buyers interested in promoting good style. They offer, among other things, a judicious selection of china, glass, pottery, furnishing and dress materials, modern and antique furniture, clothes, carpets, linen, bedding.

Liberty, Regent Street, should be an early port of call to locate real quality in goods made in leather, silk, chiffon, glass. It is among the two or three best places to look for presents, souvenirs, pretty things for the house, handbags, linen, and qualifies, to my mind, as *the* best source of silk scarves, and rugs. The famous Liberty prints are available by the yard and also made up into dresses and blouses. This store carries Britain's habit of importing good things from abroad to a fine art.

The General Trading Company, at 144 Sloane Street, pursues a policy of supplying refinements of incidental chic for the house. Go there for the nicest of waste-paper baskets, paper weights, photograph albums, visitor's books, plant holders, flower vases, bathroom accessories, ashtrays and trivia in marble, leather and gilt. Knives, dishes, aprons, cook books, wooden platters and other pretty kit abound in the kitchen department.

The policy of escape from an age of mass production and synthetics pioneered for the last half-century by stores such as Liberty is mirrored in London's smaller arts and crafts shops. The value of the hand-carved piece, a hand-blown drinking glass, a hand-woven fabric, a hand-turned ceramic, can be seen and felt at speciality shops such as Primavera, 149 Sloane Street. Betty Hope, 19 Beauchamp Place, possesses a wide range of kitchen tools made in good, old wood and scraped-pine chests and tables and chairs. Handwoven basket chairs and baskets for laundry or picnics can be got from Lord Roberts Workshops, 122 Brompton Road. As a switch of mood from appraising traditional skills you might like to look in on a permanent exhibition of some of the best-designed articles manufactured in this country. The exhibits, which are approved by the Council of Industrial Design and bear its seal, are on show at the Design Centre in the Haymarket.

One of the most fascinating aspects of London shopping is the extraordinarily wide selection of goods from abroad. For example, you want a sari, Italian shoes, Japanese paper lights, Norwegian sealskin slippers? These are usually obtainable at, respectively, Liberty; Gucci, 172 New Bond Street; Mitsukiku, 73a Lower Sloane Street; Ostmo, 23 New Quebec Street. A speciality firm which imports a treasure trove of trifles to give yourself or lucky others is Presents of Sloane Street at No. 129.

The art of table-setting is regarded as a national skill and because of it, perhaps, London's shops have accumulated a mass of covetable things for the dining table. Table silver, antique and hall marked, can best be found in the antique-furniture-shop hunting grounds. I wouldn't miss a trip to Holborn to look around the dealers' shops, and the same applies to Kensington High Street and Church Street and Gloucester Road. Georgian silver in a usable condition is a rarity everywhere but there are a number of firms specializing in the period who if they have not got what you want in stock will try to track down a suitable piece or set. The two leading fine art auctioneers, Sotheby's, 34 New Bond Street, and Christie's, 8 King Street, s w 1, are a rich source of collectors' pieces in silver, and occasionally it is possible to pick up something good at a price below the sum the lot might fetch in a shop.

Britain is a by-word for fine china, and our well-known manufacturers continue to produce a wide range of products. China by Spode, Wedgwood, Crown Derby, Royal Doulton, Worcester and Coalport is on sale in most of the department stores and some firms run their own West End showrooms. A breakfast tray laid in fine bone china hand-painted in sprigs of roses remains one of those proven indulgences which survive criticism. Thomas Goode, 19 South Audley Street, is a name synonymous with fine china and glass.

The General Trading Company, Peter Jones, Liberty, keep an enchanting collection of English and French dinner and tea services and a rather lesser known, but admirable stock of copies of traditional English designs in earthenware. Table-cloths come from Givan's Irish Linen Stores at 207 King's Road, Peter Jones and Heal's. Casseroles, coffee things, plates and serving dishes for table settings for kitchen meals can be found at Elizabeth David, 46 Bourne Street, s w 1, a small shop which specializes in serious cooks' equipment; pleasant kitchen eating kit is also at Habitat, and at Merchant Chandler, 72 New King's Road, s w 6. British beds are the most comfortable ever. Blankets, sheets, pillowcases, eiderdowns, pillows, bedspreads are among the best reasons for going to Harvey Nichols, Knightsbridge, or to Harrods or Peter Jones.

For a woman, shopping for clothes in London is character-ized by our passion for specialization. At the moment, the young have never had a better chance to be themselves, country women do as well as ever, and the rich have it made – in both senses.

As long as custom-made service remains immeasurably better than ready-to-wear service there will be people prepared to pay the price of individual attention. London's leading couturiers offer in terms of beautiful fabric, good cut, and personal service a level of clothes-designing comparable to their equivalents in Paris or New York or Rome. I would order a couture suit or a coat or a grand evening dress in London in preference to after-five or theatre clothes. Prospective clients should telephone the house and make an appointment to see the collection. Out of an exceedingly professional group I would single out Michael, 2 Carlos Place (GRO 1656), as a designer of international standing, and Hardy Amies, 14 Savile Row (REG 2436), whose graceful, wearable, appropriate clothes can be seen at nearly every leading social function in this country. Hardy Amies has a boutique with ready-made versions of his couture clothes at 2 New Burlington Street (REG 1024).

It may be useful to be reminded that London still cannot be beaten for the clothes we have always been famous for, and in addition there is a lot of new scope to be found in the work of young designers. Go to Aquascutum, 100 Regent Street, to find a dear old British mac cut in a wearable shape, or a Sherlock Holmes style cape, or tweeds of all kinds. Jaeger, with shops in Regent Street, Sloane Street and the King's Road, is renowned for sweaters, skirts, trousers, 'little nothing' wool dresses, camel hair and camel-coloured greatcoats, matching woolly outfits, and suits. Huppert, 64 Regent Street, makes exclusive sweaters and blouses. Cashmere, luckily, is everywhere.

One of the relatively few advantages a woman has on growing older is that she begins to know what she wants. For those whose conclusions lead to an appreciation of long lasting clothes I recommend a trip to Delman, 15 Old Bond Street, for crocodile shoes; to Hermes, for a crocodile or calf handbag or belt; and to the Scotch House, 2 Brompton Road, for Shetland jerseys.

The problem about advising visitors on the boutique beat is that it's always changing. There is usually a new name to try out and one that looks as if it is likely to drop out of the scene.

Established in their own individual ways are: Bazaar, at 138a King's Road and 46 Brompton Road, shops selling clothes designed by the girl who started it all, Mary Quant; Top Gear, 135a King's Road, and next door at 137, Countdown, for the briefest of mini skirts; Annacat, 23 Pelham Street; Sea and Ski, 69 Pimlico Road, for sporty clothes which can be worn on and off the sports arena; the Carrot on Wheels, 84 Fulham Road, for far-out ready-mades; the Yellow Room, 42 Elizabeth Street, for unusual hats, belts, shoes, stockings, jewellery, adornments and a hand-picked selection of day and evening clothes, Marrian McDonnell, 80 Sloane Avenue, for designs aimed at a marginally older than young age group; the Chelsea antique market, 245 King's Road, for one of the best-stocked stalls in second-hand clothes with the period flavour much admired (and worn) by the young. Marginally beyond the Chelsea beat is Biba, 19 Kensington Church Street, noted for inexpensive bang-on-now fashion and accessories.

Formal or best clothes for babies, for girls up to about eight years and for boys of all ages, are among the best things made in Britain. In terms of sheer unbridled encouragement of luxury I think that only the men's made-to-measure shirt shops in St James's have anything on the good baby counters. Ice-crisp party dresses without a ribbon too much or too few, well-tailored velvet trews and pure silk ruffled shirts, hand-smocked voiles, lawns, silks – these are the staples of luxurious baby shopping. The key names in this field are Hayford at 205 Sloane Street and Simple Garments almost opposite at 39, Fortnum's, the White House, Harrods and Liberty. A small speciality shop which imports a lot of pretty things is the Dolls House, 99a Cadogan Lane. Liberty stocks dresses made in the famous Liberty fabrics in a wide range of sizes which is a help to customers who may want to outfit daughers of various ages and sizes in the same style of frock. Shetland jerseys and lambswool sweaters and cardigans have endeared themselves to countless parents because they wash and wear so well. The Scotch House does immaculately cut rugged sweaters. Rowes, 120 New Bond Street, sells both ready-made and made-to-measure boys clothes. The cut of a Rowes's suit or coat somehow endows the wearer with an aura of effortless superiority.

Into this established world of understated good form in dress has burst a satellite of the modern pop fashion movement. Young designers are busy rethinking a child's wardrobe, and many of the designs are considerably influenced by American standards in casual wear and playclothes. Raincoats are made in brilliantly coloured PVC (Christopher Robin's Nanny, Alice, would have died rather than put him in one). Upbeat little dresses and pinafores echo the look, cut and fabric of parents' clothes. Oddball hats, baby boiler suits, pink for boys and black for both sexes, are current favourites with London parents for the pram set. Tracking down the latest place to find the latest designs can be a problem because proprietors and premises tend to change hands frequently. The best plan is to keep an eye on the glossy magazines such as *Vogue* or *Queen* and note the stockists of the children's clothes they mention.

Marks & Spencer offer a remarkably good selection of inexpensive children's clothes made in first-class fabrics and materials. Elegantly dressed Mamas from abroad are to be seen frequently in the Marble Arch branch busily snapping up bargains.

Having your face done or your hair done is probably a more restful experience here than in New York or Paris. The salons lack the atmosphere of frenzied competitiveness often found in Paris, and the pace is gentler than across the Atlantic. Elizabeth Arden, 25 Old Bond Street, Helena Rubinstein, 3 Grafton Street and Dorothy Gray, 8 Grosvenor Street, run well-staffed salons. The doyen of all cosmeticians is Countess Czaky who apart from running a personal service for a distinguished clientele produces her own beauty preparations. She compounds these herself by hand and the creams are available at Marshall & Snelgrove, Oxford Street, and Harvey Nichols. Once tried they are rarely superseded.

Hairdressing establishments share the talent for giving adaptable personal service. In general, hairstylists are prepared to adjust to the individual needs of their client and you stand an incomparably better chance than in Paris for example, of being permitted to retain your wispy curls if you wish to. On the other hand, London's standards in terms of creative styling are admired all over the fashion world. An illustration of the broadminded approach of British hairdressers is that the clientele at such well-known hairdressing establishments as Vidal Sassoon, 171 New Bond Street, and Alan Spiers, 27 Berkeley Square, includes model girls and other dollies wearing the style currently hitting the covers of the glossy magazines, and also women wearing their hair the way they have liked it for twenty years.

All in all, London remains a peach of a place for spending money. But a word of warning: don't judge shops by first appearances. By the way, if you do want a coach-built Mini, try Harold Radford, 122 King Street, w 6, and for castles, look in at Knight, Frank & Rutley, 20 Hanover Square.

More suggestions for a Saturday

There are some places that are not open every day. Here are a few which are open on Saturday, so there's a chance to see them all in one trip. You could do the whole thing by public transport, but why not go crazy and hire a mini-cab and let the driver find the route?

If you should be flying away from London on a Saturday then you could check your baggage into the West London Air Terminal before starting the trip and be comfortably at London Airport (which is quite near the last place of call) by 5.30 p.m. even allowing for a couple of delays.

The first stop is the British Theatre Museum (Leighton House, 12 Holland Park Road, W 14). It's open from 11 a.m. until 5 p.m., so arrive as it opens. Here are theatrical costumes, relics, documents and drawings. If that's not your cup of tea give it a miss. If it is, go again, it's also open Tuesdays and Thursdays. (When you do, also visit the Commonwealth Institute around the corner in Kensington High Street.)

Next door to the Theatre Museum is the Arabic style house built for Lord Leighton. It's a strange place which visitors loathe or adore at first glance. The great blue tiled hall with the fountain has a secret balcony so that the harem could see what the menfolk did. A strange thing for an unmarried English peer to incorporate into his home? Just wait till you see the rest of it.

It's virtually a straight run from here to the London Apprentice at Isleworth which is an eighteenth-century riverside pub facing across the Thames to an island bird sanctuary. Have a pint. There is a fine selection of cold roast meats, salami, Stilton, etc. Although some of the cheeses are

prepackaged the bread is fresh and crusty and the service
friendly. If it's a fine day you can sit and eat it on the terrace.
From here turn back and retrace your steps. The wall on the
right encloses the grounds of Syon House, the next stop. Turn
right into the first gate you see. The notice says that this is a
footpath to Syon House. Since today is a visiting day the
attendant should have covered up the part forbidding cars; if he
hasn't, drive in anyway. You'll see another sign saying car park
and on the right the strange, Beau Geste fort shape of Syon
House. Go in and have a look around. It's a fine stately home
although I wouldn't live there if you paid me. The highlight of
this part of the trip, for me, was the tea shop in the stables. As
fine a selection of home-made English cakes, buns, cream
sponges and fruit pies as I ever need to see. They have all been
baked that very morning so I hope you resisted that second
helping of cold tongue at the pub.

If you miss this first gate, follow the wall along, turning right
at the traffic lights and you will see the main gates. From here
visitors have to walk to the house, as cars are not permitted
through, although from the condition of the grounds I can't see
why they shouldn't be.

After seeing Syon, head back towards town by the route you
came. High Street Brentford is a stretch of road without houses
or shops; just grimy walls that enclose the gas works. You'll see
a gigantic gas holder and immediately adjacent a grey stone
building with a white hanging sign, 'Piano Museum'. The first
lecture/demonstration begins at 3 p.m. but if you arrive late,
Mr Holland will go over the bit you missed. This is a collection
of mechanical pianos, some very old, some almost new. As well
as piano-rolls that will reproduce the performance of
Paderewski or Grieg who made them, there are simple music
boxes and street organs that I used to call hurdy-gurdys until I
went to the Piano Museum. A very impressive aspect of the
museum is the help it has been given, not only by the large
companies like Imhof but also by the local vicar and a piano
tuner who gives his services free. I.C.I. donated the polish and a
local pensioner comes in without pay to keep the pianos shining.
Mr Holland will expect a 3s. 6d. donation from you for his
lecture and it's as good value as you'll get anywhere.

More suggestions for a Saturday

When you leave the piano museum by 4 p.m. you can either drive to London Airport or back to town. London is popping on Saturday evening. It's not so much a matter of where to go but whether you can get in. Perhaps you will enjoy crowding into a folk music club. They are not clubs in the strict sense of the word and will be delighted to let you in for the price of a cup of coffee and a small cover charge (there is no alcohol licence).

Bunjies Coffee House is right in the centre of town at 27 Litchfield Street, a small street off Charing Cross Road, near to Cambridge Circus. There is music at 7.30 p.m. every evening at Bunjies but at the Troubadour (265 Old Brompton Road, s w 5, very near Earls Court Road) there is music only on Tuesdays, Thursdays and Saturdays. Ten-thirty is early enough to be there. Both Bunjies and the Troubadour are worth seeing even if you don't like music. The Troubadour is hung about with ancient musical instruments, coffee pots and dusty treasures of undecipherable age or function. The music can be anything from calm social protest to the uproarious antics of Professor Bruce Lacey. The atmosphere is noisy and friendly with a good chance of spilled coffee. Dress accordingly.

No matter how late you come out of the Troubadour, walk up Earls Court Road (turn right and left after leaving) and see the only part of London that's still going at 2 a.m.

Saturday is also London's day for sport. Michael Wale will tell you how to see some.

Sport

Michael Wale

Michael Wale has been fanatically interested in sport ever since he played scrum-half for his prep school First XV and thereby avoided too close attention by his masters over his academic work. Eventually he was asked to leave because he set up a bookmaking business for fellow pupils. Educated later at Bedales co-ed boarding school, Hampshire. Became a journalist, trained on the *Northern Echo* in Newcastle-on-Tyne before joining the *Daily Express* first in Dublin and then London. Later worked for the *Daily Herald*. Resigned from the *Sun* in September 1965 to concentrate on scriptwriting. Contributes on sport to the *Observer*, is a keen player as well as spectator of football. Supports Fulham F.C.

I have spent much of my time on the terraces of London football grounds. Terraces rather than seats, because unlike Fulham's manager the eccentric Vic Buckingham, I prefer to stand and watch a match rather than sit in the clinical dissecting room of the grandstand, where all seems simple. Down on the terrace you can hear the urgings by the players to each other, tell how much dew is on the grass and why a player did not trap the ball when he should have done. It is from here you can feel the game, see the players who withdraw from the tackle in cowardice at the last moment, overhear the unprintable asides. It is from here too, packed shoulder to shoulder and sometimes swathed in a spray of unnoticed rain, that you can appreciate the difference not only in the teams on the field, but the crowds who watch them. The clinical detachment of the crowd at Chelsea's home ground, Stamford Bridge; the Establishment atmosphere of Arsenal's formal home at Highbury; the East End rebelliousness and physical feeling at The Den, the headquarters of Millwall. But for real atmosphere you must go to the other end of town, catch a train from Liverpool Street and join the thousands streaming into White Hart Lane to watch Tottenham Hotspur, the club which in the 1960–61 season won both the First Division championship and the F.A. Cup. Spurs was then captained by the voluble Ulsterman Danny Blanchflower, who was also enjoying a fair income from endorsing a brand of breakfast cereal on television. The ad always opened with the beaming, fit Blanchflower saying nonchalantly in his Irish brogue: 'Hullo there'. And every time he went near the terraces at White Hart Lane to fetch the ball and throw it in he was greeted with a round of derisive 'hullo theres' from the crowd.

White Hart Lane possesses something of the atmosphere of the old London music halls. The cigar smoke of the season ticket holders, a club whose policy is to provide the best and most expensive footballers in the land, and a crowd who when their team is leading burst forth into uninhibited song to the appropriated tune of John Brown's Body '... Glory, Glory, Hallelujah, When the Spurs Go Marching On'.

After England's victory in the World Cup in the summer of 1966 a whole new public was introduced to the game through the television coverage. Hardened rugby men who always scorned soccer as a cissy's game admitted in awe that the game had something after all, 'skill'. A learned executive of *The Times*, a man of the arts, spoke of seeing the Final in which England beat West Germany 4–2 in extra time. 'A friend switched the television on. I was reading *Jude the Obscure* for the third time and quite soon I laid it down and before I knew what had happened I'd become so engrossed my tea grew cold.' That was at Wembley watched by 100,000 people, but there were other moments during that superb competition. English crowds always love an underdog and so they took the North Koreans to their hearts. Somehow the crowd lifted them with emotional enthusiasm to beat the great Italy 1–0 and win a place in the quarter-final against Portugal. The vanquished Italians returned in deep depression to Genoa where they were pelted with tomatoes.

Before they left some of the players joined in a game in Hyde Park with coats as goals and amateurs as opponents. Even they could not escape the enthusiasm of players whose occupations range from actor, playwright or journalist, to postman, waiter and labourer. Teams based on pubs and other social meeting places fight it out every Sunday morning in Hyde Park with all the seriousness, if not the skill, of the professionals. The most unlikely men appear in shirts and shorts, like actor James Villiers who played opposite Bette Davis in *The Nanny*. On Tuesday and Thursday afternoons there is an impromptu game organized by Bill Naughton, the author of *Alfie*. Down by the river at Putney Tom Courtenay organizes a weekly game. Further down river at Teddington Tommy Steele can be found practising football on his spacious lawns. In the grounds in front of the Chelsea Hospital, home of the scarlet coated pensioners, novelist Brian Glanville, the catalyst of all this enthusiasm, will be leading out his team on Sunday afternoons. Across the bridge between the power station and the big wheel of the Battersea Pleasure Gardens, as likely as not you'll find on a Sunday morning the literary critic Karl Miller on the right flank, your correspondent on the left, practising under the watchful eye of that genius of an Irish poet, Patrick Kavanagh, if he is in London.

The 11 a.m. kick-off time of Sunday morning football in London has cost many a man a strained atmosphere with his wife, or even lost him a lover. And there are other hazards too. The British nanny, not being brought up on a diet of football, does not understand the intricacies of the game as she wheels the pram of her new charge across Hyde Park. So it is not uncommon to come racing through on the attack to find oneself challenged not only by a defender but a nanny, a pram, two other loose children and, as likely as not, a dog.

The American game of softball can also be seen in Hyde Park on a Sunday morning. Like the football it takes place at the Knightsbridge end near the site of the old barracks. The softball players tend to be more illustrious than the soccer ones mainly because there is not so much physical action, and it's an older man's game anyway. Walter Shenson, who produced the Beatles films, is often there, Harvey Orkin, and many others. A lot of shouting goes on during the game, mainly of a highly theatrical nature, and much time is spent by fielders and batters alike talking deals.

Cricket to me is Lord's seen through a half-full glass of beer from the Tavern – now demolished, but until it disappeared one of the most civilized places yet created from which to watch a game. If cricket was an Eastern game it would be a philosophy. It is to do with serenity, old-fashioned courtesies, a gentle lapping of the past in the present. These are some of the reasons the attendances for County matches in Britain over the past few years have dwindled to almost nothing. The crowds are still there, however, for the big matches; the newly instituted knock-out competition and the Test Matches every summer between England and visiting countries. Despite some additions the old-fashioned style of much of the building at Lord's gives it an air of theatre. Although the members retain a reverential decorum in an aura of county suitings and club ties, the crowd in and around the Tavern maintains a flavour of the music hall. Never have I heard such a roar of delight as when England's captain Ted Dexter was bowled third ball in the Third Test at Lord's against Australia when they were last here. What other crowd would do that? Not even a Wembley crowd, who often remain strangely detached while watching England play football, would let out a roar of delight if, say, an England player missed a penalty. Dexter stood unsuccessfully for Parliament as a Conservative candidate in Cardiff. Despite his prowess, he was felt by the popular side to be too much of the Establishment to be really accepted. More popular a hero at Lord's was Freddie Trueman, the Yorkshire and England fast bowler of the ripe language and indiscreet views. He is definitely a man of the people.

One match at Lord's no visitor should miss is that between Eton and Harrow, usually at the end of June or the beginning of July. This is one of the few ritual sporting events in England – others being the rowing at Henley and the Royal Ascot race meeting. At these it is not so much the spectacle as the spectators that catch the eye. At the Eton *v.* Harrow match sisters and girl friends wear their best clothes and parents bring champagne picnics. Watch the women rather than the play.

However, cricket, like football, is not all highly organized and official. Even on the grass before you at Lord's or The Oval small boys will be playing miniature games with the hand as a bat, lemonade bottle as a wicket and tennis or other soft ball replacing the hard variety. Many is the 'test' match I played while a schoolboy on turf one would never tread as a fully-fledged cricketer. These games are frequently suspended in favour of the headlong run to get autographs. Besides collecting those of footballers and cricketers I also collected those of jockeys, which always puzzled them outwardly but inwardly no doubt made even their small stomachs glow. Sportsmen in those days just after the war used to sign in an old-fashioned and rather chivalrous manner: 'Sincerely yours James Bloggs', 'Best Wishes Gordon McGlew', etc. I remember once looking up at what seemed the eight-foot figure of the Queen's trainer, Captain Boyd-Rochfort, at Kempton Park, and he plummeting down out of the heavens to sign briskly like a headmaster before striding purposefully on towards the paddock to nod and murmur trainer-like intimacies to the Royal Family.

English cricket started on a village green at Hambledon in Hampshire, and still the most pleasant afternoon of all is to be had within easy reach of the centre of London watching one of these local games. There is always a game to be seen at week-ends on Wimbledon Common, where you can buy an ice cream, and lounge on the grass. It is then, even more than at Lord's or The Oval, that you will come to realize that cricket to the spectator is more a therapy than a sport. It is like watching fish dart about a pool, or the sails on a windmill turn lazily around.

Rugby Union with fifteen amateurs a side compared with the thirteen professionals of Rugby League, has its headquarters at Twickenham. A Twickenham crowd on international or Oxford *v.* Cambridge days could have been laid on by the British Travel and Holiday Association, so heartily, beastly British are they. Or better still attend the Finals day of the Middlesex Sevens, usually on the last Saturday in April. Each match lasts fourteen minutes, with a twenty-minute final. Restricting each side to seven men guarantees the fast open rugby so often lacking during the preceding season. More beer is drunk at Twickenham on Sevens day than at any time during the year, and one of the most spectacular moments of the day comes just before the final in late afternoon when 4,000 young-sters are allowed to play an impromptu game of rugby on the cherished turf: a Rugby Union equivalent of the bull-running at Pamplona.

The crowds, I am glad to say, are returning to horse-racing after a lull, mainly because of improved facilities (racecourse executives were undoubtedly public-school trained and believed that a bit of hardship never did anyone any harm) and also to personality horses like the great steeplechaser Arkle. Racing is known as the Sport of Kings, and indeed it is the last of the great class-conscious sports left in England. A quick form guide to the class ratings of the Turf is provided by *The Times*. Pro-fessional jockeys are referred to by surname, trainers' names carry an initial before them, owners are honoured with Mr or Mrs, Sir or Lady, the final accolade being H.M. the Queen. I'm sure it is because of H.M. the Queen that racing men wear the bowler hat, an accessory more usually associated with gen-tlemen who live in the suburbs and work in the City. Trainers and jockeys prefer brown trilbys. For H.M. the Queen or H.M. the Queen Mother or H.R.H. Princess Margaret hats are raised as they pass. For owners jockeys touch their forelocks, and for jockeys seedy-looking men in raincoats speak out of the corner of their mouths in an effort to gain a grain of rumour of whether such and such a horse is 'on'.

Thus it all is at Sandown Park where I received my own bap-tism into the mystiques of racing first of all as a prep schoolboy. Unless you are prepared to study form as thoroughly as if trying for First Class honours at Oxford or Cambridge then it is safer to stay at home, disconnect the phone and watch it all on television, pausing only to look up as each winner passes the post and reflect to yourself that of course you would have backed it.

However there aren't many of us in these islands with the will power to continue that Lenten treatment for long, and since the Macmillan régime it has become increasingly easy to place a bet in England. Before, it was very much a right of the rich or respectable. You either had an account with a bookmaker whom you rang up or wrote to, or you did not bet unless you actually went to the course. That was all there was to it –

officially. Unofficially there was a legion of little men who would run your bet to a bookmaker and risk prosecution for doing it. In return they received commission from the bookie.

Now there is the betting shop. If you want to place a bet all you have to do is brush through the plastic strips into the smoke. Do not be put off by the *mystique*. If you want to place a bet simply write on any piece of paper the name of the race meeting, the time of the race, the name of the horse and how much you want to stake. Either x to win or x each way, which means you'll get paid out if the horse comes first, second, or third. You hand it in at the counter and they hand you a slip recording the bet. Voices are seldom raised above an inaudible mutter in a betting shop. The tobacco smoke is thick despite the air extractors, and men move furtively as they scribble their bets because it is not done to crib another man's wager, although if you asked him outright for advice you'd never shut him up. A voice direct from the racecourse intones what the odds are on the course and these are also chalked up beside the name of the horse on a board at one end of the betting shop. The voice will intone 'They go 3–1 the field at Sandown', which, interpreted, means the favourite in that race at Sandown is 3–1. The voice will then give a somewhat unemotional commentary on the race. Often, within five minutes of placing your money you can be back on the street light a few pounds or plus a few, according to whose advice you took.

Far better, however, to go to the course itself, and Sandown Park in particular. It is one of the most beautiful courses in England and a place such as to soften the blows of the hardest betting losses or add elation to the smallest of wins. There are regular meetings here throughout the season and good prize money ensures a high standard of entry, all of which makes for good racing and betting. The flat racing sprint course runs down the centre of the park and it is quite pleasant to walk out to the finish on a good day. The grandstands at Sandown, being on a hill, give a superb view of the course, although at least once during the afternoon I recommend a walk down to the start. Women often find the thirty-minute interval between each race rather tedious so both visits help to break the afternoon. Not many people ever bother to go down to the start of a race.

At Sandown the 1¼-mile start is within easy walking distance of the stands, and so too is the three-mile starting gate during the jumping season. It is at the start of a flat race that you get its real atmosphere. You must also not mind the language. Jockeys, who in England traditionally receive 10 per cent of the prize money as a present, are not given to niceties as they hustle to get a good start. You will also swear before the actual 'Off', when the wire mesh gate goes up with a hiss, that you have heard every jockey in the race ask the starter to 'Wait, sir'.

This is automatically shouted as soon as a jockey feels his horse would not jump out of the gate immediately. A draw is made for starting positions for each race so this also complicates matters as the starter and his assistant sort out a highly nervous group of two-year-olds into an exact starting order.

On the way back to the start, and after watching the finish, it would be as well to pause on the popular side, where you will now be able to hear the tipsters at work before returning to the sophistication of the grandstands. Tipsters are an incredible breed of men, peculiar to British racing, who have spent their lives travelling to every race meeting with 'advice' for the punter. This 'advice' is usually sold at 2s. 6d. a time. Their approach varies. One will lay out on the grass, propped up against a battered cardboard suitcase, faded photographs that show various horses being led into the winning enclosure, from the look of it nearly 100 years ago. The tipster will claim that the man on the animal's back is himself in his great and distant riding days. Quite how he has swapped the winner's enclosure for a non-combative view of the racing on the popular side is never quite clear. He addresses the crowd in confident extrovert terms and often claims to have given the winner of the last race, pointing, as he does so, at an anonymous looking person and shouting: 'Ask him'. At which the man nods agreeably and we are all silently impressed and feel it is our duty to buy a tip for the next race.

Then there is the really smooth operator. He comes over to the popular side from the members' enclosure dressed in a dark suit with his members' badge ostentatiously dangling from his lapel. He wears an incongruous bowler hat and his accent is second-class public school at the very least. He often raises his hat and speaks firmly but in rather more hushed tones than the ex-jockey. Sometimes, it must be recorded, he unaccountably drops his H's: 'I don't have to come over 'ere you know. In fact at any moment I shall be returning to where the money is at this very moment – the members' enclosure. But I have come over 'ere specifically to give you one winner. It will cost you 5s. but will be worth every shilling. I can tell you that at this very moment over there (jerks manicured hand violently in direction of members' enclosure) those IN THE KNOW are falling over themselves TO GET ON this one.' 'To get on' I might add does not mean literally a whole lot of people trying to ride the next winner, but a whole lot of people endeavouring to get their bets on it.

The Minister of Sport, Mr Dennis Howell, told me last year that his biggest problem was to align the mentality of the people who control sport in this country to our dreadful climate. They carry on as if it never rained. Well, at the dogs, at least you can have a reasonably warm and dry night. Greyhound racing is one of the few British sports to take account of the British weather. At most London tracks the patrons are under cover and at many you can actually eat a very good meal while watching the racing from behind plate glass. Losing does not seem quite so hard if accompanied by a pleasantly cool hock instead of the racecourse's obligatory lukewarm light ale. You can witness betting at its most intricate as the giant totalisator board flicks up the units placed on each dog. Unlike the racecourse crowd the dog men don't find getting the winner so hard. What they are really interested in is getting the first and second to seize the Forecast. There is a bet, fruitily named Quinella, linking the winners of several races together. Apart from the restaurant crowd in evening dress, spectators at greyhound racing's bigger events like the Derby at the White City are less dressy than their horse-racing equivalent. Personally I find the whole thing lacking the human element of, say, Epsom or Sandown Park. The best sight is six thoroughbred greyhounds pulling up after a race, muzzling the 'hare' and wagging their tails. Somehow this puts the sport into a true perspective.

Croquet is a game apart. Very British, very beautiful to watch because of the surroundings of the Hurlingham and Roehampton Clubs (Hurlingham has an air of the Athenaeum about it). It is at these two clubs that Britain's major croquet tournaments are played. It's a fascinating game and the players taking part will be only too ready to explain it to you. You may be lucky and see London's world champion, John Solomon, a remarkable man who retains his title by playing a mere three weeks' croquet a year. He puts it all down to a natural swing.

Croquet has a peculiar English image of being played upon vicarage lawns by genteel old ladies who also provide cucumber sandwiches, and it is true that it used to be like that. But Mr Solomon abruptly dismisses the sort of croquet you play at home on a lawn as 'golf croquet'. Nowadays it is all highly complicated tactics, and many of those taking up the game come from the universities. The lawns of Roehampton and Hurlingham are pampered to a degree by vigilant groundsmen so that the slightest tap of the mallet sends a ball skimming across the surface.

Croquet players are slightly cool at the mention of Wimbledon. This is not because of any aversion to tennis, for in fact many ex-tennis players become especially good croquet players. The reason is that Wimbledon was the croquet centre of England until the demands of the tennis players gradually eased it out. Wimbledon now means tennis, and in particular that fortnight in mid-June when the world's best amateurs compete for the British titles. Wimbledon is one of those peculiarly British sporting institutions with the ivy-encrusted buildings of the Centre Court, the presence of members of the Royal Family to whom players bow or curtsy, the ball boys from Dr Barnardo's homes for orphans, who scamper expertly around the court; and, behind the Centre Court, the excellent lawns where strawberries and cream are traditionally served and the tea stews in a silver urn.

Twelve miles or so from the centre of London you can go hunting with the foxhounds of the Enfield Chace. Northerners wishing to sneer at the insularity of Londoners often say that we have no knowledge of anything taking place beyond Potters Bar. It is therefore appropriate that the Enfield Chace secretary, Miss Angela Graham, should live at Potters Bar. It underlines the fact that this is London's own. And in return the hunt holds its annual Hunt Ball in a West End hotel and its point-to-point (hunt-horse steeplechases) at Enfield, which is on the tube. The thing about hunting in England is not so much the art of riding to hounds (prohibitively expensive for most people) but the art of following by foot and car. There has in the past been slight feeling between huntsmen and followers but the new hunt supporters' clubs provide the modern hunt with much of its revenue. If you intend to follow a hunt you need two things: a copy of *Horse and Hound* to find where the Meet is to take place, and an ordnance survey map to prevent you getting lost.

London is the arena for other sports too numerous to discuss here. There is, for example, professional wrestling, featuring such splendidly-named gentlemen as The Ghoul or Doctor Death, who do battle regularly in town halls or on the stages of suburban cinemas. Their steps look strangely choreographed, especially if the bout is being televised, but there are moments of real rage which set old ladies screaming for blood. In contrast there is the quieter and more serious game of darts, whose world champion is a printer working in the middle of Covent Garden. You can find a game of darts in progress in many London pubs and every year Britain's darts players have their championships, sponsored by the *News of the World* newspaper, at the Albert Hall. Or, in an atmosphere of even greater concentration, the nation's best snooker players can be seen throughout the winter season in the centre of London (Burroughes and Watts Hall, Soho Square). With the darkened hall and brilliantly lit table, the smell of chalk and the dull squeak as players chalk their cues, this outwardly calm sport can have an air of high tension.

Here is a list of London's major sporting centres and some suggestions for getting there. Enjoy yourself!

ASSOCIATION FOOTBALL

First Division clubs and their home grounds:
Arsenal: Highbury Stadium (Piccadilly Line to Arsenal).
Fulham: Craven Cottage (District Line to Putney Bridge then short and pleasant riverside walk to ground).

Chelsea: Stamford Bridge (District Line to Fulham Broadway or any bus down Fulham Road).

West Ham: Upton Park (District Line to Upton Park).

Tottenham Hotspur: White Hart Lane (British Railways train from Liverpool Street to White Hart Lane).

Normal kick-off times during season: Saturday, 3 p.m., evening matches 7.30 p.m. Consult local evening papers. When travelling by tube or train always buy a return ticket. This saves much queueing on the return journey.

RACING

Alexandra Park. London's most central course (Piccadilly Line to Finsbury Park, then bus 212; or by train from Paddington to Wood Green).

Ascot. (Trains from Waterloo to Ascot Station. By road take A329 Virginia Water–Reading road.)

Epsom. (Trains from Victoria, Waterloo, to Epsom Town, Epsom Downs, or Tattenham Corner. Road travel not advised.)

Kempton Park. (Frequent trains from Waterloo to racecourse station.)

Sandown Park. (Trains to Esher from Waterloo. By car take A3.)

Windsor. (Trains from Waterloo or Paddington to Windsor. By car M4 motorway spur leads to course.)

CROQUET

Hurlingham Club. (District Line to Putney Bridge.)
Roehampton Club. (Train Waterloo–Barnes; bus 72.)

CRICKET

Lord's: St John's Wood (Bakerloo Line to St John's Wood).
The Oval: Kennington (Northern Line to Oval).

TENNIS

Wimbledon. (District Line to Earlsfield.)

MOTOR CAR and MOTOR CYCLE RACING

Brand's Hatch. (Trains from Victoria to Swanley. By car on the

A20, twenty miles south-east of London between Swanley and Wrotham.)

RUGBY UNION

Twickenham. (Trains from Waterloo to Twickenham.)

SPORTS CENTRE

National Recreation Centre. Crystal Palace (trains from Victoria and London Bridge to Crystal Palace).

WEMBLEY

For Stadium, Empire Pool and Bowling Alley. (Bakerloo Line or Metropolitan Lines to Wembley Park then short walk.)

GREYHOUND RACING

Major and most pleasant tracks:

Wimbledon. (Fri. and Wed. 7.45 p.m.: District Line to Wimbledon or train Waterloo–Wimbledon. Then express bus.)

White City. (Thurs. and Sat. 7.45.: Central Line to White City.)

Wembley. (Mon. and Fri. 7.45 p.m.: Bakerloo or Metropolitan Line to Wembley Park.)

Soldiers, sailors and aeroplanes

London has always been something of a soldier's town, not because the British are martial * but because, as Trevelyan said in his *English Social History*, 'England's army . . . was a part-time occupation of the governing aristocracy'. The activities of the fashionable regiments became a part of London's social scene. Few tourists come here without seeing the Changing of the Guard. This ceremony is a slightly more elaborate business when the Queen is in London and if you check to find out if the soldiers are from Chelsea Barracks you can follow them all the way. The alternative – Wellington Barracks – is just across the road from Buckingham Palace. The guard-changing times are posted up outside its gates. For an overall view of the ceremony, head straight for the Victoria Memorial. The earlier you get there the higher you'll be able to climb. You'll get the best view of the ceremony, but you won't exactly be rubbing shoulders with the red tunics. So if you have binoculars and telephoto lenses, take them with you. I prefer however to watch the guard forming up in the barrack yard across the road to watching an empty Palace yard.

The times of the guard-changing don't always remain constant and it's a good idea to check with the British Travel Association's Information Centre. When you see the ceremony you will see the new guard marched to the Palace by a regimental band. The various regiments – Scots, Irish, Grenadiers, etc. – are distinguished by the colour and position of the plume in the bearskin caps. The Scots are distinguished by not having one at all. The Grenadiers wear a white plume on

* And indeed of all the Roman bits and pieces found in London only two (shield bosses) have military origin.

the left. Watch out for a drummer in the band wearing black
armbands in mourning for Charles II. If the Queen is in London
the Queen's colour – it's crimson – will be carried. If not they
will be carrying the regimental colour.

By the time the new guard are positioned in the Palace
forecourt the old guard are formed up facing them. The new
guard march – in slow time – toward the old guard. The keys
of the palace are handed by the captain of the old guard to his
counterpart. The band plays while they position the sentries
and then it marches the old guard away.

While you're standing there snapping away, the Horse Guards
are pulling a switch down in Whitehall. If you skip the last half
of the show at Buckingham Palace, and sprint like mad across
St James's Park you can catch the last half of their
performance.

But it's better to leave the Horse Guards for another morning.
Turn up early, and you can get a close-up view of the whole
thing from inside the courtyard.

The Buckingham Palace changing ceremony is at 11.30 a.m.
while the Horse Guards changing is at 11 a.m. on weekdays and
10 a.m. on Sundays. It's easier to see both changing ceremonies
on Sunday but possible to see both on a weekday if you really
hurry.

Real fanatics might even write to the Resident Governor of
the Tower of London months in advance for permission to see
the ceremony of locking up the Tower at 10 p.m. It only
takes ten minutes (visitors must be in position by 9.40 p.m.)
but I'm told it's worth the trouble.

More leisurely military fanatics might content themselves
with the museums. There is a regimental museum – the Royal
Fusiliers' – right there in the Tower of London. See also the
national collections of arms and armour.

For most of the year there is a long, long queue waiting to
get to see the Crown Jewels. One of the officials told me that the
only way to get in without a long wait is to go into the Tower
at the moment it opens (10 a.m.) and hurry immediately to the
Wakefield Tower where the jewels are. If you are keen to see
the jewels take his advice – it's a long miserable queue.

Not far from the south side of Westminster Bridge is the

Imperial War Museum. It has a large collection of relics, paintings, documents, films and photos of two world wars. There are fine models, real aircraft, tanks and submarines, and by the time this is published a regular cinema will be in daily operation. The museum is open 10 a.m.–6 p.m., Sunday 2 p.m.– 6 p.m. (library Monday–Friday only).

The Artillery Museum is in the suburbs at the Rotunda, Woolwich Common, S E 18 (about twenty minutes by car without heavy traffic). It has guns, muskets, artillery, etc., and is open 10 a.m.–5 p.m. in the summer (Sundays 2 p.m.–5 p.m.). In winter it closes one hour earlier.

The most important Army collection is the national one at the Royal Military Academy, Sandhurst. This is just outside London (a thirty-minute train journey to Camberley from Waterloo Station) but then I warned you this was just for fanatics. Incidentally there are ninety-three other military museums in Britain. They are all listed in *Museums and Galleries in Great Britain and Ireland* (Index Publishers, 3s. 6d.).

The Wallace Collection (Manchester Square, W 1, quite near to Oxford Street and Baker Street) is a private hoard of art treasures in a fine house. It includes a selection of armour, with a particularly fine suit of fifteenth-century south German armour.

I make no apology for mentioning the National Maritime Museum again. See the ship models, and the coat Nelson wore at Trafalgar. The museum is open 10 a.m.–6 p.m. Sundays 2.30 p.m.–6 p.m. There is a vast library of books, plans and pictures but you must apply in advance to use it (G R E 4422).

Trooping the Colour, one of the most notable ceremonial events in the military calendar, is at the beginning of June. Also in June, on the Horse Guards Parade, the Marines' Massed Bands beat Retreat. The Royal Tournament, a military display ranging from mountain artillery to massed bands and motor cycles, takes place every evening during the second half of July.

One most remarkable place of interest which no guide book has ever mentioned as far as I can trace is 'the secret place'. This was the complex of 150 rooms under Whitehall from which

Churchill conducted the British war effort, known officially as the Cabinet War Rooms. Six rooms are now open to the public. There is the room where the War Cabinet met and the control room crammed with phones and maps covered in marker pins. On the wall are maps showing the disposal of military defences in May 1940. The smallest room is a tiny soundproof one from which Churchill spoke on the transatlantic line to the White House. On its door a toilet lock prevented anyone blundering into this top-secret telephone box when the place was 'occupied'. During the war, armed marines constantly patrolled these underground corridors and flashing lights and signs warned the occupants of enemy bombers or the chances of light snow. Churchill's desk has been left much as it was during the war. There are two visits each day and you should phone WHI 5422 Extension 96 to be included on one. At the time of writing there is no delay or waiting list. My friend Jack (*The Finest Hours*) le Vien told me that he won a reputation as an *eminence grise* by arranging this trip for visiting friends while carefully implying that he was probably the only man in Britain with enough pull to get them in there.

Military books are available from Francis Edwards, 83 Marylebone High Street, W1, but they are expensive and I have never discovered a bargain there. Jack Beaumont runs his little shop at 11 Bath Street, EC1, which is near Old Street Underground station. Beaumont Aviation Literature is open all the week, but the regulars who like chatting go there on Saturdays. It's the only bookshop in the world devoted exclusively to aeronautics. Jack is an ex-R.A.F. and airline pilot and still a flying enthusiast. He'll talk for hours if you ask him and it's the only bookshop I know where if you stand gazing on the books long enough they will put a cup of tea in your hands. You'll meet some fascinating people at Jack's shop: the Soviet Air Attaché might be rubbing shoulders with editors of aero magazines or Hollywood stunt flyers. In the past Jack has answered questions that encyclopedias haven't done. And when you think you've seen it all he might let you go down to the cellar where he has thousands and thousands of aero magazines from every country in the world.

Near Jack Beaumont's (but with only a small interest in military affairs – a selection of model armoured vehicles) is Auto Models Ltd, at 70 Finsbury Pavement, E C 2. They have all kinds of model cars, kits, motors, etc., and deal wholesale as well as retail.

If you are going to be in London during the late part of the summer, remember that September is the anniversary of the Battle of Britain and some R.A.F. stations (including historic ones connected with the battle, e.g. Biggin Hill) are open to the public. Often vintage aircraft of both wars are displayed and flown. Also at this time on alternate years the Farnborough Air Display takes place quite near to London. The newest British aircraft are displayed on the ground and demonstrated in flight. For the best view go on the days reserved for press and commerce if you can convince the organizers that you are a newspaperman at heart. On the days when the public are admitted the place is overcrowded and uncomfortable as well as very expensive.

For model soldiers – beautifully painted replicas – see Norman Newton, 49 Hertford Street, w 1, who also sells ancient arms and armour of all kinds. The soldiers are under £5 but the arms and armour can be a pretty expensive investment in these dangerous days.

Milton Shulman suggests entertainment less dangerous and less expensive.

Theatre

Milton Shulman

Milton Shulman has been the theatre critic of the London *Evening Standard* since 1953. He has also been an executive TV producer specializing in current affairs programmes and has written film and TV criticism.

He was born in Canada where he practised law before coming to Britain with the Canadian Army during the Second World War. His books include *Defeat in the West, How to be a Celebrity, Kill 3,* and two children's books, *Preep* and *Preep in Paris*. He is married to Drusilla Beyfus, and they have three small children.

Snap. Snap. Snap. Tripping over the prostrate or crouching forms of photographers from *Paris Match, Life, Der Spiegel* or *Esquire* has now become one of the accepted hazards of London streets.

The world, it seems, is fascinated by British fashion, British night life, British gambling, British restaurants, British films, British tradition and, of course, British girls. Magazines and newspapers throughout the world are determined to gorge their readers with every detail of the strange goings-on in Britain's capital.

The phenomenon of London – once the epitome of all that was dowdy and square – as the with-it, swinging, bouncing, jumping town of the sixties is still as incongruous to many as the image of Queen Victoria doing the can-can.

In Chelsea, the girls in their breathtaking short skirts, their outrageous dresses inspired by anything from *art nouveau* to the Union Jack, their mad stockings and kinky boots, their oblivious acceptance of the stares of stunned, gasping males, are so tantalizing and so beautiful that any account of entertainment in London must inevitably give them pride of place.

Sociologists and historians will no doubt soon be offering academic explanations for this explosion of fashion and frivolity. The confusion resulting from Britain's changing world role; the release of working-class energies into the arts; the recruitment of middle-class brains and talent – previously exercised in diplomacy, the clergy or the armed services – into the entertainment field; the need to earn foreign currency through tourism – take your pick.

But whatever the causes of what one might call The Gay Revolution, there is no doubt that the theatre has been one of its vanguard forces.

Some three million tourists visited Britain in 1966 and most of them came expecting to visit one or more of London's theatres. The West End ranks with historic sights and the countryside as one of the nation's main attractions for tourists. The prospect of seeing Sir Laurence Olivier or Vanessa Redgrave or Peter O'Toole on the stage is as alluring for visitors as the Tower of London or the Changing of the Guard. It has been estimated that if something happened to seriously shrink the number of London's theatres – there are about forty-five in the capital alone – we might lose as much as 25 per cent of our tourist trade. And since this is one of our major foreign currency earners – perhaps our biggest single earner of dollars – this would have a disastrous impact on the nation's economy and our balance of payments problem.

But it was not always so. Only ten years ago the British drama was cocooned in the cosy, undemanding world of Noël Coward, Terence Rattigan and Agatha Christie, with the criterion of a successful play being whether or not Mr Rattigan's Aunt Edna had enjoyed it. Matinée taste dominated management enterprise.

The date the modern millennium came to the West End is commonly said to be 8 May 1956. That was the first night of John Osborne's play, *Look Back in Anger*, at the Royal Court Theatre. In the sense that the financial success of this play saved the Royal Court from possible extinction – it was going through a rough patch – the new British theatre certainly owes much to Osborne. For it was in this theatre – under the guidance of the late George Devine – that many of the playwrights

227

of a fresh generation got their chance. John Arden, N. F. Simpson, Ann Jellicoe, Arnold Wesker, Willis Hall, Edward Bond were a few.

But by merely listing those names one realizes how little they have in common with the uninhibited, passionate cry of protest about the arid future of England's youth contained in *Look Back in Anger*.

Even less likely is it that Osborne's play inspired the work of Brendan Behan, Peter Shaffer, Henry Livings, Alun Owen, Harold Pinter, John Mortimer, David Mercer and David Rudkin.

These writers were not spawned at the Royal Court but got their chances in Joan Littlewood's Theatre Workshop in Stratford East, the Arts Theatre and, most significantly, in television.

But who should or should not get credit for lighting the fuse is less important than the fact that an artistic explosion took place. Young writers had something to say and wanted to say it in new ways – by manipulating speech rhythms, by experimenting with fresh forms, by probing the potential of unfamiliar regional accents, by shocking audiences and ridiculing conventional attitudes and institutions. There were new writers in Britain. Lots of them. And the theatre tingled with their vivacity and enthusiasm.

But along with this bursting activity came the realization that experimentation can be a costly business. Notoriously disinterested in the arts, British governments began belatedly to listen to the rumblings of a society demanding the right to cultivate minority tastes. And the government-controlled Arts Council was slowly given more funds with which to sustain ballet, opera, music and the theatre.

And it is because of this Government support that there are now flourishing in London three theatres that have become havens for everything enterprising, adventurous, daring and exciting on the British stage. Any visitor to London who is conscious of the theatre as being something more than a giggle emporium for tired businessmen or a relaxation for leisure hours should try to get tickets for anything being shown at the Aldwych, which houses the Royal Shakespeare Company, the Old Vic which is the temporary home of the National Theatre, or the Royal Court Theatre which puts on the plays of the English Stage Company.

Not everything they do is successful. Indeed, sometimes they have had bleak and dismal failures. But whatever these companies present comes from a passionate and sincere desire to make the stage worthy of the highest and most stimulating aspirations of the dramatic form. Let us consider these theatres in turn.

The Royal Shakespeare Company has for decades presented the works of the Bard at Stratford-on-Avon. It still does so and it is safe to say that nowhere in the world are the productions of Shakespeare so stunningly and imaginatively treated as they are at the birthplace of Shakespeare himself. A visit to this gentle tourist town and a chance to see any of these productions in the magnificently equipped Memorial Theatre will linger in the memory for many years.

Under Peter Hall's energetic guidance, the Royal Shakespeare Company opened a London branch at the Aldwych Theatre and began to diversify into the works of playwrights other than the Bard. In the last few years this theatre has seen some of the most exciting productions not only in Britain, but in the world. There was, for instance, the *Marat/Sade* by Peter Weiss which was produced with staggering effect by Peter Brook and won the New York Critics' Award as the best play of the year when it was seen unaltered on Broadway during the 1965–6 season. Then there was the brilliant comic interpretation of Gogol's *The Inspector General*, starring Paul Scofield; Peggy Ashcroft oozing maternal venom, greed and possessiveness as the she-wolf mother in *Days in the Trees* by Marguerite Duras; and an omnibus production of Shakespeare's histories called *The Wars of the Roses* which brought a staggering new dimension to these often-neglected plays. And though seats at the Aldwych for their most successful productions are almost unattainable, it needs something like £150,000 of Government money to keep the company out of the red.

The other formidable and major achievement of the English stage is the establishment and dazzling success of the National Theatre. In less than five years, it has, under the directorship of Sir Laurence Olivier, become a national institution that can compete with, and out-shine, such hallowed companies as the Moscow Arts Theatre and the Comédie Française.

Its production of *Othello*, starring Olivier, was such a critical and popular success that it has been preserved intact in the form of an exciting film. Shaffer's *The Royal Hunt of the Sun* (which was seen on Broadway), a revival of Coward's early comedy *Hay Fever*, Arthur Miller's *The Crucible*, Sean O'Casey's *Juno and the Paycock*, Shaffer's delirious farce *Black Comedy*, *A Flea in Her Ear* by Feydeau (in my opinion the funniest event in the West End for almost a decade) and John Osborne's steaming adaptation of a Lope de Vega play, *A Bond Honoured* (which resulted in one of the fiercest squabbles between artists and critics seen for many years), are some of the invigorating and delightful productions recently produced by this company.

Housed in the cramped quarters of the small Old Vic Theatre, the National Theatre's greatest failure has been its inability to cater for the eager audiences clamouring to get in. In the summer of 1966 a supplementary theatre, the Queen's, had to be taken over for ten weeks in order to siphon off some of this overflow public outraged at their inability to see these dramatic treasures. After all, since the Government and the G.L.C. foots an annual bill of over £290,000 to subsidize the National Theatre, every tax-payer feels he has a right to get a seat. If you are planning to get to London in the near future, it would be advisable to write several months in advance for a seat at the National Theatre and take gratefully whatever you can get.

The Royal Court Theatre, which also gets some state money as well as contributions from private donors, has fared less happily recently than either the Royal Shakespeare or the National Theatre. Under its latest artistic director, William Gaskill, it has gone over to the repertory system of a permanent company with a roster of alternating plays. Its aim seems to have been to recapture the experimental spirit of the Royal Court's pioneering period of twelve years ago. But little has come right for it.

Relying upon the work of some of its earlier discoveries – Ann Jellicoe, N. F. Simpson, John Arden – it has had two successively disappointing seasons that merely emphasized the capricious transience of theatrical taste. Its preference for plays that make unusual demands upon an audience's tolerance and understanding has not deserted it. There were, for example, Edward Bond's *Saved*, which included a horrific scene in which an infant was stoned to death and which involved the theatre in a court action with Britain's official censor, the Lord Chamberlain; Keith Johnstone's *The Performing Giant*, a weird play about the exploration of a giant's physical and sexual functions which was received with general disdain by the critics; and Jarry's *Ubu Roi*, an elaborate production of this rarely done, early *avant garde* French play.

But these three state-subsidized theatres, although they have contributed to most of the sparkle, outrage and adventure in the British drama today, represent only a small minority of London's forty-five-odd theatres. The bulk of the West End is not supported by public money and it must be admitted that those managements depending on box-office receipts for their survival have not been able to compete with the subsidized theatre in terms of drive, daring or novelty.

Most of the plays that do succeed on the commercial stage are comedies and amongst the recent best, one would note *The Killing of Sister George* (a winner of a number of best-play awards), *Spring and Port Wine* (a raucous north-country comedy), *Say Who You Are* and *Beyond the Fringe* (a satirical revue that has been going through successive versions from year to year).

Another staple ingredient of the commercial theatre is the vehicle play in which plot, dialogue and action are largely tailored for the talents of an individual star. There are always two or three of these productions running in London and some recent examples of this genre include Noël Coward in his trilogy of plays – *Song at Twilight, Shadows of the Evening* and *Come into the Garden, Maud* – Diana Sands in the American comedy, *The Owl and the Pussycat*, and the beautiful *tour de force* of Vanessa Redgrave as the fey, romantic heroine of *The Prime of Miss Jean Brodie*.

Stylish revivals of the classics with a cluster of star names often lured back from the lush pastures of the cinema is another way in which the commercial theatre earns its keep in the West

End. There have been lately available in London such successes as Turgenev's *A Month in the Country* with Ingrid Bergman, Michael Redgrave and Emlyn Williams, Shaw's *You Never Can Tell* with Ralph Richardson, Arthur Miller's *Incident at Vichy* with Alec Guinness and Anthony Quayle, Chekhov's *Ivanov* with John Gielgud, Claire Bloom and Yvonne Mitchell, and Oscar Wilde's *An Ideal Husband* with Margaret Lockwood, Richard Todd and Michael Denison.

It is the great fortune of London that at any moment of time some of the greatest actors in the world can be seen by theatre-goers. While the names I have just listed may be shining in the West End, the subsidized theatres could be matching them with the work of Laurence Olivier, Albert Finney, Joan Plowright, Maggie Smith, Peggy Ashcroft, Paul Scofield, David Warner or Ian Holm.

And if you're looking for something really baffling in London's theatre there is always Agatha Christie's *The Mousetrap* which has been running for fifteen straight years. A tired, old-fashioned, obvious thriller, the mystery is no longer who-did-it but who still wants to see it?

British musicals have acquired the vivacity and bounce of the American product in recent years and there have been some notable hits such as *Oliver!* (the longest running musical in the West End's history), *Half-a-Sixpence* (which pleased Broadway) and *The Black and White Minstrel Show* (a long-running version of a B.B.C. television show whose melodic songs and corny routines seem to have an irresistible appeal to family audiences). But the three most successful musicals in London for a long time have been American – *The Sound of Music, Hello Dolly!* (which began with Mary Martin and continued with Dora Bryan) and *Funny Girl* with Barbra Streisand (which closed after a short run because Miss Streisand had to go home and become a mother).

Although the music halls have been finding life difficult against the competition of the cinema and television and very few of them still survive, there is still the Palladium which offers a haven for variety acts whether in the form of straight vaudeville or more elaborate and sumptuous revues.

If you are looking for dexterity on the trampoline, ventriloquists, pretty girls balancing tables and chairs on nimble toes, pop groups and an occasional dog act, the Palladium is probably one of the last remaining places in the world where you can see them outside of a circus. The bill is usually topped by a broad comic like Ken Dodd (a sort of Lancashire Ed Wynn), Michael Bentine, Frankie Howerd, Charlie Drake, Harry Secombe or Benny Hill. It was television that brought many of them their fame and the parochial nature of many of their gags may be somewhat baffling to the uninstructed visitor.

In addition to the theatres of the West End, there are a number of well-known little theatres that cater for a specialized audience wanting something more experimental and less commercial. These theatres offer the equivalent of the off-Broadway type of dramatic entertainment and any list of them can be only tentative since the chances of them actually functioning at any specific time of the year are largely problematic. The Lyric Theatre in Hammersmith (about a half-hour taxi drive from Piccadilly) and the Theatre Royal, Stratford East (about three quarters of an hour from Piccadilly), have recently had a rather chaotic career and it would be wise to check on the kind of play they are offering before setting out on a safari to these remote corners of the London theatre world.

A somewhat unique aspect of London theatrical life is the club theatre. These come and go like fireflies in the night, but some have managed to wedge themselves into a relatively permanent place in the affections of London audiences. Only members can attend and it usually needs something like forty-eight hours notice before you can go through the necessary formalities to make you eligible. The fees for joining are not very large (something between five and ten shillings) and almost all applications are welcomed. The chief advantage of a club theatre is that it is not subject to the strict censorship requirements of the Lord Chamberlain and it is in club theatres that some of the most daring breakthroughs in subject-matter and the most liberal experiments with taboo language have taken place.

The most successful club theatre is probably the Player's Theatre, located in the arches beneath the busy railway lines running into Charing Cross. It offers old-fashioned Victorian music hall – comics, sentimental singers, hoofers, acrobats and Christmas pantomimes – to a convivial audience that is familiar with every routine and takes considerable pleasure in heckling the master-of-ceremonies and howling in unison with him the exact words of his predictable introductions. You can drink beer and have sandwiches while the show is on and as an aspect of nostalgic Britain it is, indeed, worth a visit.

Other club theatres that have survived the vagaries of public demand are the Arts and the Hampstead Theatre Club but their careers have had the sudden ups and downs of a yo-yo and it would be prudent to read the notices before deciding to invest in a membership fee and a ticket to either.

Every ballet-lover has, of course, heard of the Royal Ballet Company and its home in Covent Garden. This astonishing theatre, surrounded by the ugly warehouses of London's vegetable and flower market, is always jammed to capacity on the nights when Fonteyn or Nureyev dance. The queues sometimes start forming two days before the box-office opens and getting to the theatre means not only dodging the hand-pushed carts full of tomatoes or hyacinths, but avoiding being tripped up by sleeping bodies waiting for a ticket.

Getting tickets for plays you want to see is not always easy. If they are hits, you may have to book as much as a month or six weeks in advance. One of the more exasperating features of trying to get into a theatre is contacting the ticket box-office. Most of them do not start functioning before 9.30 a.m. and if the show is popular the telephone is nearly always engaged. Even if you do get through, and get a pair of seats, you will probably be asked to pick them up at the theatre at least an hour before curtain-time. This means an extra trip to the theatre or arriving an hour early and hanging about the foyer in a desultory fashion regretting the fact that you didn't go to the cinema instead.

Of course, you can always book seats through ticket agencies by paying a little extra. Most large hotels have representatives of these agencies on the premises. Or you can telephone them. It is not a good idea to rely upon the recommendations you get from the girls who sell you these tickets. Too often their enthusiasm for a show tends to coincide with the interest the agency has in the particular play or musical. Agencies often guarantee certain shows a specific number of sold seats, and it is perhaps natural that they should push these entertainments on customers too lazy or indifferent to care about what they are going to see.

It is not always wise, either, to rely upon the enthusiastic phrases snipped out of critical reviews to determine your choice. Not only are words like 'a hit ... flippin' marvellous ... spine-chilling' meaningless unless one has read the whole notice and recognized the context in which they have been used, but you ought to be warned that some critics are more responsible and authoritative than others. Too often, indeed, you might be lulled into the theatre by the spasms of enthusiasm of an uninformed reporter who happened to be around the office when the regular critic was on holiday or suffering an attack of jaundice. It is best to be guided by these critical extracts when the actual name of a critic is quoted rather than merely a paper. A name is a surer guarantee of the authenticity not only of the quote but also of the spirit of the entire notice.

There are a large number of critics functioning in London because the metropolis has so many daily and Sunday papers. Some of these papers take their responsibilities towards the theatre more seriously than others. At the moment, the most authoritative notices in the daily papers come from *The Times*, the *Guardian,* the *Daily Telegraph,* the *Mail,* the *Express,* the *Sun*, the *Financial Times,* the *Evening Standard*, and the *Evening News*. Only three Sundays provide informed reviews – the *Observer*, the *Sunday Times* and the *Sunday Telegraph*. Amongst the weeklies, the best notices appear in the *Statesman*, the *Spectator* and *Punch.*

All London theatres are equipped with bars. They vary from the luxurious to the doleful. Some are large and well attended; others are cramped cubby-holes supervised by elderly ladies who function at the speed dictated by the more advanced forms of rheumatism. If the bar is small, it would be a wise precaution to order your drinks before the curtain goes up and then you will at least be sure of having them without the need to gulp them down just before the last bell for the end of the interval starts to ring.

The English weather, notoriously fickle, does not usually become warm enough to justify the installation of air-conditioning in most theatres. However, if you are in London on a very hot day in July or August I think a more comfortable way of spending the evening would be in a boat on the Thames or at the Open Air Theatre in Regent's Park, rather than in the muggy confines of most West End theatres.

Food has always had a mysterious association with the theatre. Because plays are usually performed in a time segment between an early supper or a late dinner, their enjoyment is often conditioned by the digestive after-effects of a gulped supper or the enticing vistas of a meal yet to come. I often spend the latter part of a bad third act contemplating the relative merits of an avocado or a smoked trout as the first course of the dinner soon to be enjoyed.

Because the evening performances of most London theatres begin about 7.30 p.m., which means leaving your hotel before seven to get there on time, it is best to plan an after-theatre dinner rather than hurry through a few sandwiches at six o'clock. Britain's reputation for indifferent food has been untrue for many years and London particularly has restaurants to delight the most exacting gourmets in the world.

The only restaurants I intend to discuss here are those that cater for a theatrical clientele and where you are likely to find some of the actors you have just seen on the stage munching an *entrecôte* beside you. There is no specific theatre restaurant like New York's Sardi's in London but rather a number of places varying in size and popularity that undergo shifting waves of favour with their notoriously fickle customers.

The most respectable in terms of prestige and longevity are the Caprice, the Ivy and the White Tower, where the food is always of the most impeccably high standard and where patrons wearing polo-neck sweaters and jeans are not exactly encouraged. The Caprice, where I once saw Epstein, Somerset Maugham, the Maharaja of Baroda and Noël Coward all dining on the same evening at different tables, tends to be patronized by the older and more established figures in the theatrical world. Reigned over by its gracious host, Mario, it is still the restaurant used to celebrate first-night parties and at lunch-time it is a favourite haunt for agents and impresarios to meet, introduce prospective stars and genially conclude deals.

The White Tower, which concentrates on exotic and memorable Greek dishes, is jammed nightly with celebrities and when they are in town you might catch Charlie Chaplin, Ingrid Bergman or Alfred Hitchcock dining at an adjoining table.

Less demanding in terms of dress and price are a number of small, gay restaurants located on the periphery of the West End which offer pleasing menus and the chance of seeing the younger theatrical set relaxing after work. Again it is impossible to predict how long they will remain in favour with a clientele always ready to drop an in-place for something more tantalizingly 'in'.

I would predict, however, that restaurants like Daphne's, the Casserole, Le Carrosse, Nick's Diner, the Garden and Alvaro's – scattered between Covent Garden and Chelsea – will for many years yet be patronized by producers, critics, writers, directors and actors like Albert Finney, Maggie Smith, Sarah Miles, Nicol Williamson, Peter O'Toole, Robert Stephens and others of the new crop being spawned at the Royal Court, the Aldwych and the National Theatre.

There are, too, a few club restaurants which concentrate exclusively on pleasing the members of the entertainment world. Perhaps the best known is the Pickwick Club, where the food ranges from delectable to depressing depending upon the presiding chef, and where you can dance to records or a lively pop group in the pleasingly claustrophobic room downstairs which has for some inexplicable reason been done up with Russian décor. You won't get in, however, unless you have a theatrical friend who is a member or unless your theatrical associations are legitimate enough to qualify you for temporary or full membership.

Another source of entertainment that no survey of this kind should neglect are London's pubs. Unique drinking places which at their worst can be grim and dreary and at their best rollicking centres of conviviality, there are a number of pubs that offer up with the beer and the gin, music, variety acts and pop groups. The most dedicated to this kind of fun are those with Cockney customers who are uninhibited, noisy and gloriously vulgar. These musical pubs, with their open spaces of Victorian décor, are located chiefly in the East End and in south London.

Since there are something like seven thousand pubs in London, and since their atmosphere can change overnight with a change of proprietor, it is best to make inquiries about the prevalence of musical entertainment before setting out on a safari to hunt them down. Recommended for the variety of its groups from trad to pop is the Green Gate in Bethnal Green Road; the Deuragon Arms in Shepherd's Lane, Homerton, which can feature anything from a regular band to local talent; the Hercules Tavern in Lambeth which features beat groups, well-known singers and a youngish clientele; the King's Arms in the Old Kent Road which offers modern rhythmic groups; and The Castle in Tooting which features a succession of ear-splitting groups.

One other way of taking in the theatre while in London is tasting the offerings of near-by provincial towns. Some organize festivals from time to time which tempt some of the biggest theatrical names to these delightful places. The large apron stage at Chichester has provided splendid productions of Chekhov, Anouilh and Shakespeare, starring such formidable personalities as Laurence Olivier, Joan Plowright, Albert Finney and John Clements. Then there is a summer season of special plays at the Yvonne Arnaud Theatre in Guildford which in its short life has seen the work of such actors as Michael Redgrave, Emlyn Williams and Ingrid Bergman.

You can drive to either Chichester or Guildford in less than two hours, but if you are planning to go by rail it would be wise to study the times of the last trains to London. A late curtain and you could find yourself stranded without transport back. And any visit to Stratford-on-Avon, where you can always be sure to see the best Shakespearian productions in the world, will mean an overnight stay or a return to London in the very small hours. And you can only get back by car. British Railways packs up very early at Stratford.

Theatre

At the moment London's theatre is the envy and wonder of the world. Fresh ideas, new faces, daring innovations, shocking language – these are the ingredients that have pushed the stage to the forefront of the Gay Revolution that is now transforming this old, bewildered and rapidly changing land. Its end is nowhere near in sight. But gaiety, abandon and irreverence never survive for long in Britain. The Elizabethans had a spell of it. And there was the Restoration romp under Charles II. But the British feel much more comfortable being conventional, orthodox and institutional. The forces of conformity could close in at any time. But while the fun lasts, it would be a pity not to enjoy it.

Don't just stand there, learn something

Although you don't need any lessons in English or you wouldn't be reading this book many people come to London with just this purpose. Full- and part-time courses are run by the London Education Authorities. They have a booklet called *Classes in English for Students from Abroad* which lists all the courses that are available. The names of private schools that give lessons in English can be obtained from Truman & Knightley Ltd, 93 Baker Street, W1 (HUN 0931).

Perhaps you would like to spend some of your time in London improving your English accent? Speech tuition is regularly advertised in the *Stage*. It comes out on Thursdays; you can get it at many West End bookstalls, but ask early; every copy is sold by the middle of the afternoon. There are adverts offering lessons in singing and dancing. If you want to go back home and tell the theatrical group how you studied acting in London you'll find acting tuition is also available by the hour, day or week.

For a longer stay try contacting one of the theatre schools which run weekend and evening courses in writing and designing as well as acting. The Mountview Theatre Club, 104 Crouch Hill, N8 (MOU 5885) has a fully equipped theatre to work in and has special teenage acting tuition but is only interested in longer courses.

A visitor who intends to study here should buy *The Student Guide to Britain* by Helen Pickthorn (5s.). Other visitors might be interested in more casual learning, e.g. museum lectures.

There are regular lectures at the incomparable British Museum, Great Russell St, WC1. They are usually given at 3 p.m.

and, as well as specialized subjects – 'Hebrews in history', 'Persian painting' and 'Chinese antiquities' – there are lectures for the general visitor in which some selected items from the museum are discussed. These latter are often on Saturday afternoon.

There are also lectures at the Victoria & Albert Museum, Cromwell Road, sw 7. They are at 1.15 p.m. and on Saturdays at 3 p.m. The museum authorities will also, without charge, provide a lecture on anything within their compass if you let them know well in advance and provide a group of interested people to listen. The V. & A. is devoted to Fine and Applied Art, which covers everything from costume (including armour), musical instruments and book design through to oriental textiles. They also have the largest art library in the world. Just in case some swinging young designer decides to have them organize a lecture on New York advertising design I should tell you that in my estimation the museum does not excel in books, information or artifacts of recent origin and is essentially historical in outlook.

The V. & A. is in the heart of London's museumland. Across Exhibition Road is the Natural History Museum, where the lectures – at 3 p.m. every day except Saturday – are particularly suited to children. It sometimes has film shows. Subjects include: 'Man the hunter', 'Frogs and toads' and 'Coral reefs'. I have spent a lot of time in this building, for reasons that I won't go into, and I still find new exhibits there each time I call by. If you want to draw the exhibits they will lend you a stool. Don't miss the full-size whale.

In Exhibition Road there is also the Geological Museum – a specialist museum with some popular exhibits – and the Science Museum. Lectures are at 11.15 a.m. and 3.15 p.m. and often involve a conducted tour of selected exhibits. As with most museums there are no lectures on Sunday. The Science Museum is an endless source of amusement, with lots of working models, as well as real vintage motor cars and aeroplanes.

If looking at stationary racing cars isn't your speed and you'd like to have a try at pressing the right foot down don't take to one of Britain's new motorways, for they have a nasty habit of coming to pieces in your hand. Drive instead down the

A20 to the International Motor Racing School at Brands Hatch circuit near Farningham, Kent. Phone West Ash 404, and arrange a visit. There's no obligation to go again. They will analyse your driving as you go around the circuit three times in a Lotus Elan. Then, after a briefing, they will pop you into a racing car for five high-speed laps all on your own. In fact those Lotus Formula 3 cars are so small there's hardly enough room for one.

If you are even half as good a driver as you keep telling your friends you will be graded straightaway into grade 6, and then make rapid progress up to class 1. Meanwhile you can join the club, which entitles you to drink in the bar, try your own car around the Brands Hatch circuit, slide around the skid pan and on the dance floor on club nights, which also include film shows and dinners. Club membership extends to two other circuits. What's more you'll get discounts on various bits of motor equipment, up to and including a Lotus racing car.

You don't need mechanical knowledge or even a driving licence. They will lend you a pair of goggles and a crash helmet but do wear a comfortable pair of lightweight shoes with little welt.

The charge is £1 a circuit and you have to do at least ten circuits before they will upgrade you a class. When you are in class 2 they'll let you enter a race as a school entry. When you think of what it costs to keep a racing car in first-class nick it's pretty sensational value, especially since you can buy your instruction lap by lap, as and when you want it. Training, by the way, goes on during rain just as a motor-racing Grand Prix does. You'll learn the finer points of pole position, clipping points and slip streaming.

For the rules governing motor racing buy a copy of the R.A.C. *Motor Sport Year Book*, which gives all the regulations about this sport. No need to be a member to get this book; order it by post or buy it at 31 Belgrave Square, s w 1. It costs 5s. (plus 1s. post and packing).

Brands also teaches high-speed driving other than racing driving and will arrange instruction for putting you into Aston Martins and Jaguar E types. Bururururmmmmmmmmmmmm!!

If your interest is motor rallying you must join a club.

Contact the British Automobile Racing Club at 5–6 Argyll Street, w1 (G E R 2533) or the British Racing and Sports Car Club at 6 Buckingham Street, w c2 (T R A 1351).

In Britain the motor car is a manifestation of class warfare. A man buys a car of the class image with which he wants to identify. Once in it, going somewhere is a secondary objective. Bentleys scream down the highways pursued by wolf packs of Minis and M.G. sports cars. Ancient Ford Populars purr unerringly down the centre of the road while sabre-toothed Jaguars snarl behind. On Sundays cars are washed and stroked and adorned with leopard-skin pattern steering wheel covers, dangling dollies and badges.

Perhaps to prove their consummate dexterity with their car controls, British drivers put an arm out of the car whenever an opportunity occurs. These arm movements are signals (derived originally from the whip signals used by horse transport drivers) taught to the British at driving schools. They might mean 'It's just a shower' or 'That's where they do an egg and chips for only five bob', but more probably mean 'Did I surprise you when I slowed up and started to turn just now?'

If you are more interested in looking impressive in your motor than learning how to drive it, Les Leston is the shop. There are white overalls, skid lids, wooden steering wheels and switches and dials enough to make a London bus into a tall red sports special. Les Leston's is at 314 High Holborn and there are more car accessories – less specialized but including some great bargains – at the large store, Gamage's, just down the road. In this same street in the other direction (i.e. west) is the Weather Office, and at No. 284 across the road, the H.M.S.O. or Government Bookshop, as it is called.

Perhaps you don't know that *bona fide* students of any kind can get discounts on magazine subscriptions (e.g. *Punch, Economist, Listener, Spectator*), *The Times*, and airline tickets. Sometimes they can also get cheap theatre tickets – usually about 5s. – by turning up twenty minutes before the shows starts. You'll need an N.U.S. card. Details from the National Union of Students, 3 Endsleigh Street, w c1, who also have a lot of publications about training, etc.

If you want to learn to play a musical instrument the

Orchestral Association at 13 Archer Street, w1 (G E R 1588), will put you in touch with an instructor. For pottery in a private school try the Chelsea Pottery, 13 Radnor Walk, s w3 (F L A 1366).

For evening classes during the normal academic year the Inner London Education Authority runs an astounding number of classes from archaeology to yachtsmanship through angling, Egyptology and tape-recording techniques. The classes are remarkably cheap. For details get the booklet called *Floodlight*, price 6d., from the Education Officer, County Hall, s e 1. From this same office you can also get details of day lectures and courses.

For a day without any lectures at all the nudist resort Spielplatz at St Albans on the outskirts of London welcomes day visitors for swimming and sunbathing but they must undress completely. For a long or short visit phone Garston (Watford) 2126.

Home

Nick Tomalin

Nick Tomalin was born in Highgate, in 1931 (his mother heard Bow Bells ringing to celebrate the triumphant election of Ramsay Mac-Donald's National Government). During the war he was shipped off to Canada for four years. Until 1951 he spent holidays from boarding school beside Primrose Hill, and holidays from Cambridge in a converted railway hotel in St John's Wood. Before he married he lodged in a basement in Holland Park, but celebrated matrimony by moving back to Primrose Hill. Then he bought an astoundingly cheap, beautiful house in Greenwich and lived there for five years – but really that was only to make enough profit to move back to Camden Town, where he has lived ever since. He has worked largely in E C 1 (Fleet Street) and W C 1 (*Sunday Times* and now the *New Statesman*) with the occasional excursion to W 12 (B.B.C.) and W 2 (*Town* magazine).

Who invented the myth of rootless Metropolitan man? Of all rural propaganda the idea of featureless conurbations filled with anonymous scurrying ants is the most fatuous. No one is more inexorably bound to his birthplace, conditioned by his landscape, than today's middle-class Londoner. His roots may be overlaid with Mexican carpets, Irish linen, Italian coffee-machines, Swedish furniture, German cars and French cooking pots, but he is tied to his few square yards of asphalt, linoleum and dusty geraniums in a way no Breton peasant, Highland laird or Kansas sharecropper could comprehend.

Perhaps it is the tribalism of the modern Londoner that conceals his passionate identification with his surroundings. The city is such a diverse place, which can be pushed to mean so many different things to different people that overall London patriotism is resistible, at least in its more blatant forms. A

Londoner's loyalty is to the sub-division, like the public school-boy's to his house, the regimental soldier's to his battalion, the undergraduate's to his college.

Thus if I am far away and someone whispers 'London' in my ear, my reaction is one of stock nostalgia, without real passion. But if he whispers 'N W 8!' then I am caught. And if he clothes these initials in words ('Belsize Park', 'Inner Circle', 'Chalk Farm') then I am gripped to the vitals. It was born in N 6, bred in N W 1, reached puberty in N W 8, and adulthood in N W 1, a slow logical progression down the hill from Hampstead towards the Zoo. My patriotism is therefore towards that professional middle-class cake-slice between Haverstock Hill and Finchley Road, bounded on the north by Whitestone Pond and the south by Prince Albert Road. In its centre, the *mons veneris* of my lust for identification, is Primrose Hill.

I feel at home here; I feel deprived when taken away. Wherever I may be I can instantly recognize a fellow North Londoner by the way he holds his bones, his clothes, accent and intellectual predilections. Within minutes we are swapping shibboleths: the cabman's pull-up on Rosslyn Hill; the Technicolor-Egyptian Black Cat cigarette factory now turned office block at Mornington Crescent; the Tavistock Clinic (where, like as not, we were psychoanalysed together at the age of two); the Young Communist League Dances at Hampstead Town Hall; French films at the Everyman; the 187, 31 and 74 bus routes; the Camden Town pet shop where boa-constrictors once cost only 1s. 7d. a yard; the yellow motorboats on Regent's Park boating pond; the secret army (to foreigners, the Royal Horse Artillery, barracks in Ordnance Hill) that would waken us with the rattle of hooves and gun carriages at five o'clock on summer mornings; the crenellated towers of the Mekay shirt factory, or the distant prospect of King's Cross gasometers; the Giraffe House, the Penguin Pool, feeding time for the sea lions; the two tube lines – Bakerloo (that evocative Twenties coining!) with its elegant Bauhaus modern stations stretching out to Swiss Cottage, and the dear old Northern (so much *smoother* than the bumpy Central) with stations tiled in dried-blood, culminating in Hampstead, where most of us learnt about girls on London's longest, and most deserted, circular staircase.

Another Londoner, from another district, could produce his own incantatory list. If I happen to think my bit is better this is because district patriotism, as all genuine patriotism, is nourished by real intellectual attitudes, for which the streets, buildings, and institutions are only elaborate metaphors.

I can express this linkage best, again, in terms of my own part. In public reputation the quintessence of my North London is Hampstead. And Hampstead still (despite its period quaintness and the dead hand of invading advertising executives) means Bohemianism: talent, freedom, immorality and red rebellion. Even the non-Londoner knows all about Hampstead Bohemia, as we know about the Left Bank in Paris or Greenwich Village in New York. What he can't be expected to know with any precision is exactly what kind of Bohemia it is.

Possibly he lumps it together with the more fashionable Chelsea Bohemia, unaware that Chelsea is basically opposed to Hampstead. Hampstead is profoundly different from Chelsea because it developed earlier. It became institutionalized in the 1930s, largely thanks to the influx of Jewish refugees from Europe. And largely thanks to them it will always bear the imprint of earnest purpose, social democracy and left-wing do-gooders.

Not so Chelsea. It only became an institutionalized Bohemia after the last war. Chelsea rebels were therefore rebelling against austerity and the Labour government, anarchists rather than communists. They gathered in coffee bars and boutiques rather than kaffeeklatsches or comrades' 'demos'. They fled from Tunbridge Wells, Wilton House, or Alice Springs rather than Auschwitz or Dachau. The tyrant they defied was Daddy, not Hitler.

This difference is not so detectable nowadays, with the spread of mass culture and improvement of communications. The passage of time has deposited a Chelsea patina on the Hampstead metal and the second generation, in the form of the executives' rebellious children, drink in newly established coffee bars along the main streets. But the old spirit still lurks in the alleyways and garrets. It could scarcely have been more convincingly demonstrated than in the 1966 election. When Hampstead amazingly rejected Henry Brooke, the sitting Tory member, because he had infringed all its left-wing liberal values as Home Secretary (as well as all its Bohemian values as a square old buffer), what did Chelsea do? It re-elected a Tory, or rather elected a brand-new, dynastic young Tory called Marcus Worsley, by a scarcely depleted majority.

This difference, incidentally, obeys a basic anthropological law. It is not by chance that Chelsea is to the west, and to the south of Hampstead. Success tends to follow the setting sun in cities. By an almost inflexible rule the further west one travels within – and indeed without – London the more worldly, with-it, conformist, prosperous and newly established are the citizenry and buildings. This is true in the centre (compare Bishopsgate with Kensington Church Street), in London as a whole (compare Bethnal Green with Kew) and in the Home Counties (compare Brentwood with Kingston).

Even so, the Hampstead that runs to writing, psychoanalysis, progressive schools and free love has the same social geography as the Chelsea of painting, theatre, good food and promiscuity. Both have, at their inner edge, neighbourhoods of unbelievably stuffy ritzyness (Hampstead has St John's Wood; Chelsea has Kensington) where the Bohemians tend to move once they've made it. Both have, just beside this ritzy area, a kind of raffish lower-middle-class neighbourhood artificially depressed by railway lines (Hampstead has Camden Town; Chelsea has Pimlico) where the Bohemians tend to move if they haven't made it. Both have a 'poor relations' neighbourhood nestling beside them where the more downtrodden of the refugees huddle together for comfort and vicarious participation (red-brick Hampstead; Fulham). And both have at their outer edge, semi-suburbs whose total lack of distinction is emphasized by the contrast (Hendon; Putney).

As a North Londoner I have a chauvinistic dislike of other areas corresponding, in its mindless disdain, to racial prejudice. Many of my best friends are West Londoners, but despite the occasional condescending foray into that area I cannot overcome a conviction that the district is simultaneously corrupt and dingy, a universal Bayswater on the wrong side of the park,

composed of brothels for American airforce officers, residen-
tial hotels for dying ladies, love-nests for squalid industrialists
and communal flats for unattractive secretaries.

Then there is South London for which, like an oppressed
minority, we all have a condescending affection. This area,
spread lavishly beneath – in a manner of speaking – the river,
deserves a book of its own. It has nothing to do with London
as a Capital. It is a totally separate city, linked only by a large
commuter population. Because it has virtually none of the
buildings, institutions, tube trains, aristocracy (save the odd
Earl who has wangled a penthouse in a G.L.C. block) or
criminals (save the villains of the old Elephant and Castle or
the Spades of the new Brixton) that mark a Capital, it is un-
cannily like a provincial city, such as Leicester or Nottingham.
Like them it has a series of town halls, rather than parliaments
(culminating in that most provincial of all buildings, County
Hall), specialized folk museums (the Horniman, the Bethnal
Green, the Imperial War), surprisingly *avant garde* music and
theatre (the Festival Hall, the Old Vic), a second-rate cathedral
(Southwark) and a palatial Bishop's residence (Lambeth). Like
them it has, instead of the ironic social mix of the Capital, little
besieged pockets of embattled gentry (at Blackheath, Dulwich
and Wimbledon) and instead of institutionalized Bohemias
defiant artistic hermits, glorying in their ingenuity.

South London has a relaxing innocence that is lacking north
of the river. Those who have never lived there despise it; those,
like myself, who have for a time deserted North London retain
a respect for it as a refuge from keeping up. They usually discover it round about the time their first baby is due, move there
and pass through a period of local jingoism during the ger-
mination and birth of three or four children. This tends to
dwindle as a burgeoning salary (or the profits from the subse-
quent discovery by the rest of the world of their South London
neighbourhood) enables them to move back into the North
London mainstream. Some remain, to become professional
South Londoners making a steady living by writing articles
about how happy they are not to be surrounded by their peers.

Those who only know South London by driving through it
may also think it featureless, a two-storey, two-up-two-down

desert with the odd oasis of broken down Georgian ribbon development. This again is untrue. The differences are expressed in another language, they need more delicate antennae to detect, but they are as distinct as North London tribal patterns. The impoverished bookish intellectuals who live round Denmark Hill, the newspaper sub-editors who gather in Petts Wood (because of the late trains), the insurance clerks of Lewisham, the H.G. Wellsland around Bromley or Sidcup would hate to be lumped insensitively together. 'Sidcup,' said Wally Fawkes, clarinettist and cartoonist, 'is the Athens of South-east London.' It would deserve a master's degree in social nuance to know the difference between Bermondsey and Deptford, between Peckham and Camberwell, or West Greenwich and East Greenwich. But a lady I know in Greenwich still feels these are the most important distinctions in the world.

Having emphasized the native Londoner's sense of place and identity I want to make a second fundamental point which, although it apparently contradicts my first, is not ridiculous – only paradoxical. London is fascinating because it is unique; it is wonderful because it isn't. In many ways it is more like Paris, New York, Rome, Rio de Janeiro, Nicosia, Dublin than anywhere in England outside the green belt.

This is a new aspect, caused both by immigration of foreigners and a change in the pattern of British society. Traditionally the Capital of the British Isles was the epitome of Britishness and the pinnacle of the class structure. It offered by example and embodiment the essence of what we should all aspire to. Just as Luton made straw hats, and Sheffield cutlery, London made the English Gentleman, the acknowledgement of authority. Provincials came to town to see the Houses of Parliament, the Changing of the Guard, Pall Mall perhaps, the opening of the Royal Academy, *The Second Mrs Tanqueray*, and Ascot. Whenever the gentlefolk enjoyed themselves, the poor would gather on the pavements to catch an intoxicating glimpse as they passed haughtily from carriage to red-carpeted doorway.

Nowadays, if a rich man holds a party there is no crowd of the poor watching his guests arrive. Even the gossip columns ignore his junketing. If you attend the Changing of the Guard you will find the crowd is almost entirely foreign or juvenile, and neither foreigners nor juveniles could grasp the real propaganda nature of the ritual.

If a provincial tourist comes to London, what does he come to see now? Real Madrid, perhaps, playing Tottenham Hotspur. Or the World Theatre Season. Or Duke Ellington playing at the Hammersmith Odeon. Or Miss Candy Barr from Albuquerque, New Mexico, stripping in Soho. Or the Boat Show. Or to shop at Casa Pupo, Galeries Lafayette, or to eat Italian or Hungarian as a respite from the everlasting beanshoots of the British provinces.

So much for theory. In practice it is difficult to recommend a concrete series of sights to embody these ideas. My major, imperative suggestion is that you must see the Grand Union Canal, known for the most part in London as the Regent's Canal, which arches across the northern part of the city from just south of Uxbridge to Limehouse, where it debouches into the Thames (there is a short branch to Brentford where at one point you enjoy the unique pleasure of a three-layer sandwich bridge, road above canal above rail).

The historic importance of this canal is that it offers you a genuine, unaffected slice through Industrial Revolution London. If you seek this on dry land you will find it sullied by launderettes, lemon-yellow doorways and all the other signs of continued vigour and tasteful restoration. But because the canal is wet, noisome, inconvenient and uneconomic no one has bothered to keep it up to date. The beauty of the canal depends partly on its elegance and integrity of structure, imposed by the mechanics of water and tow-ropes, and partly on the incredible grotty picturesqueness that a hundred years of neglect have created.

Because modern aesthetic corruption shies away from it, the canal can meander past such plasticated horrors as the Heinz, the Nestlé's, the Wall's and the Guinness factories in the wasteland suburbia of Middlesex and still remain weathered, handsome and bathed in picturesque scents.

By Kensal Green Cemetery the canal has on one side the rural charm of the biggest and most bosky of London graveyards (Isambard Brunel is buried there), and, on the other side, the

Gothick *Götterdämmerung* of one of the largest gasworks in England. For a considerable stretch you float along 200 ft above Thames level, peering down at faraway streets of Chelsea. At one point you suddenly discover, with an intense shock, the contemporary honkeytonk of the North Circular Road, crammed with impatient Jags, below your dripping olde worlde aqueduct.

For a short stretch from Maida Vale to the Zoo the canal becomes almost well-known. But from Camden Town locks to the Thames there is an utterly disregarded stretch where once again its sludge-green incorruptible nature reasserts itself. Add to it the Piranesi tangle of weeds and steel that is the King's Cross railway yards, strange yellow fires that burn day and night on the cinder towpath disposing of shavings and glue from furniture factories, the white-tiled backside of London's biggest bakery, the A B C, and the Islington tunnel, three quarters of a mile long, fifty yards deep, pitch black, beautifully proportioned, and more dramatic than any blue grotto in any Capri. Why the Islington tunnel is not clogged with the mouldering bodies of Victoriana fans drawn irresistibly to its dark satanic depths I cannot fathom.

Alas the canal is only visited with difficulty by water. The tourist narrow-boat Jason (19 Blomfield Road w 9; telephone c u n 3428) and special water-buses ply the hackneyed stretches from Little Venice, and Jason does the more interesting Middlesex trip each summer Saturday evening. It can also be hired, but otherwise it's difficult to get aboard boats within London. You could buy a canoe and do it that way (avoid the tunnels) or you could walk or bicycle along the towpath after a simple act of trespass over sagging chicken wire broached by little boys at countless points. If you must be legal, buy a permit from British Waterways in Little Venice.

As for dry sights, I recommend secret gardens. Beautiful as they are, I don't include Syon House in Isleworth and its grounds among these, or Kew itself, although the bluebell woods around the western end, if trespassed into, possibly constitute a secret garden.

My own favourite is the Astronomer Royal's Garden, which is tucked just behind his Observatory. Take the railway from

Charing Cross or the river boat to Greenwich (stop for a drink at the Saloon Bar of the Station Hotel on your way; red and green navigation lights, incense, brass warming pans, buxom wenches and fat prosperous scrap-metal dealers, who will sell you *anything* on discount), walk through the park to the Observatory, then nip round the back by a path through a sort of kissing gate and you curve down to the garden. It specializes in spring shrubs.

The second secret garden is in Regent's Park, a rose-garden attached to the old Nash villa variously known as St John's Lodge or the Institute of Archaeology. It extends in a series of hedged circular chambers, each one more mysterious than the last, and ornamented with odder statues. This should be sought in June or July. Go via the Inner Circle in Regent's Park, walk twice round and you can't miss it. When the sun goes down walk a little along the road till you find a metal gate, push it open and visit Clement Freud's food tent for the Open Air Theatre. Lovely food under canvas, décor by Mrs Freud, general atmosphere like a camp church fête. A visit to the adjoining theatricals is not absolutely necessary.

Postman's Park in the City officially known as the churchyard of St Botolph's Without, just by the G.P.O. Headquarters in King Edward Street, has few flowers, but is chiefly interesting for its situation, for the charm of those who visit it, and for an enchanting little cloister to one side where porcelain *art nouveau* plaques have been erected to brave heroes and heroines of ninety years ago:

George Stephen F U N N E L
Police Constable
December 22nd, 1899
In a fire at the Elephant and Castle,
Wick Road, Hackney Wick, after rescuing
2 lives, went back into the flames, saving
a barmaid at the risk of his own life.

Frederick M I L L S, A. R U T T E R, Robert D U R R A N T
and F. D. J O N E S who lost their lives in bravely
striving to save a comrade at the sewage pumping works,
East Ham, July 18th, 1895.

William D R A K E lost his life in averting
a serious accident to a lady in Hyde Park,
April 2nd, 1869, whose horses were unmanageable
through the breaking of a carriage pole.

William D O N A L D, of Bayswater, aged 19,
Railway Clerk, was drowned in the Lea
trying to save a lad from a dangerous
entanglement of weed.
July 19th, 1866.

Kensal Green Cemetery I have already mentioned. More
central and in some ways more interesting is Highgate Cemetery where, among others, Karl Marx, George Eliot, Herbert
Spencer, and Mr Koon (father of the modern London Chinese
Restaurant) lie buried. The charm of Highgate cemetery lies in
its landscaping, its general state of total disrepair (monu-
mental angels lie tumbled hither and thither, immortal dust
seeps through the gaping cracks in the mausolea) and the busload after busload of Russian tourists in their gaberdine mack-
intoshes. It makes a perfect Sunday outing (get there before
four), a short walk down Swain's Lane from Highgate Village.
Don't miss the upper section, with its catacombs.

While in London you should try junk collecting, a classic
local diversion. The rules are, at present, in confusion. Until a
couple of years ago junk was mandatorily Victorian, now the
twenties and thirties are in favour and pop art signals the
arrival of yesterday's cigarette coupon as an art object. The
devotees of junk collecting now move in such tight circles of
self-parody they are searching their own dustbins. Participation
by the casual visitor is problematical, almost impossible. He
should, perhaps, go to the Portobello Road to catch a faint sniff
of the real pungent atmosphere of acquisitive muck. But I warn
him that I know of two expensive antique dealers who
double their prices before taking *objets* out of the neat surroundings of the nicely arranged shops and setting them upon
dingy stalls in Portobello.

The twin temples of junk used to be the two emporia, Sim-
monds in Gower Street and Austin's in Peckham Rye, s e 15.

Both have gone off a bit, decimated hourly by ravenous Italian and American dealers, but every now and then nice bits and pieces survive. For cheap utilitarian furniture I recommend the auction rooms, Sotheby's, Christie's and Bonham's. Otherwise there is a stall run by a man called Reg in Inverness Street by Camden Town which is the cultural nexus of an area stretching for three-quarters of a mile around. Reg is a *totter*; he collects the entire contents of houses vacated by the dead. He is beginning to learn the value of his stock, but the legendary story of the china figurine –

'How much for this?'

Reg: 'Sixpence.'

'But you *fool*, it's Meissen!'

Reg [hurt]: 'Oh, all right then, a shilling.' –

brings him customers from all over the world.

No one can say Reg is undiscovered. He figures powerfully in the folklore of North London, and is second only to obscenity as the sure-fire topic local hostesses hold in reserve to bridge awkward conversational gaps at dinner parties.

There is an excellent shop in Nevada Street, Greenwich, called Spreadeagle Antiques, run by a bearded tycoon called Richard Moy; the Caledonian Market in Bermondsey every Friday; Deptford Market on Saturdays and the Antique Supermarket in Barrett Street near Oxford Circus for overpriced (but not impossibly overpriced) junk. Nineteenth-century postcards which retail at a penny on Reg's stall can cost as much as 5s. at the Antique Supermarket.

A good way to see London, and for locals to see it afresh, is to set up a series of arbitrary challenges. Why not collect Corners? There are scores of named corners in London, and properly planned it should be possible to visit every one of interest within a week: Staple's Corner, Bradley's Corner (now known as Chepstow Corner), the four Henlys Corners, Hyde Park Corner, Speaker's Corner, Apex Corner, Gardner's Corner to name just one or two. Get a street guide and go to work. Or see if you can eat lunch in the B.B.C., Time-Life, International Telephone and G.P.O. canteens; very good subsidized nosh.

You could compare every swimming pool in central London.

Or skate at Richmond in the morning, Streatham in the after-noon and Queensway in the evening. The all-night bowling rink at London Airport is said to attract a nice type of customer. See if you can run *up* every *down* escalator on the Northern Line. Try to use every luxury hotel lavatory, or telephone kiosk, in one morning. Or visit each of the Royal Parks after dark. Their fences are derisory, and at Hyde Park they always leave one gate unlocked each night in a secret sequence so there is some exit for lovers' cars.

Why not try profession spotting? Or celebrity spotting? All through London there are pubs, for instance, which have evolved into everlasting parties for particular specialist groups. The Salisbury in St Martin's Lane is always crammed with camp theatricals, sometimes with some well-known camp theatricals. The Marquis of Granby in Smith Square is full of politicians. So is St Stephen's Tavern in Bridge Street, West-minster. The Coach and Horses, in Old Compton Street, houses brilliant young satirists, munching their austere snacks each lunchtime (elbows well in), and every Wednesday there is a high-powered lunch upstairs when they entertain distinguished rumour-mongers secretly. Try the Prospect of Whitby, which I always find a wonderful pub for looking at tourists; it has by now gone right through fakery to a glorious real identity of its own. Try the various Finch's Wine Houses in Chelsea for fortune-hunters, con-men and heiresses, the Dover Castle by the B.B.C. for forties poets, El Vino in Fleet Street for journalists (avoid the grey-faced men with black jackets and dandruff, they are lawyers and devoid of interest, the fat red-faced men at the door tend to be editors).

Restaurants can also be enjoyed in this fashion. Try Wheeler's in Old Compton Street for journalists and trade-union officials living off each other; the Gay Hussar in Greek Street for left-wing agitators; Wilton's in Bury Street for dukes; old-guard publishers upstairs in Bianchi's, Frith Street, or L'Escargot Bienvenu, Greek Street; new guard in the Trattoria Terrazza's Positano Room. A select group of evil-doers and raffish ladies gather in Muriel's, Dean Street, otherwise known as the Colony Room, which is nicer, and less classy than it sounds.

A real discovery is the *Chinese* Chinese Restaurant. It is only penetrated at the cost of embarrassment and hostility from the other customers. If you invade it the Chinese clientele will undoubtedly desert it for some new hideaway and the pre-cooked sweet-and-sour pork will arrive in place of the Chinese hors-d'oeuvres, and musty noodles of deep subtlety, but it was too fragile a bloom of *esoterica* to survive anyway, and you might as well enjoy its decline. The place is clearly favoured by the owners and chefs of every other Chinese restaurant in London; it only begins to fill up at 3.30 in the afternoon, and 11.30 each night. It hides itself on the first floor of an indifferent Chinese café (what a magnificent cover for a good restaurant, a *bad* one!), the Universal, in Tin Pan Alley, otherwise known as Denmark Street, by St Giles Circus.

It is to Mr Murray Sayle, an Australian author, that we owe its discovery. Mr Sayle was ploughing rather disconsolately through lunch at the Universal when he noted a succession of Chinese gentlemen edging past his table to use the telephone, and *not returning*. By the time a large busload had entered the kiosk he investigated, and found the secret stairway leading upstairs.

Similar proper national cooking can be savoured around Camden Town, where countless Greek Cypriot restaurants thrive. All about as good as each other, all wonderful for lunches after hangovers. Take your own beer, and don't mention Turkey, as feelings about partition are still strong. They go to the length of serving Greek coffee, and Greek Delight; one man is even contemplating serving roast Greek at Christmas. I would recommend a place with the un-Greek name of the Golden Arm Social Club in Bayham Street if you're coming from the north (it's a one-way street). Don't miss the multi-coloured crazy-paving at Emilia's Hair Fashion in Pratt Street round the corner. If you're coming from the south try the Athenian Club in Delancey Street. In Catford, of all places, ten miles from the West End, there still exists probably the finest survivor of the classic Soho Italian Restaurant, Cominetti's, 129 Rushey Green, SE 6. It is run by a wonderful family who, thank God, still lack the worldliness to come up to the West End.

Living in London has a special quality because you can get

anything here, and because of the anarchy of random behaviour patterns which this open endedness inspires. Whereas most small societies are made up of hidebound traditionalists occasionally throwing off the traces on cosmopolitan sprees, London is made up of cosmopolitans occasionally throwing on the traces in hidebound sprees. It is in this interplay of innocence and artifice, local and foreign, of direct and ironical enjoyment, that the real art of London life resides. It is difficult to take part in it, but worth a try. And remember that while you are doing so, you are yourself one of the most extraordinary and fascinating sights of all.

Let them eat cake

By now you might be short of money. This won't help you save a penny but it might help you spend less. Stop eating, stop drinking and start walking. Lyons, an extensive chain of restaurants, serve plain and inexpensive food. In London at various strategic places they have huge eating palaces called Corner Houses. They are landmarks and anyone will direct you to those near Marble Arch, Piccadilly Circus or Tottenham Court Road Underground stations. Somewhat tarted-up lately, they still have the ocean-liner-of-the-1930s-tourist-class atmosphere. There are a number of restaurants in each Corner House and the one named the 'Grill and Cheese' provides just that, as cheaply as it can be bought in similarly clean and comfortable conditions anywhere in London. The Corner Houses are very English in style and design, sociologists please note. Corner Houses open on Sunday: the one in the Strand opens at 8 a.m., the one at Coventry Street, near Piccadilly opens at 10 a.m. and the Marble Arch and Oxford Street Corner Houses open at 10.30 a.m. and 11 a.m. respectively. Make a note of this in case you find yourself midtown and hungry on Sunday.

At one time London excelled in tea-shops which had windows glittering with home-made cream cakes, eccles cakes, scones and currant bread. They would serve you lavish teas at 4 p.m. arrayed with best china and supervised by grey-haired old ladies who would give you detailed recipes at the drop of a compliment. Now they are replaced by hamburger joints.

Although the olde worlde tea shoppes have virtually disappeared there are some great 'cream tea' places still around.

The House of Peter, 18 Gloucester Road, s w 7, sells

259

home-made cakes and coffee and also does inexpensive lunches and early dinners. It is open from 9 a.m. to 9 p.m. every day. Yes, including Sunday.

Gloriette calls itself a Café-Konditorei and is opposite Harrods at 128 Brompton Road, s w 3. This is a continental-style coffee shop selling croissants and a wide selection of cream pastries and serving full-scale lunches too. It's one of my favourite places to break training with a plate of cream cakes, and what's more it's next door to a well-stocked bookstall that has lots of English and continental magazines.

Derry & Toms is a department store that has a famous roof garden where teas are served. It's a curious place full of old ladies complaining about their servants and smart debs boasting about their hairdressers. It's at 103–105 Kensington High Street, w 8, and certainly worth a visit if you like tea, gardens, old ladies or roofs.

Fortnum's Fountain, Piccadilly, is an anglicized American drugstore serving rickeys, milk shakes and complex sundaes as well as lobster salads. At lunchtime you can get beaten to death by old ladies' umbrellas.

Bertaux, Pâtisserie Française, 28 Greek Street, w 1, is in the heart of Soho (if Soho has a heart). The ground floor sells fine pâtisserie and croissants and you can order any you fancy and have coffee or tea too on the first floor. Friendly service, twenties style décor. Closed Mondays.

Pâtisserie Valerie, Old Compton Street, is a Belgian cake shop, and we all know how those Belgians nosh. Fine cakes, croissants, etc. Rather like Bertaux although I sometimes think that I'm the only person who goes to both places since they each have such loyal customers. Both make excellent places to ease your shoes off looking at Soho and it's less expensive than a restaurant meal.

If you are so short of money that you cannot afford coffee and a cake go for a walk in one of London's parks. The whole town is dotted with open spaces ranging from the ugly little children's recreation grounds to the sylvan splendour of Hampstead. There are few 'don't walk on the grass' signs in London parks and when they do appear at seeding time they are apologetic in tone. The Londoner likes his parks to look

like an unplanned open space and they are artfully contrived
to do so. Hampstead Heath for instance pretends to be
neglected open countryside and as you walk across it seeing
sudden pastoral patterns and arrangements of trees and hillocks
it's easy to think no one saw it or planned it. Go there and see
for yourself. All told there's about eight hundred acres
beginning four miles from Charing Cross. The Londoner has
always relished his parks and when Charles II exercised his dogs
his subjects were delighted to pretend they didn't recognize him.
Pepys entertained ladies in the park and lay down and took the
sun there as Londoners do now whenever a trace of sunlight
shows. Couples kiss there and princes play polo. Typists eat
sandwiches there and admen play cricket. Guards officers go
riding, old gentlemen sail boats and young ladies fly kites. All
quite oblivious of each other.

When Billy Graham remarked on the sexy behaviour of
Londoners in their parks, London was shocked. It was
considered rather bad form to watch your neighbour; to
comment seemed unforgivable.

To see a West End play at lowest possible cost find out if the
theatre has unreserved seats. They are hard and uncomfortable
but it's the same show.

Two establishments that have catered on a large scale for
intimate low-cost entertainment are the Talk of the Town (next
door to Leicester Square underground) and the Pigalle in
Piccadilly. Both provide lavish floorshows, sometimes with
international star names. Both places will provide a large and
acceptable meal, wine and floorshow without too much damage
to the wallet. (Dinner at the Talk of the Town, including show
and dancing, is under £3.) They will give you value for money
and a chance to see the Londoner having a night out.
So will the Poor Millionaire at 158 Bishopsgate
(B I S 3311). To get into the Playboy Club you must be a
member. The same goes for gambling clubs like Crockford's
or the Pair of Shoes and for discothèques like Sibylla's,
9 Swallow Street (Beatle-backed discothèque for incognito jet-
set), or Samantha's (flashing lights and a musical E-type).
There's plenty of variety, and a copy of *Queen* magazine will
brief you on the current fads and fancies. In my experience

difficulty of access to any club varies in inverse proportion to its success. In the words of Groucho Marx, 'Who wants to join the sort of club that will let me in?'

You'll need to be a member to get into Ronnie Scott's jazz club at 27 Frith Street in Soho. Join. It's good service, good food and great music. Most of the world's great jazz musicians have appeared at Ronnie Scott's and the atmosphere is just right. Ronnie Scott apart from being one of our great jazz musicians and a tolerant and affable host is a master of the one liner. 'That's the end of the music ladies and gentlemen. But you don't have to go home yet. As long as you get out of here.'

When you get out of Ronnie Scott's follow Steve Race.

Jazz

Steve Race

Steve Race's career as a jazz writer goes back to the jazz revolution in the late 1940s, when 'be-bop' divided the old critics from the new, and only two critics (of which he was one) opted for the new movement. Later for twelve years he wrote a weekly jazz column for the *Melody Maker*, meanwhile appearing regularly on radio and TV. His reputation as a pianist, composer and arranger firmly established, he contents himself now with writing only when he has something to say. His weekly B.B.C. World Service programme 'The Jazz Scene' is heard everywhere, oddly enough, except in Britain.

One evening in 1966 – admittedly rather a special evening – it was possible, within a mile radius of Piccadilly Circus, to see Erroll Garner, Earl Hines, Buck Clayton, Bud Freeman, Rex Stewart and Jimmy Witherspoon, as well as a dozen English groups and God knows how many folk singers. There is hardly a major jazz star alive who hasn't played in London.

No wonder, then, that jazz fans laugh when all and sundry dub London the 'swinging' city, just because it's easy to play chemmy all night and watch strippers all day. For London really does swing – in the original, jazz sense of the word.

There are two things to do before your London visit begins. Drop a line to Harold Davison Ltd at 235 Regent Street, w 1, and ask what concerts are on. You may well find Thelonius Monk at the Royal Festival Hall or the Herman Herd at a cinema in Victoria. Write also to the Ticket Unit, B.B.C., London, w 1, in case there should be any jazz radio or television programmes being recorded during your stay. All B.B.C. tickets are free, but they like you to enclose a stamped addressed envelope with your inquiry. In case you have any ideas about attending a jazz L P record session, they scarcely exist, and they're never open to the public.

When you arrive buy the current issue of *Melody Maker*, which lists the clubs, addresses and fixtures lists. If you need further information, Roy Burchell of the *Melody Maker* staff (F L E 5011) knows the scene well and won't mind a brief phone call.

Some of the best live jazz is to be heard in pubs. *My* favourite is the Bull's Head at Barnes Bridge – well worth the journey if you can spare a whole evening. You can get there by tube via Hammersmith and then a No. 9 bus, or by driving south over Hammersmith Bridge and turning right at the first traffic lights. There'll be no parking problems on arrival.

Though the Bull's Head fronts on the Thames it isn't a river-side pub in the chi-chi sense. Indeed, when landlord Albert Tolley took it over it was little more than a derelict billiard hall. He's turned it into a seven-nights-a-week-plus-Sunday-mornings jazz spot that many musicians rate among their favourite rooms anywhere. You may find Tubby Hayes in session, Mark Murphy, Jimmy Witherspoon or the driving quartet of Dick Morrissey. Occasionally there's a big band. The music starts each night around 8 p.m. and ends some time after 10; average door admission is 3s. 6d., rising somewhat for the big names . . . naturally, since they cost the guv'nor more.

The music lounge at the Bull's Head is full of atmosphere, thanks in part to contemporary paintings from near-by Hammersmith Art School. The wall seats are worth elbowing for, but you'll find a good supply of casual stools dotted around the floor. There's no dancing; nowadays jazz musicians like (and deserve) to be listened to properly.

Across a courtyard is a charcoal grill, where the décor is smart and intimate, the food reasonably priced and the wine list unusually enterprising.

The Bull's Head is high on my pub list but there are quite a lot of jazz pubs nearer to central London. A typical one is the Tally Ho, managed by Jim and Lilian Delaney, at the junction of Fortess Road and Highgate Road, a step or two from Kentish Town tube station. The quality of the music is quite high, the prices quite low and there's no extra admission charge to the jazz room. Atmospherically speaking, the Tally Ho's pre-posterous 1920s hunting décor, its shortage of chairs, ghastly acoustics, and the fact that the bass drum rests half on the stage and half on a beer crate, combine to give the place a strong sawdust charm. Bix Beiderbecke would have loved it.

Jazz holidaymakers in London usually suffer from too many days and not enough nights. All the more reason to go to Dobell's Jazz Record shop at 77 Charing Cross Road. There, crammed within two tiny rooms, are 20,000 new and second-hand jazz L Ps, the folk and folk-blues discs being housed separately next door, presumably because they attract a kinkier clientele. In spite of the space shortage at Dobell's there are private listening rooms – a rare luxury at a record store these days. The pallid gentleman you may glimpse through the venetian blind at the far end of the shop is Doug Dobell himself, one-time trad pianist, now the Onassis of jazz-record retailers.

The real fun is to plunge down the perilous, almost vertical staircase into Dobell's bargain basement, which John Kendall runs as a cross between a jazz discussion group, a news agency and a secondhand record store. The display boxes here are in-furiatingly full of bargains, and behind the monstrous centre pillar – what wouldn't Doug Dobell give to be rid of that – are about a thousand 78s listed alphabetically under artists: Albert Ammons' wonderful old piano boogies, Chris Barber learning to play his first trombone on weird forgotten labels, Bob Crosby's Bobcats, Tommy Dorsey.... Sentimental jazz collectors in their forties grow hysterical in this Corner of Memory Lane and have to be led out weeping happily at closing time. Jazz devotees from all over the world crowd into Dobell's; several international jazz friendships have been forged here following a brisk argument over a mint-condition 'Miles Ahead' at 22s. 6d.

In the unlikely event of Dobell's not having what you want, Jimmy Asman offers 7,000 almost-half-price records only a step away at 23a New Row, opposite the New Theatre. Asman's has one slight advantage over Dobell's in that your girl friend can browse through some secondhand Presleys (or, for that matter, Mozarts) while you get stuck into the M J Qs.

Manager Pete Payne knows a lot more about jazz than his mine-host appearance would indicate. Get talking to him, and he'll probably tell you about the City of London Jazz Society, which sponsors record recitals by star critics on alternate Tuesdays at the Mail Coach, Camomile Street, E C 2. Admission is 2s. 6d. – but with a curious, commendable gallantry all wives and girl friends are admitted free.

Awaiting you at Dobell's or Asman's are records from Armstrong to Ayler and Zawinul to Zurke. But what about the vintage jazz collector whose blood races at the mention of the California Ramblers on Banner, or the King Oliver Gennetts? Where can one buy a copy of '19th Street Blues' played by 'Stinking Socks' Seraphic Duo, half of which, as any discographer knows, was 'Dodds, J. (clt)'? The answer entails a trip into north London to meet the most knowledgeable vintage-jazz collector of our day, Brian Rust.

Brian is a phenomenon, a true eccentric and a walking reference book. His memory is uncanny. He can give you instant details, including recording date, catalogue and matrix numbers, of practically any record issued between 1895 and 1940. At his home-cum-showroom are thousands of historic 78s. If he doesn't have a duplicate for sale he can dub an early record to tape for you at a modest price.

To contact Brian Rust, ring him first at H A T 4452. He'll then tell you how to reach 38 Grimsdyke Road, Hatch End (you'll identify the house from its 1902 horn gramophone in the window). Brian's records cost from 2s. to 30s., but remember that he cares only for 78-type music. Babble eagerly of John Coltrane or Stan Kenton and you'll be sent back to town in disgrace without even being offered a chair, let alone coffee.

So to the night time and the clubs. If you're a foreign visitor to London you may not know who our best local musicians are. Most of all we seem to specialize in good tenormen: Tubby Hayes, Don Rendell, Tony Coe, Art Ellefson and Dick Morrissey are all worth going some distance to hear. So, on their respective instruments, are Ian Carr (trumpet), Harold McNair (alto), Ronnie Ross (baritone) and Johnny Scott (flute); all Grade-A, forward-looking modernists. The Graham Collier Septet will reward you with *avant garde* (but non-angry) sounds.

For mainstream jazz moving back towards Dixieland, watch out for Humphrey Lyttelton, Alex Welsh or Chris Barber. Ken Colyer's Band deliberately revives the almost-exact sounds of Storyville. Bruce Turner leads a Jump Band which is deliciously reminiscent of 52nd Street days, and on the fringe of the pop scene watch out for Alexis Korner's Blues Incorporated.

You'll find Dixieland Jazz, sometimes with superb American guests like Earl Hines or Ruby Braff, at the 100 Club on the north side of Oxford Street, not far from Tottenham Court Road station. This is the sort of atmosphere in which jazz grew up: a stifling, bare cellar where the sweat of the dancers glistens through the steam rising from the players. The glare of light over the bandstand will remind you of a police identification parade; elsewhere in the room there's no light at all. It costs 6s. to get in (7s. 6d. at weekends); you can drink, dance, or sit on a hard chair just listening to the non-stop jazz. The place is open every night from 7.30.

Every Londoner has his own favourite among the jazz clubs, depending on the type of music featured and on whether his idea of heaven is rotgut at Murphy's Irish House or champers at the Hotel Splendide. My favourite club is undoubtedly Ronnie Scott's, at 47 Frith Street, Soho. It's not just the best in London or Britain. It's probably the best jazz club in the world.

Ronnie Scott couples a flair for management with a clear knowledge of what jazz fans and jazz musicians like, since he himself is both. There are no 'Closed on Monday' signs at Ronnie's; no nonentities filling in during the slack summer months; no touts at the door or thirst-crazed hostesses at the bar. Ronnie's is always open, always civilized, always exciting.

It's a true night club, opening each evening at 8.30, warming up about 11 and closing at 3 a.m. You can reserve a table by ringing GER 4752. Ask to be put on one of the tiers, unless of course you're there to find out how Sonny Rollins fingers an F-sharp, in which case you'll want one of the candle-lit tables directly in front of the stand. From there you can practically take his pulse if you've a mind to.

The average admission price is 15s. (less for members of the National Union of Students) but when big stars like Stan Getz are appearing Ronnie charges a bit more.

You're not compelled to drink anything, but the prices are reasonable, rising from Coke at 1s. 6d. and bottled beer at 2s. 6d. If you're with a small party and have a taste for wine try sharing a bottle of the Piesporter Riesling, served nicely chilled at 24s.

Among twenty main dishes the menu lists a fillet steak at 14s., spaghetti at 6s., and two very popular West Indian curries at 12s. 6d. each. There's a 10 per cent service charge on all food and drink but the waitress will like you better if you add an extra bob or two.

Scott's is ideal for seeing, listening, eating, drinking and generally enjoying the world's most superb modern jazz soloists in sophisticated, air-conditioned surroundings. There are always two guest stars, one of them a singer – Ernestine Anderson perhaps, or Carmen MacRae – while Ronnie's guest instrumentalists are legendary jazz figures. Sonny Stitt, J. J. Johnson, Sonny Rollins, Stan Getz, Bill Evans, Ben Webster, Roland Kirk, Horace Silver – the list reads like a world jazz poll.

As my favourite blues singer says, have a good time, baby, have a good time. In London nowadays the jazz fan can hardly miss.

Telephones and radios

Not even the most fervent Anglophile living could describe
Britain's telephone service as anything but appalling. The
visitor – and the resident too – is best advised to avoid contact
with it. This is however a counsel of perfection, for you will
have to make arrangements, book restaurant meals and inquire
about timetables. Ask your hotel to do this whenever you can,
it will save you hours of wasted time and all the agonies of
getting no answer or wrong numbers.

When you are forced to use the phone handle it carefully
and dial slowly and precisely, for many of the wrong
connexions are due to antiquated equipment. Dial 100 to
connect with the operator and I N F if you want information. In
an emergency dial 999 and state whether you want Police, Fire
or Ambulance. You will be asked your name and where you are
phoning from first – in case you are cut off, a frequent mishap –
so be ready to supply that information. The 999 service answers
rather quickly. I cannot say the same for any other number
mentioned. It's quite possible to spend hours trying to get the
operator.

To report a fault dial E N G. To get someone's phone number
dial D I R for directory. To send a telegram within Britain dial
T E L, for an overseas telegram 557. (The last time I wanted to
send a telegram it took me two hours to get through to 557.) If
you are lucky enough to get a ringing tone, hold on. There is
an automatic queue. It may take a long time but I know that
eventually they will answer; the G.P.O. press office told me.

To phone Austria, Germany, the Netherlands or Scandinavia,
dial 105. For any other part of Europe dial 104. For places
outside Europe dial 108.

To hear the main tourist events of the day phone A S K 9211. For the same thing in French, German and Spanish, dial A S K 9311, A S K 9411 and A S K 9511. For a London weather report dial W E A 2211 (there are other numbers for other districts, ask I N F). For a general meteorology inquiry phone T E M 4311 and you will find the Met. Office very helpful. During the summer when there are Test Matches, cricket scores, etc., are available from U M P. During the winter, information on road conditions for fifty miles around London is available from A S K 6611.

To find people in a trade or service there is a classified telephone directory listing phone numbers by trades. Ask to see the 'buff book' at any post office.

The B.B.C. is as good as the phone service is bad. On sound radio there are three stations operating all day each day. The Light Programme broadcasts record programmes, comedy shows, short news bulletins, soap opera and the odd easy-to-take play, from 5.30. a.m until 2 a.m. The Home Service (6.30 a.m. till midnight) is more serious in content; good plays, symphony concerts, discussions and programmes of minority interest like bird-watching, historical reconstructions and archaeology. The Third Programme broadcasts serious music all day (some of it in stereo) from 7 a.m. till about 6 p.m. when it changes first to an educational programme – languages, literature and art – and then to a real minority programme for erudite lectures and experimental music and drama. The only departure is on Saturday afternoons, which are devoted to sports broadcasting.

There are also commercial stations beamed from outside Britain and pirate radio stations – most of which broadcast the Top Twenty and pay no royalties to the artists – situated on ships anchored beyond the territorial limits. The music is London 1967 but the chat is Greenwich Village 1945.

The B.B.C. instituted the world's first public T V service in 1936. Now there are three T V channels available in London, none of them colour and none of them broadcasting for more than half the day. The commercial channel – I T V – broadcasts a predictable amalgam of superficial drama, Westerns and pop shows, with an occasional serious play or news discussion programme. The B.B.C. has two channels, both putting out a more serious standard of material but with generous allowances of trivia and soap opera. Commercial T V programmes are announced in a weekly journal called *TV Times*. All B.B.C. broadcasting is announced in the *Radio Times*. A visitor truly interested in getting the taste of Londoners' London should see and hear some T V and sound broadcasting. The best T V programmes in any week are superb, and surpass any television I have seen abroad. The B.B.C. sound broadcasting is, if anything, better.

Guide books and maps

In London there's a great temptation to walk out of your front door and just maunder around. If you've got a year or two to spare, sooner or later you'll see everything in the guide books.

But if you've only got a week or two, you'd better get a guide book.

Because there are now so many guide books and maps here are my comments. An asterisk (*) means I have used it a lot while preparing this book.

Street Maps in book form

Geographia. 3s. 6d. *Geographers' A to Z* *London*. 3s. 6d.	Black and white, very small type. These pocket-size books are what the average Londoner uses to find his way about.
Phillips ABC. 10s. 6d.	A slightly bigger and better, coloured version of the two above guides. If you want a street guide and can afford it, get this one.
* *Geographer's Greater London Atlas*. 25s.	Large hardback coloured street plan book. Won't go into the pocket, it's intended for the car shelf. Get this if you are staying a year or two.
Bartholomew's London Street Atlas. 50s.	Grandest street atlas but very expensive. This is the one the police cars have on board.

Street Maps folded (i.e. not in book form)

Buy one from a petrol station (Shell, Esso, etc.). They are not only the best and most up-to-date, they are also the cheapest, at 6d. each. I found that several of the more expensive street maps were not only unchanged for decades (in the case of one map a building destroyed in the blitz was still marked and named), but some publishers have a nasty habit of putting a publishing date on the map to suggest that the map itself was accurate at that date.

* Geographers' City of London, 3s. 6d.	Super detailed, 18 ins. = 1 mile, map of the oldest part of London (not the West End). Shows the small alleys, street markets, churches and selected City taverns. In spite of omissions like the Jamaica, George and Vulture, and Anchor pubs, it's all you need to explore the most fascinating part of London.
London Underground, Bus and Railways *Underground* *Central Buses* *Country Buses*	All these four are available free from London Transport or British Travel offices. While you are at it get the other pamphlets too.
London and Surrounding Area. 5s. 6d.	(Ordnance Survey ½ in. = 1 mile.) The best map for the environs.

Pamphlets, Brochures, etc. from Information Offices

Conducted Coach Tours, Royal London, Know your Animals, Opera and Oranges, Village Life, Town and Country Houses, Country Churches, and the series of pamphlets of suggested day trips, e.g. *Day at Greenwich, Guildford, St Albans, Day on the River,* etc. These are available free of charge from London Transport, as is *The Passenger's Guide* and a clever leaflet called *London from the top of a bus* which, in diagrammatic form, shows how to link some trips on London buses so that you see the most important tourist sights. An excellent idea for people who can't stand tourist bus trips.

Books from the British Travel Association

London; Maps and Information. 3s. A straight-up-and-down 58-page booklet with fold-away map and a couple of coloured photos. Has lists of restaurants and hotels with prices, phone numbers, etc., but obviously cannot state preferences. Maps show some walks, including a list of things to see if you are in London only for one day.

Excursions from London. Companion to above. Lots of black-and-white photos. Well designed, clearly printed and has full travel instructions under each entry. Great value at 3s.

* London from the River. Clearly printed on fine paper, as are the previous two books. Lots more colour than either and more slanted to be a pictorial account of the history of London's river. Price 2s. 6d.

Hotels and Restaurants in Britain: Official Guide. 8s. Multi-language charts show at a glance what each hotel has to offer and what it charges.

Books and Pamphlets from Greater London Council

These are not normally available at tourist information offices. Write or go to the Greater London Council, County Hall, s e 1.

Open Air Entertainment. This is the most fascinating book they do. It's 100 pages thick and is illustrated. It costs 1s. and lists all the goings on in the London Parks (or nearly all the goings on): tennis, dogs shows, concerts, motor-cycle racing, beat groups, fairs, steel bands and sculpture. They also do several coloured pamphlets about parks, the *Enjoy your Parks* series, which detail routes and even the best time to go to see which flowers in bloom.

As well as these there are many pamphlets about education, each one specializing in a subject, e.g. *Commerce and Law, Languages, Banking*, etc.

London Guide Books

London: a Geographia Guide. Geographia, 3s. 6d.
Famous Guide to London. Geographers, 3s. 6d.
These guides are very similar in shape and style and even the publishers' names are similar. They each efficiently list the sights of London and show them on small black and white maps with numbers on. Either will do for someone who wants this sort of guide book. The former appeals to me more by having more historical information but they are both rather dull.

* *London Night and Day* by Sam Lambert. Architectural
Press, 6s.

The great classic London guide book: witty, stimulating,
brilliant. Full of fascinating facts and erudite comments. This
is the Londoner's favourite guide book by far, and rumour has
it that it will never be reprinted. If you see one grab it. Please,
Mr Lambert, whoever you are, do it again, just for the eight
million of us.

Nairn's London by Ian Nairn. Penguin Books, 8s. 6d.

London seen with an architectural eye; fussy and pedantic, but
also chatty and amusingly biased. It's a very formidable list and
I don't think a tourist could digest it unless he was fanatically
building-bent.

* *London for Everyone* by A. Ogden. Dolphin Paperback
Original, 7s. 6d.

Written by an American who knows London remarkably well
and makes it all the more fascinating by showing it through a
visitor's eyes. Good potted history and super walks which you'll
be inspired to take, book in hand, as I was. Highly detailed
and highly readable.

Penguin Guide to London by Frank Banks. Penguin Books,
7s. 6d.

Straightforward, rather dull guide book. If you want an
exhaustive catalogue of London this is good value.

**Companion Guide to London* by David Piper. Collins, 30s.

The ultimate in the 'everything about everything' style of
guide book. Urbane in style and reliably objective in manner,
its 450 pages of closely printed text are something to dig into
well before arriving on a two-week holiday.

Visitor's London by Harold Hutchison. London Transport, 5s.

An exquisite little book, on fine white paper and decorated with
excellent illustrations (Ravilious and Bawden among them).
The introduction says it's a Ready Reference to buildings and
places, which it is, but being in alphabetical order makes it of
limited practical use. However it makes a cheap present for the
folks back home.

* *London on a Pound a Day* by Betty James. Batsford, 12s. 6d.

If *London Night and Day* disappears then this might well
become the best informal London guide book. Ignore the pound

a day bit, it's just a first-class book by a painstaking guide.
London on Sunday by Betty James. Batsford, 12s. 6d.
A follow-up to *London on a Pound a Day*. Buy this one too,
it's excellent value.
London à la mode. Drawings by Paul Hogarth, text written by
    Malcolm Muggeridge. Studio Vista, 36s.
Hogarth is one of the best illustrators in the world. His former
books on New York and Ireland were full of masterpieces.
This one is almost as good and it could be a good deal worse
and still be worth my money any day. Muggeridge supplies a
brilliant but all too short commentary.
New London Spy by Hunter Davies. Blond, 30s.
Various writers on topics from homosexuals to sermons. Some
fascinating facts mixed with some far-fetched fiction. Good
fun. There are also lists of goods and services.
Offbeat in London by Geoffrey Fletcher. *Daily Telegraph*,
    2s. 6d.
Bright, well-illustrated (by drawings) guide to lesser-known bits
of London. Any books by Fletcher are fascinating. This is a
bargain but look at the more expensive ones too.
The London Walkabout by H. J. Deverson and Guy Gravett.
    Wolfe, 3s. 6d.
A bright idea crudely carried out. Scrawled over photos is a
step-by-step walk through Central London. The authors suggest
that a child would like to guide an adult by means of this book;
that's a good notion. More walkabouts are promised.

Districts of London

* *Soho Night and Day* by Frank Norman and Jeffrey Bernard.
    Secker & Warburg, 42s.
For more about Soho buy this book by Frank Norman (who
contributed the piece on slang). The ins and outs of modern
Soho by a man who knows it well. The book is lavishly
illustrated with fine photos by Mr Bernard. More a super
souvenir than a guide book.
A Literary Guide to the City by Rachel Hartley. Queen Anne
    Press, 3s. 6d.
Published by the City of London Corporation, this is a small
booklet concerned only with the City. There is a potted

biography of literary figures from Adam, Joseph to Wycherley, William, and fourteen maps to show where their feet trod.

Food and Drink Guides

* *Egon Ronay B.M.C. Guide to Hotels, Restaurants, Pubs and Inns* by Egon Ronay. Four Square, 25s.

As well as rating and describing restaurants, etc., throughout Britain, it has useful lists of pubs, e.g. wine-conscious London pubs, pubs in beautiful villages and outdoor pubs. Ronay is one of our top gourmets and I'll follow his advice any day.

Good Food Guide by Raymond Postgate. Consumer's Association and Hodder & Stoughton, 18s.

Instead of using inspectors this guide uses the reports of its members. Otherwise it's like the Ronay Guide. Many people buy both to compare results.

Good Cuppa Guide by J. Routh. Wolfe, 3s. 6d. A witty and comprehensive guide for tea drinkers. Strongly recommended.

Museum and Gallery Guide Books

* *Museums and Galleries in Great Britain and Ireland*. Index Publishers, 3s. 6d.

A remarkable book listing with all details, addresses and opening times all Britain's museums, together with many photos of interiors and exhibits. Museums are cross-indexed and subject matter ranges from a Museum of Witchcraft at Looe to Aerial Photography at Cambridge.

Guide to London Museums and Galleries. H.M.S.O., 3s. 6d.

A paperback book giving details of the 17 most important London museums together with a listing of more. Many photos.

Specialist Books

Shell Nature Lovers' Atlas by James Fisher. Ebury Press, 7s. 6d.

Beautifully designed book of coloured maps showing nature and animal reserves throughout Britain with a brief description of each one.

A Book of London edited by Ivor Brown. Collins, 10s. 6d.

This is not a guide book but a delightful anthology of writing about London; snatches of Shakespeare and verses of Victorian music-hall songs. Well chosen with a few excellent photos.

Guide books and maps

What's Where in London by Denys Parsons. Kenneth Mason,
  5s.

This has been going a long time now and no library however
small is complete without a copy. Although really a reference
book, the bizarre things Parsons finds on sale make it easy to
read. This book is published for B P, for whom the same
publishers do *Angling with B P*, 5s., and *Motorboating with
B P*, 3s. 6d.

Children's London

Exploring London by Isobel Barnett and Ronald Searle. Ebury
  Press, 8s. 6d.

Delightful book with bright Searle drawings designed to show
many ways of entertaining children in London.

Seeing London by Dale Maxey. Collins, 16s.

Lots and lots of two-colour drawings, with a text written by the
artist. Some elements of fantasy but a great deal of very useful
(and sometimes offbeat) information. This book, unlike the
previous one, is directed to children rather than parents.

Students' London

The Student Guide to Britain by Pickthorn. Pan Piper, 5s.

A handbook giving details and addresses that any student
needs, with quite a lot of attention to foreign students.

The Student Guide to London. Published annually by the
  National Union of Students, 3s. 6d.

Intended for the visitor with little money who plans to stay a
long time. Details of discounts, cheap shopping, museums,
bookshops, etc. Much more racy in its attitude than the more
serious Pickthorn book.

History of London

*London: The Unique City by Steen Eiler Rasmussen. Penguin
  Books, 5s.

Danish architect's view of the history of London. A popular
history book, with an emphasis on city development and why
London differs from all other towns. There are 48 pages of
excellent photos and 32 drawings. A classic book and an
erudite souvenir to take home.

Georgian London by John Summerson. Penguin Books, 7s. 6d.
Just as many illustrations and photos as the previous book but
this one deals only with what many would regard as London's
most elegant period: 1714–1830. Books which use history as
their theme seem much easier to read and enjoy than the ones
that list one building after another like a walk down the street.
You may not agree, but at this price these Penguin books are
fabulous value.

London Life in the Eighteenth Century by Dorothy George.
  Penguin Books, 16s.
A very excellent and scholarly work; almost one third of the
book is notes and appendices. No illustrations, strictly for the
serious reader.

Historic London by G. E. Eades. Queen Anne Press, 42s.
The City of London Society do research and provide guides
and lecturers to people who want to know more about the City
of London. They have endorsed this book, which has been
written by a history lecturer from Goldsmiths' College. It is a
very good history for the general reader.

* *London from the Earliest Times to the Present Day* by John
  Hayes. Black, 12s. 6d.
This is a school book and is not elegant enough to be a souvenir
gift, but what fantastic value. It has nearly 300 illustrations –
photos, prints and reconstructions of historic scenes. It is
written by an official of the London Museum and is packed with
information in a clear direct style without 'talking down'. They
also have a limp cover edition at 6s. 6d. which makes it just
about the best value on my list.

* *London: an Illustrated History* by Ivor Brown. Studio Vista,
  £3 10s.
A lavishly illustrated, careful history of London. Prints,
drawings, plans, photos and paintings, many of them in good
colour. This is the ideal souvenir or present. It isn't cheap but
unlike so many picture books this one has lots of information.

* *A History of London Life* by R. J. Mitchell and M. D. R.
  Leys. Penguin Books, 5s.
No illustrations in this highly entertaining book that unearths
all kinds of curious behaviour by rich and poor from ancient
times till the present day.

Illustrated English Social History (4 volumes) by G. M.
 Trevelyan. Penguin Books, 8s. 6d. per volume.
I'm cheating by including this but it's such a lavishly illustrated
and excellent account of the life of the English from Chaucer
to Victoria's funeral that I urge you to buy it anyway for
London plays a large part in the story.

And before you write and tell me that there's a guide book
I've left out let me tell you I'm up to my ears in London books
and there are dozens I've missed out. Some of them are
excellent and some of them are awful. Many of them repeat
and repeat completely wrong information copied from other
guide books. I'm beginning to hate guide books.

Newspapers

More newspapers are sold per head in Britain than anywhere
else in the world – twice as many as in the U.S.A.

London is about as loaded with newspapers as one city can
possibly become in an age of T V. They vary from the pompous
to the preposterous.

The Times. The Thunderer. With a circulation somewhat under
300,000 it remains the most influential paper. Conservative in
policy, it has a historical tendency to support the party in
power and can be quite radical at times. Between the wars it
adopted rather strange postures. Recently it has had a face lift
and news was put on the front page to replace the traditional
classified adverts. Immediately after this it was bought by
Thomson Newspapers. Useful to the tourist, it has
entertainment and state functions listed each day. On Saturday
it lists sermons.

Guardian. *The Times* designed to be read as literature.
Originally a Manchester paper, its circulation is about that of
The Times but it is far less predictable in its political views,
e.g. it opposed Suez.

Financial Times. A small circulation, high prestige daily paper
for big business. No publication has more highly regarded
reviewers for stage, films, books and art.

Daily Telegraph. Big, 1·3 million circulation daily with strict
Conservative politics. Read by people who think the *Guardian*

is radical. Excellent reporting, good layout. On Friday there is
a lavish colour supplement included which makes it just about
the best value obtainable in newspapers anywhere in the world.
Daily Express. An extraordinary newspaper that is the first to
be condemned and the first to be read. Brilliant typography,
brilliant journalism; its principal flaw in the past was the
occasional cruel vendettas against public figures. If you want to
see British journalism then buy the *Express.* Circulation
4 million.
Daily Mirror. The only mass circulation daily (5 million) with
left-wing politics. Big headlines, big breasts, big pictures.
Outspoken editorials had a reputation for fearless blunt
speaking even during the war.
Daily Sketch. Like the *Mirror* this is a tabloid. Conservative in
outlook, its circulation is below a million, which might prove
that conservatives like large newspapers.
Daily Mail. Another popular-style Conservative newspaper,
rather like the *Express* but with differences. Its circulation at
time of writing is about 2·4 million, but of all the newspapers
this is the one that has gained most in reputation among
newspapermen. Saturday's edition has news of the weekend's
events of interest to the tourist.
Sun. This is the *Herald* – a trade-union-backed newspaper –
with a new name. Rather muddled in design and falls between
the *Mirror* and *Express* in manner. In spite of selling only 1·3
million it has kept going through many predictions of
demise.
Morning Star, previously the *Daily Worker.* Strict Communist
policy runs through this 60,000 circulation paper but it is
important for the clues it furnishes to international politics.
Some of the reviewers are well worth reading and the sports
forecaster has a reputation second to none.
Evening Standard. The newspaperman's newspaper if there is
such a thing. Great blending of news and features, highly
readable and highly informative with prestigious political
commentators. Comparatively small circulation (650,000) and
pop manner belies its power and influence.
Evening News. London's most popular evening paper (biggest
evening circulation in the world: 1·2 million) with all the

ingredients needed after a long day at the office. Good news reporting as well as short stories, etc.

Sunday Times. Egg-head Sunday. Conservative in policy but can hit hard in all directions. Started a department ('Insight') that used teams of reporters and turned up some memorable stories and horrifying scandals, e.g. Rachman the slum landlord. Included in the price is a business section, an arts section using top reviewers and a full-size colour magazine that is worth double the price of the whole paper. This was the first of Britain's colour supplements. Tourists should note the entertainment adverts. Circulation one and a quarter million.

Observer. A more liberal but less successful version of the *Sunday Times* – circulation 824,000. It has superb reviewers and a literary touch with news coverage, a great deal of which is exclusive. The *Observer* also has a colour supplement no less readable than the *Sunday Times* but emphasizing historical subjects and women's interests to a greater degree. Tourists should note 'Briefing', a section about entertainment and events.

Sunday Telegraph. Since the *Telegraph* steals a march on the other two egg-head Sundays by issuing its colour supplement on Friday, Sunday's paper has more difficulty in competing in spite of some excellent contributors. Circulation 650,000.

Sunday Express. Not quite the Sunday version of the *Express* although it has the same publisher and a slightly larger circulation. Mixes pin-ups and puritanical tough talk into a magic formula.

Sunday Mirror. Gay, youthful pop weekly, heir to a hot-blooded Sunday tabloid. More human interest features than news, with a circulation topping 5 million.

News of the World. Once banned in Ireland, its gigantic circulation – over 6 million – is based on coverage of divorces and what the scoutmaster was doing in the woodshed. It also indulges in cheque-book journalism, or the buying of memoirs like those of Christine Keeler for enormous fees.

People. When the *News of the World* is bidding for the memoirs of notorious newsmakers the *People* man is likely to be at their elbow. It published the story of Lonsdale the Soviet

spymaster. Beloved by over 5 million who buy it and see it as a
champion of the little man victimized by authority or landlord.
It has uncovered many scandals and, with the *Daily Express*,
has the best crime coverage.

Weekly Periodicals
Times Literary Supplement. Extensive book reviews dealing, as
might be imagined, with more serious and educative books.
Times Educational Supplement. A review of education from
techniques to vacancies.
New Statesman. A weekly of politics and literature viewed from
centre, or left of it. Influential and hard-hitting. Highbrow
competition pages are a prime egg-head pastime.
Spectator. Another weekly of considerably smaller circulation
than the *New Statesman* and of more conservative outlook. It
has reviews of art, books, theatre and films as well as political
commentaries.
Listener. A weekly published by the B.B.C. which prints –
often in full – talks and other items that have been broadcast
that week.
Illustrated London News. A rather lavishly illustrated magazine
dealing with the news of the week, from archaeological finds to
a royal visit to a plastics factory.
Private Eye. A satirical magazine capable of delivering a bite
that proves fatal. Endlessly involved in litigation, each time it
seems about to perish a most catholic and unlikely cross-section
of the British Isles rallies round it. The last time it had to raise a
few thousand, for things it said about Lord Russell (not the peace
one, the other one), it staged a benefit called *Rustle of Spring*.
Stars ranged from Manfred Mann's pop group to Peter
Sellers via David Frost and many members of the group that
initiated the 'new satire' and in so doing liberated and put new
lead into the pencil of Britain's journalists and commentators.

Bookshops

For maps, guides and books about London I can recommend
the Times Bookshop at 42 Wigmore Street, which also stocks a
general selection of books from best-sellers to paperbacks. Lots

of children's books here too. See Mr Edgecombe if you want to talk about military books, as he is an expert.

Among other notable bookshops I would count several opposite the British Museum, particularly Collet's at 39 Museum Street, WC1, who have foreign books (specializing in Russian). Just around the corner, catering for students from London University, is Dillon's at 1 Malet Street. H. K. Lewis at 136 Gower Street has medical and scientific books; there's a good secondhand department, and the shop also operates a loan scheme. Janson at 44 Great Russell Street has natural history books (particularly entomology). Luzac at 46 has oriental books and other shops in that street have Japanese prints and all sorts of African and Eastern books.

Grant & Cutler at 11 Buckingham Street, Strand, WC2, have new and secondhand books in most European languages but if you want only French language books go to Hachette, 4 Regent Place (just off Regent Street), or to the Librairie Française, 34 Rosslyn Hill, NW3. There are also books *about* France in English.

German books are at Libris, 38a Boundary Road, NW8, and Polish books at Orbis, 38 Knightsbridge.

Scientific and electronic books are stocked at Lamley, 5 Exhibition Road, South Kensington, and also at the Modern Book Co. in Praed Street, W2. Go into the basement of Karnac's, 56 Gloucester Road, SW7, for all kinds of secondhand books especially art and architecture books. For economists there is The Economist Bookshop at Clare Market, Portugal Street, WC2. Personally I am not an economist and have never been near the place.

A place I do frequent however is Her Majesty's Stationery Office. There are two branches in London, one at 49 High Holborn, WC1, and the other at 423 Oxford Street. H.M.S.O. publishes books and periodicals for the British Government as well as for museums and other official bodies. It publishes about 6,000 new items each year and has books, pamphlets and reports on everything from secret service operations in France in World War II to diseases in poultry. It has cookery books, war histories, illustrated books on art treasures and various museum guide books. It also acts as agent for foreign official publications and international bodies such as the World Health Organization, Council of Europe and U.N.O.

A visitor with specialized interests should take a look at the magazine racks of a big newsagent. Periodicals such as *Billiards and Snooker*, *Boxing News*, *Golf News*, *Horse and Hound*, *Judo*, *Lacrosse*, *British Lawn Tennis*, *Motor Cycle*, *Yachting World*, *Tenpin Pictorial* and *Motor Sport* will tell you exactly what events might be worth seeing during your stay.

You

To even out the score I asked a lot of Londoners what they thought of tourists. They said you were very clean in appearance and the men's hair was trim and short. You refrain from comparisons with things in your own country even when this must take a lot of self-restraint. You are kind and complimentary about the things you see, but you overtip and you don't complain enough.

You do, I'm told, spend most of your time with your fellow tourists. You eat tourist food and pay tourist prices in places where the service is so bad that only tourists (who tend to be ill at ease and unfamiliar with local standards) would tolerate it without punching the staff on the earhole.

The only Londoners you meet are people in the tourist industry; waiters, guides, cabbies and porters, who, my brief survey showed, are not warmly regarded by their fellow Londoners. You resent paying top prices but avoid lower-priced places, where the natives go, for fear of dirt, disease or xenophobia.

The Londoners interviewed wished tourists would see more of 'the real London', which transpired to be 'ordinary places' and 'not tourist places', and not to go to pubs in bus loads.

There's lots to see in London and it is still one of the least expensive towns on the tourist circuit. Many Londoners live here on £10 a week and still get to a theatre and a concert once a week. With your sort of money you can live like a king. If this book has given you a few ideas on how to get more for less we'll all be delighted because that's the only object of it.

For a final word on London let me quote (and this time

acknowledge) John Salmon, who has helped me put this book together.

'The way to avoid petty frustration on a visit to London is to look before you leap. Check the weather before you decide where to go. Check whether it'll be open when you get there. And find out how to get there and back before you leave.

'I always do. And I've lived here the best part of thirty years.'

Index

Index

kebab, 39, 49
Kebab and Homous restaurant,
49, 53
Kenco Coffee Houses, 31, 52, 53
Kensal Green Cemetery, 251
Kensington Gardens, 132, 141
Kensington Palace Hotel, 47
Kenwood, 89, 155
Kenwood House, 89, 155
King's Arms (pub), 238
King's Restaurant, 47, 53
King's Road, 30–31, 88, 152–3, 195
kitchen tools, 199, 200
Knight, Frank & Rutley (estate
agents), 204
Knightsbridge, 194
Kodak (photographic equipment),
148
kooftahs, 39
Korma curry, 39, 47
kosher market, 81
kosher restaurants, 118–19
Kuo Yuan (restaurant), 40

Lacey, Professor Bruce, 207
Ladbroke's (turf accountants), 111
Ladies Directory, 161
lager, 58, 62
lakeside concert, 89
Lambeth Bridge, 145, 149
Lambeth Palace, 149
lambswool, 192
latkes, 49
launderettes, 179
laundry, 12
Law Courts, 123, 154
Leadenhall market, 45
Leather Market Street, 152
Leicester Square, 151
Leighton, Lord, 205
Leston, Les (shop), 243
Lewis, H. K. (bookshop), 283
Liberty (department store), 198–9,
200, 202
Librairie Française (bookshop),
283
library, art, 241
Library, London, 108

library, military, 223
licensed hours, 58
Lillywhite's (department store),
141, 191, 197
Lincoln's Inn, 154
Listener, 282
Literary Guide to the City, 275–6
Little Venice, 126, 252
Littlewood, Joan, 228
London Airport, 14, 131–2
London Apprentice (pub), 60,
205–6
London Bridge, 69–70, 154
London fashion houses, 192, 201
London guide books, 273–9
London Health Centre, 50
London Library, 108
London Museum, 132
London Season, 113
London Stamp Exchange, 103–4
London Steak Houses, 52
London Transport, 9, 10, 16, 18
(*see also* buses, Underground
railway)
Look Back in Anger, 227
Lord Robert's Workshops, 199
Lord's (cricket ground), 110, 111,
211–12
Lotus Elan, 242
Lotus Formula 3, 242
Ludgate Hill, 125
lunchtime gramophone concerts,
94, 144
lunchtime music, 94, 98, 143, 144
luxury goods, 103–14
Luzac (bookshop), 283
Lyons Corner Houses (restaurants),
47, 48, 53, 119, 259
Lyric Theatre, 233

Madame Tussaud's, 136
Madras curries, 39, 47
magazines, 33, 87, 260, 282
Maggs Brothers (rare books), 104
Magpie and Stump (pub), 143
Mail Coach (pub), 266
Malay Satay, 50
Mallet (shop), 195

Index